Teaching Large Online and Blended Classes

Teaching Large Online and Blended Classes

edited by

Selma Koç
Cleveland State University

Marius Boboc
Cleveland State University

INFORMATION AGE PUBLISHING, INC.
Charlotte, NC • www.infoagepub.com

Library of Congress Cataloging-in-Publication Data

A CIP record for this book is available from the Library of Congress
http://www.loc.gov

ISBN: 978-1-64802-678-2 (Paperback)
      978-1-64802-679-9 (Hardcover)
      978-1-64802-680-5 (E-Book)

Copyright © 2022 Information Age Publishing Inc.

All rights reserved. No part of this publication may be reproduced, stored in a retrieval system, or transmitted, in any form or by any means, electronic, mechanical, photocopying, microfilming, recording or otherwise, without written permission from the publisher.

Printed in the United States of America

CONTENTS

Preface vii

1 Reflecting on Two Decades of Online and Blended Learning at an Australian Multi-Campus University 1
   Steven Pace

2 Teaching Large Online Classes: Strategies to Structure and Support Supersized Learning 15
   Peggy Semingson and Karabi Bezboruah

3 Building a Better Large Blended Course 33
   Jami Nininger and Miriam R. Abbott

4 Using a Blended Learning Approach in a Large Community Engagement Course 51
   Martina Jordaan and Dolf Jordaan

5 Physically Distant but Socially Connected: Building Community in Large Online or Blended Courses 71
   Michael Porterfield and Jennifer McKanry

6 Strategies for Collaborative Learning in Large Online Classrooms 89
   Marcus Schultz-Bergin and Erin Avram

7 Engagement and Critical and Ethical Thinking—Effective Online Teaching With Large Online Student Cohorts: Anti-Racist Pedagogy and First Nations Studies 111
Mary Frances O'Dowd

8 Instructional Design and Faculty Partnership for a Standards-Aligned Online Course Design for Large Classes 127
Manuella B. Crawley and Vivian LeAnn Krosnick

9 Faculty Learning About Teaching Large Online Classes Remotely: Reflections of Faculty Developers 153
Joanne E. Goodell, Judith Ausherman, Marius Boboc, Shamone Gore-Panter, Selma Koç, Sarah Rutherford, and Marcus Schultz-Bergin

10 Building an Adaptive Online Learning Environment: Learners' Perspectives and Satisfaction 169
Emre Emrah Özkeskin and Cengiz Hakan Aydın

11 Building a Human–AI Framework for Teaching Large Online Classes 189
David Stein and Shen Ba

About the Editors 205

PREFACE

This book aims to provide practical assistance to those who have taught for a while or who are new to teaching large online and blended classes. The authors who contributed chapters to the book include faculty, instructional designers, facilitators in providing faculty development, and researchers with years of experience and understanding as well as interest in improving the effectiveness of large online classes. We hope that these chapters add to the relevant literature by continuing conversations started before the COVID-19 pandemic but brought to the forefront by it. Moving forward, it is our intent to provide readers with examples of how instructors around the world have adapted to the new reality of teaching online since early 2020. Distilling what has worked and why from areas that require further analysis would benefit us all by identifying strategies, structures, support services, and policies that could augment online education with a particular focus on large virtual classes.

Chapter 1 by Pace, "Reflecting on Two Decades of Online and Blended Learning at an Australian Multi-Campus University," examines the evolution of online and blended learning at an Australian multicampus university over the past 20 years. In order to provide a well-rounded picture, this chapter considers several practical aspects of teaching online and blended classes, how those practices have changed over time, and the reasons for those changes.

Chapter 2 by Semingston and Bezboruah, "Teaching Large Online Classes: Strategies to Structure and Support Supersized Learning," examines the challenge of designing effective personalized learning for teaching large online classes while providing concrete research-based solutions that focus on collaboration, predictive analytic tools, and the issue of cognitive load. The overarching guiding question that focuses the chapter is: "What evidence-based strategies can instructors use to reduce learner cognitive overload, foster strategic virtual outreach, and support collaborative learning through both structure (course design) and teacher presence in large online and blended courses?"

In Chapter 3, "Building a Better Large Blended Course," Nininger and Abbott, explore and discuss the standards and design elements for building a large blended course. The authors conclude that appropriate integration of instructional tools and the development and disclosure of sound course policies provide support for design.

In Chapter 4, "Using a Blended Learning Approach in a Large Community Engagement Course," Martina and Dolf Jordaan describe how a community-based course with an annual enrolment of between 1,600 to 1,900 students is facilitated by only one lecturer and one administrative staff member using the university's learning management system, among other forms of educational technology.

Chapter 5 by Porterfield and McKanry, "Physically Distant but Socially Connected: Building Community in Large Online or Blended Courses," uses the frameworks of community of inquiry (Garrison et al., 2000) and community of trust (Palmer, 2005) to break down the idea of community into its key components and provide practical, evidence-based examples that can help faculty build a learning community in their large online classes.

In Chapter 6, "Strategies for Collaborative Learning in Large Online Classrooms," Schultz-Bergin and Avram discuss the importance of collaborative learning in large online classrooms and then examine a variety of techniques and tools to identify general guidelines and best practices for effectively establishing collaborative learning environments.

Chapter 7, by O'Dowd, "Engagement and Critical and Ethical Thinking—Effective Online Teaching With Large Online Student Cohorts: Anti-racist Pedagogy and First Nations Studies" extends discussions on fostering engagement, deep critical and ethical thinking in large online teaching classes. The chapter details four critical periods in the semester and specific strategies for each of period: (a) Preparation; (b) Engagement by week three; (c) Assessment and feedback; and (d) Final two weeks and Improving evaluations.

In Chapter 8, "Instructional Design and Faculty Partnership for a Standards-Aligned Online Course Design for Large Classes," Crawley and Krosnick discuss the benefits of a partnership between the instructional designer and faculty member throughout the course design, implementation and evaluation process for online course design for large classes. The authors argue that intentional design with emphasis on learning outcomes, pedagogy, course alignment, and the potential value of the online learning environment itself supports a student-centered approach to virtual learning. They provide strategies and suggestions for engaging students in their learning particularly in large online classes.

Chapter 9, by Goodell et al. titled, "Faculty Learning About Teaching Large Online Classes Remotely: Reflections of Faculty Developers," describes and reflects on how three professional development courses at a higher education institution were implemented. These professional development courses included over 60 full-time and part-time faculty participating in each course during the summer of 2020. The courses focused on flipping your remote classroom, small teaching online, and engaging students in online learning. In addition, the authors discuss the future impact of such faculty development and future lines of inquiry.

Chapter 10, "Building an Adaptive Online Learning Environment: Learners' Perspectives and Satisfaction," by Özkeskin and Aydın, focused on a research study related to testing the effectiveness of an adaptive learning environment and a MOOC course and the participants' persistence to complete as well as exploring their reactions to and perspectives on these notifications.

In Chapter 11, "Building a Human–AI Framework for Teaching Large Online Classes," Stein and Ba explore recent developments in artificial intelligence as pedagogical agents in the online classroom. They introduce a human–AI framework about how pedagogical agents can serve learners in large online classes and help faculty manage social, teaching, and cognitive presence in large online classes.

We wish to thank the authors for their contributions and innovative strategies they shared with respect to teaching large online and blended classes.

—**Selma Koç** and **Marius Boboc**

REFERENCES

Garrison, D. R., Anderson, T., & Archer, W. (2000). Critical inquiry in a text-based environment: Computer conferencing in higher education. *The Internet and Higher Education, 2*(2/3), 87–105.

Palmer, P. (2005). The community of truth. In C. Anders & L. Runciman (Eds.), *Open questions: Readings for critical thinking and writing* (pp. 627–636). Bedford Books.

CHAPTER 1

REFLECTING ON TWO DECADES OF ONLINE AND BLENDED LEARNING AT AN AUSTRALIAN MULTI-CAMPUS UNIVERSITY

Steven Pace
Central Queensland University

ABSTRACT

This article examines the evolution of online and blended learning at an Australian multi-campus university over the past 20 years. Central Queensland University is based in regional Australia, but it has campuses and study centers across the country. The university has served a large population of on-campus and off-campus students since 1972—well before the advent of online learning. This chapter focuses on developments in online and blended learning within a single course at Central Queensland University, the Bachelor of Digital Media, which was established in 1997. The discussion is presented from the perspective of an insider who co-founded the course and coordinated it for most of its existence. In order to provide a well-rounded picture, this chapter considers several practical aspects of teaching online and blended classes, how those practices have changed over time, and the reasons for those changes.

This case study examines the evolution of online and blended learning at an Australian multicampus university over the past 20 years. Central Queensland University (CQUniversity) is based in regional Australia, but it has campuses and study centers across the country. The university has served a large population of on-campus and off-campus students since 1972—well before the advent of online learning. This chapter focuses on developments in online and blended learning within a single course at CQUniversity, the Bachelor of Digital Media, which was established in 1997 as the former Bachelor of Multimedia Studies. Some readers might refer to a bachelor's degree as a *program*, but at CQUniversity it is referred to as a *course*. The Bachelor of Digital Media prepares students for a career in the media and communications industries. It is a generalist qualification focusing on a range of disciplines associated with design, technology, and media, but it allows students to pursue specializations in graphic design, interactive media, animation, or screen production. This discussion is presented from my perspective as an insider who co-founded the course and coordinated it for most of its existence in the role of head of course. In order to provide a well-rounded picture, this chapter considers several practical aspects of teaching online and blended classes, how those practices have changed over time, and the reasons for those changes.

BACKGROUND

The Bachelor of Digital Media currently has more than 300 active students, one-third of whom study online. The remaining students are enrolled at one of six campuses across Australia in Cairns, Mackay, Rockhampton, Bundaberg, Brisbane, and Sydney. On-campus students study in a blended learning mode—attending face-to-face classes, but accessing resources, interacting with each other, and undertaking learning activities in an online environment. The size and structure of the Bachelor of Digital Media has varied throughout its 24-year history. At its peak in 2004, the course had 774 active students who were either studying online or at one of eight campuses. The learning outcomes for the Bachelor of Digital Media encompass both discipline-related and generic outcomes, including knowledge and skills required for employment and further study. The course learning outcomes have been mapped to the Australian Qualifications Framework (AQF) to ensure that they are consistent with the relevant AQF level, and they have also been mapped to the individual units of study that comprise the course to ensure that they are consistent with the unit content and learning activities (Australian Qualifications Framework Council, 2013).

Like all courses at CQUniversity, the Bachelor of Digital Media is made up of learning components called units of study, or simply *units*. At other higher education institutions, units might be referred to as *courses* or *subjects*. For example, DGTL11005 Web Design is a foundation unit that provides a practical introduction to Web design and development. All digital media students complete this unit as part of their first year of study. A full-time student in the digital media course completes four units of study per term. Each term consists of an orientation week, 12 weeks of classes, and a 2-week assessment period. The academic year at CQUniversity consists of three terms separated by vacation periods, but digital media units are generally only scheduled in two of those terms. Each unit that contributes to the first year of the Bachelor of Digital Media typically has between 120 and 200 students enrolled in a single term. Most of these students will be completing the unit as a requirement of the Bachelor of Digital Media. The remainder of the class will be students from other courses who are taking the unit as an elective. Units that make up the second and third years of the digital media course have smaller numbers of enrolled students than the first-year units.

Staffing arrangements within the digital media course have been designed to support its complex blend of face-to-face multicampus delivery and online delivery. Each unit of study in the Bachelor of Digital Media has a single unit coordinator who is responsible for the curriculum, assessment, learning resources, teaching, administration, and general oversight of the unit. Each unit coordinator also supervises a geographically dispersed team of tutors who teach the unit at various CQUniversity campuses across Australia (see Figure 1.1). In most units of study, both the unit coordinator and the tutors teach face-to-face classes, but only the unit coordinator teaches the online classes. For example, the unit coordinator for DGTL11005 Web Design who is based at the Mackay campus might supervise five tutors located at the Cairns, Rockhampton, Bundaberg, Brisbane, and Sydney campuses. Each tutor teaches the classes for that unit at their local campus. The unit coordinator teaches the DGTL11005 classes at the Mackay campus and the online classes for distance students in that unit.

As part of CQUniversity's quality assurance measures, digital media students are invited to complete an anonymous online evaluation form for each unit of study at the end of each term. The evaluation form asks students to rate their satisfaction with the unit in categories such as overall satisfaction, unit Web site navigation, learning resources, assessment tasks, and more. Students are presented with a positive statement about their satisfaction with each category and are asked to indicate their level of agreement with the statement on a 5-point Likert scale ranging from s*trongly disagree* (1) to s*trongly agree* (5). In 2019, evaluations were conducted for

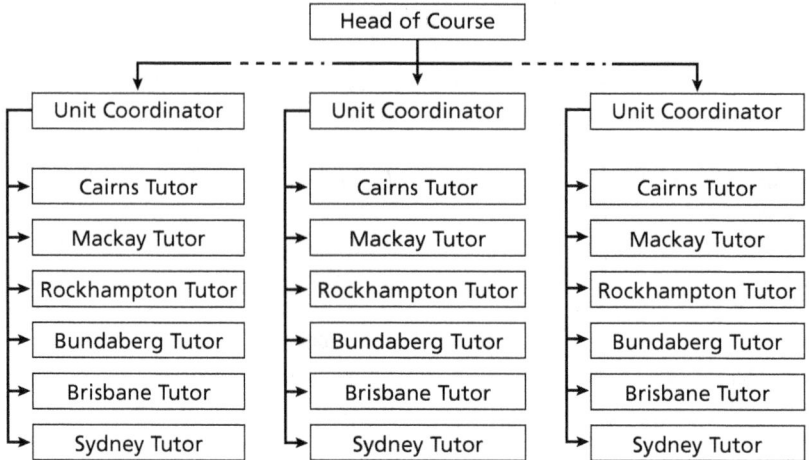

Figure 1.1 This organizational chart illustrates the supervisory relationships between the head of course, the unit coordinators, and the tutors in the digital media course.

23 digital media units. The average response rate for each unit was 40%. Twenty of the 23 units (87%) achieved an average overall satisfaction score of more than 4.0 out of 5.0. The remaining three units achieved an average overall satisfaction score of 3.7 or 3.8 out of 5.0. These results indicate that students are generally satisfied with the quality of digital media units. In most cases, students are very pleased with the quality of digital media units. Thirteen of the 23 units that were evaluated in 2019 achieved satisfaction scores of more than 4.0 out of 5.0 in every category.

MODES OF INSTRUCTION

When the digital media course was first established in 1997, on-campus students participated in a weekly lecture and tutorial for each of their units of study. The lectures were delivered by the unit coordinator to students at multiple campuses via videoconference. Small classes with fewer than 10 students gathered around a PictureTel™ videoconferencing unit that resembled a cathode ray tube (CRT) television with a camera module on top of it. PictureTel was one of the first commercial providers of videoconferencing systems. Large classes sat in a lecture theater fitted out with a projection screen, speakers, multiple cameras controlled remotely by the presenter, and microphones at each seat which drew the gaze of a camera when they were activated. Face-to-face tutorials were conducted at each campus by a local tutor in either a computer lab or a traditional classroom, depending on the needs of the class. In those early days, online students had no scheduled interaction with teaching staff. They relied predominantly on supplied learning resources and ad hoc interactions with the unit coordinator by phone or email.

Over time, academic staff recognized the need and the opportunity to provide greater support to online students. One of the enabling factors was the invention of asynchronous digital subscriber line (ADSL), a technology that increased the bandwidth of copper wire and enabled Internet connections of up to 6 Mbps over the existing phone network. ADSL was significantly faster than the dial-up Internet services that preceded it. As ADSL services became widely available to students across Australia, unit coordinators gradually replaced their weekly lectures with prerecorded online video presentations that students could download and watch prior to their tutorial classes. Software tools such as Camtasia were used to prepare the video presentations and demonstrations. Rather than continue with the traditional format of 1-hour lectures, unit coordinators prepared collections of shorter videos covering the same content, which students seemed to find more palatable. Guo et al. (2014) have since demonstrated that "shorter videos are much more engaging" than longer instructional videos. Their large-scale study of video engagement was based on data from 6.9 million video-watching sessions across four courses on the edX MOOC platform.

Years after its adoption by the digital media course, this pedagogical model became widely known as the "flipped classroom" because of the way it "flipped" the traditional classroom on its head (Bergmann & Sams, 2012). Traditionally, instructional content was presented to on-campus students in the classroom in the form of a lecture, while exercises and projects were completed at home. Under the flipped classroom model, students considered instructional material such as readings and video presentations at home, which freed up class time for them to work on exercises, projects and discussions with the help of their tutors and peers. Although the digital media course introduced prerecorded online video presentations primarily for the benefit of online students, on-campus students also benefited from this arrangement.

Like the lectures, tutorial classes also changed in response to advancements in pedagogical tools and methods. On-campus students continued to receive support through weekly face-to-face tutorials in computer labs and other facilities at their local campus, but those classes were typically restructured as a sequence of short presentations interspersed with practical exercises, group discussions, video clips, and other activities involving the prescribed software and equipment. This new approach was consistent with the advice of Medina (2008), who claimed that audience attention steadily drops 10 minutes into a presentation. To regain audience attention at that point, tutors need to change gears by telling a relevant story, showing a relevant video, or doing a relevant activity—essentially buying another 10 minutes. More recently, Bradbury (2016) has claimed that "the available primary data do not support the concept of a 10- to 15-min attention limit" (p. 509). However, many academics within the digital media course continue to use this approach because of the positive response it receives from students.

These changes to the format of on-campus lectures and tutorials were accompanied by the introduction of dedicated tutorials for online students, which were conducted by videoconference. Real-time videoconferencing tools, Blackboard® Collaborate, and later Zoom™, were used for this purpose. Zoom's current array of features include support for both computers and mobile devices; a chat function for students who don't have access to a webcam or microphone; a screen-sharing function for displaying documents or demonstrating software; the ability to record tutorials for later playback; and the ability to split the class into separate sessions called breakout rooms, where individual students can receive private assistance with their work.

Initially, these videoconference links proved to be unreliable because of the limited bandwidth of the remote participants' Internet connections. Teaching staff tried to cope with these limitations by applying workarounds, such as asking students to mute their microphones and switch off their webcams when they were not speaking. Problems with low-bandwidth Internet connections slowly began to improve when the Australian government committed to the deployment of a National Broadband Network (NBN) in 2009. The Rudd Government announced that the NBN would combine fiber-to-the-premises (FTTP), fixed wireless, and satellite technologies to deliver Internet speeds of up to 100 Mbps to 90% of Australian homes, schools, and workplaces (Rudd, 2009). Unfortunately, the NBN became a political football, and the reality did not live up to the promise. After a change of government in 2013, the NBN was redesigned to reduce costs. A mixed copper/optical technology known as fiber-to-the-node (FTTN) replaced FTTP as the preferred approach for providing most NBN connections (Conifer, 2016). The resulting connection speeds were significantly slower than the 100 Mbps that was originally proposed. Nevertheless, by 2016 the service was available to most digital media students at CQUniversity, and online video tutorials had become commonplace.

While most units of study in the Bachelor of Digital Media employ the modes of instruction that have just been described, project units are an exception. Project units are typically completed in the final year of the course. In these units, students undertake a digital media project of their choice in consultation with academic and workplace supervisors. The project may involve the development of a digital media product that demonstrates advanced production skills; the development of a portfolio of digital media work to show prospective employers; a digital media-related work placement with an approved organization; or an academic research project with a digital media focus. Some project units require students to work as part of a team on a substantial project for an external client over a period of two terms, while other project units allow students to work as individuals on smaller single-term projects. Project teams may include a blend of on-campus students and online students who communicate via phone, email, and videoconference with their clients, supervisors, and each other. Project units illustrate that the modes of instruction used within the digital media course are not mandated but are flexibly applied to suit the needs of each individual unit.

LEARNING RESOURCES

The strong practical component of the digital media course has always required students to have access to specific hardware and software tools to support their learning. All current digital media students need access to a computer and prescribed software, such as the Adobe Creative Cloud™ applications. Some units also require students to have access to additional hardware such as a mobile phone, graphics tablet, camera, or video production equipment. On-campus students typically access these resources through their local campus, while online students must have access to their own computer, software, and production equipment at home to complete the same activities as on-campus students.

Learning resources in the digital media course have changed significantly over time, but the unit website has consistently served as the central hub for accessing those resources in CQUniversity's model of blended and online learning. Study guides, prescribed readings, instructional videos, interactive courseware, files for tutorial activities, open source software, and other learning resources are all delivered to students in electronic form through the relevant unit website. In addition to these downloadable items, discussion forums on each unit website are used to support communication between students and academic staff about topics related to the unit. The first unit websites that were used within the digital media course were custom-made by individual unit coordinators. Within a few years, these sites were replaced by a learning management system named Webfuse, which had been developed in-house (Jones, 1999). Webfuse®, in turn, was replaced by a series of externally developed systems including Web CT™, Blackboard, and most recently, Moodle®.

Learning resources were not always delivered online to students in the Bachelor of Digital Media. In the early years of the course, printed study guides and prescribed readings, lectures recorded on videocassettes, and DVDs containing software, were posted to the homes of off-campus students. The change to online delivery did not occur until broadband Internet services became widely available. Once again, the theme of technology as an enabler of change in teaching and learning is evident in this discussion. In the early years of the digital media course, unit coordinators had to contend with many technology-related concerns when preparing learning resources, not just the bandwidth of their students' Internet connections. For example, the software tools that students used for digital media production were not always affordable or available for both the Mac and Windows platforms. When prescribing software tools for their classes, unit coordinators had to consider a range of factors such as cross-platform compatibility, affordability, usability, and de facto industry standards. Another technology-related issue of concern was the visual fatigue that students experienced when reading from low-resolution computer screens (Köpper et al., 2016). In the days of CRT screen technology, students commonly expressed a preference for reading from paper rather than reading from a screen, and some students objected when printed study materials were replaced with electronic equivalents. In time, these and other concerns were resolved by advances in technology. Issues such as affordability and access to suitable technology still persist today, but they are not as pronounced as they once were.

ASSESSMENT

Unit coordinators within the Bachelor of Digital Media have always endeavored to assess student performance using methods that are both engaging and effective. The assessment tasks within each unit of study are mapped to the unit learning outcomes and to CQUniversity's generic graduate attributes to ensure that they are aligned and capable of validly assessing student progress. Examinations typically are not used for assessment within digital media units. Instead, students are assessed using assignments that involve a combination of academic tasks and authentic real-world tasks. Examples of academic assessment tasks include writing essays, writing reports, maintaining reflective journals, delivering oral presentations, conducting research, completing online quizzes, conducting peer reviews, and participating in online discussions. Examples of authentic assessment tasks include activities within the realms of video production, audio production, illustration, visual design, Web design and development, user experience design, coding, photography, social media management, animation, 3D modeling and animation, motion graphics, game design and development, and app design and development. Authenticity has long been recognized as an important element of good assessment design, and digital media staff have tried to incorporate that into their practice (Gulikers et al., 2004).

In the case of project units, which were described earlier in this chapter, teaching staff act as project supervisors and work with the students to devise assessment tasks that are aligned with both the requirements of the project and the learning outcomes of the unit. Each student confirms the details of their project early in the term with their project supervisor and client, and they submit a written project proposal that outlines their intended course of action for the term. Assessment tasks in project units vary depending on the nature of the project, but they typically involve the production of a creative artifact, some form of reflective writing by the student, and appraisals by the project supervisor and client.

One of the challenges of assessing student performance in a large class is minimizing the risk of marking inconsistency. This issue is particularly pertinent to assessment tasks in Digital Media units, which are generally marked by multiple tutors working across geographically dispersed campuses. Each tutor marks the work of their own local students to ensure that students receive feedback promptly and the unit coordinator is not overwhelmed with marking responsibilities. One drawback of this approach is that it increases the chance of inconsistent marking. To maintain accuracy and consistency in the assessment process, each unit coordinator provides their tutors with the published assessment criteria and marking guidelines to follow. Tutors are also asked to send samples of their marked assignments to the unit coordinator for a quality assurance process known as moderation. The unit coordinator checks the sample assignments to ensure that student performance is being assessed fairly, and provides each tutor with feedback about any adjustments they need to make to their marking. Records of the moderation process are kept by the unit coordinator for later independent checking.

In recent years, one of the biggest challenges to ensuring valid assessment of student performance has been the rise of contract cheating. This term refers to "a form of academic dishonesty, where students contract out their coursework to writers or workers, usually found via the internet, in order to submit the purchased assignments as their own work" (Walker & Townley, 2012, p. 27). A study involving 14,086 students from eight Australian universities revealed that 814 students (5.78% of all respondents) had engaged in a range of behaviors that could be classified as contract cheating (Bretag et al., 2019a). These behaviors included obtaining a completed assignment to submit as one's own, providing or receiving exam assistance, taking an exam for another student, and arranging for another person to take one's exam. CQUniversity has implemented several strategies designed to promote and uphold academic integrity. For example, all CQUniversity students must complete a mandatory annual online educational program about academic integrity before they can access any of their unit websites.

Unit coordinators in the digital media course have also adjusted their assessment designs to counteract contract cheating. Digital media teaching staff have traditionally used authentic assessment tasks that engage students in real-word problems or scenarios as a standard part of their assessment design. Some researchers have described authentic assessment tasks as useful tools for discouraging plagiarism (MacAndrew & Edwards, 2002). However, Bretag et al. (2019b) have demonstrated that authenticity alone provides no protection against the more challenging problem of contract cheating. Consequently, digital media teaching staff have started making greater use of assessment tasks that are personalized and unique, tasks that have a reflective component, and tasks that involve peer review either in person or online. In the study conducted by Bretag et al. (2019b), assessment tasks with these characteristics were perceived by students to be among the least likely to prompt contract cheating.

STUDENT SUPPORT

The challenge of successfully teaching large online and blended classes at CQUniversity (2020) is heightened by the fact that it is one of Australia's most inclusive universities, with a higher-than-average proportion of students from disadvantaged, mature-age, Aboriginal and Torres Strait Islander, and first-in-family backgrounds. CQUniversity invests considerable resources into support services for its diverse student base, but this was not always the case. Around the time when the digital media course commenced, Cuskelly et al. (1995, p. 7) observed that student support mechanisms at CQUniversity were "tacked on" to courses rather than incorporated into the overall student experience. They correctly suggested that distinctions between on-campus and distance learning would blur in the future, and that the nature of student support would have to change to accommodate this blending. "The type of support offered will have to take into account students' locations, age and experience and also course design decisions, the cost and accessibility of technology and the actual subject area and its specific requirements," they proposed (Cuskelly et al., 1995, p. 15).

CQUniversity's efforts to provide this kind of personalized support for individual students has improved significantly since the commencement of the digital media course. Today, a sophisticated real-time learning analytics system named CQUni Success provides important insights into how students are progressing and how they may be helped to do better. CQUni Success uses data from multiple sources, machine learning, and predictive analytics technology to identify students who may require early intervention strategies to improve their chance of success in a particular unit or course. When a student is identified as being at risk, a unit coordinator or student advisor will phone the student to initiate an intervention. The aims of these phone calls are to establish personal contact with the student; to demonstrate interest in their progress; to subtly gather information about their circumstances, concerns and potential problems; to offer immediate advice and support where possible; and to arrange referrals for further support where necessary. Examples of the support that might be arranged for students include individual consultations with teaching staff; adjustments to submission dates for assessment tasks; structured peer-assisted study sessions; private counseling on academic and personal matters; appointments for learning support with the Academic Learning Center; appointments with the Indigenous Student Engagement Team; or the development of an individual accessibility plan for students with a disability, illness, medical condition or mental health condition. Although unit coordinators also contact individual students and demonstrate interest in their progress as a matter of routine, CQUni Success provides an effective way of identifying and addressing emerging problems early. Access to CQUni Success is restricted to staff with specific roles, and any eligible person who wishes to use the system must first complete mandatory training in the ethical use of data.

FUTURE DIRECTIONS AND RESEARCH

In 2020, the global coronavirus disease (COVID-19) pandemic had an unprecedented impact on teaching and learning activities at CQUniversity. Shortly after the commencement of the Australian academic year, all face-to-face classes were replaced with online classes as part of social distancing measures designed to slow the spread of the disease (Pillhofer, 2020). In some respects, the transition for the digital media course was straightforward because online learning was already an integral part of the university's operations. But the transition still presented challenges for staff and students alike. New students who had only commenced the course 2 weeks earlier had to abandon their expectations of face-to-face classes and adjust to an online learning experience they did not choose. Although most full-time academics were well-prepared for the transition, casual tutors who had only ever taught face-to-face classes needed to quickly learn how to teach online classes via videoconference. The challenge of keeping online students engaged with their course was exacerbated by the economic hardship, loss of services, travel restrictions, and general turmoil that permeated society. Videoconferencing services and telecommunications networks struggled to cope with the surge in demand that occurred as a large proportion of the population was forced to work from home (McCarthy, 2020). Despite these challenges, the transition from blended learning to online learning was relatively seamless for the digital media course. CQUniversity did not have to suspend classes for a period, as many universities did, to prepare for the change. All face-to-face classes ceased on Friday 20th March 2020, and online classes commenced the following Monday.

Although the pandemic created many challenges and hardships for the CQUniversity community, it also created a unique opportunity to explore student experiences of online learning. For the first time in the history of the Bachelor of Digital Media, all students were studying all units online. An anticipated backlash from on-campus students did not eventuate. Instead, anonymous student evaluations that were conducted for the digital media units offered during 2020 Term 1 indicated that students were more satisfied than they were during the previous offering of the same units in 2019 Term 1. The evaluation form asked students to rate their satisfaction with each unit in categories such as overall satisfaction, unit website navigation, learning resources, assessment tasks, and more. Students were presented with a positive statement about their satisfaction with each category, and were asked to indicate their level of agreement with the statement on a 5-point Likert scale ranging from s*trongly disagree* (1) to *strongly agree* (5). Between 2019 and 2020, the proportion of *strongly agree* responses in student evaluations of digital media units increased from 51% to 63%—a remarkable 12% improvement. During the same period, *agree* responses decreased from 29% to 20%, *neutral* responses decreased from 14% to 11%, *disagree* responses remained steady at 4%, and *strongly disagree* responses remained steady at 2%. Thousands of responses were collected in each reporting period. Why did students report greater satisfaction with digital media units in 2020 despite the replacement of all face-to-face classes with online classes? Why did these evaluation results defy expectations at a time when surveys at many other institutions reported widespread student dissatisfaction with online learning (College Pulse, 2020)? Will this trend be repeated in the data from future unit evaluations if the social distancing measures continue? These interesting questions warrant further investigation.

At the time of writing, the outcome of this global experiment in online learning is far from known. Will this period become a watershed moment for education, demonstrating that online learning is much more than a stop-gap or contingency plan? Alternatively, will the rushed efforts of unprepared academics lead to substandard learning experiences for students, and ultimately increase resistance to online learning? Whatever the outcome may be, it will not change the fact that blended and online learning are highly developed pedagogical approaches that have much to offer students, teachers, and administrators when they are executed well. The collective experiences of blended and online learning in schools, tertiary institutions and corporations around the globe has produced a rich body of knowledge, skills, and practices that we can all benefit from.

REFERENCES

Australian Qualifications Framework Council. (2013). *Australian qualifications framework* (2nd ed.). https://www.aqf.edu.au/sites/aqf/files/aqf-2nd-edition-january-2013.pdf

Bergmann, J., & Sams, A. (2012). *Flip your classroom: Reach every student in every class every day*. International Society for Technology in Education.

Bradbury, N. A. (2016). Attention span during lectures: 8 seconds, 10 minutes, or more? *Advances in Physiology Education, 40*(4), 509–513.

Bretag, T., Harper, R., Burton, M., Ellis, C., Newton, P., Rozenberg, P., Saddiqui, S., & van Haeringen, K. (2019a). Contract cheating: A survey of Australian university students. *Studies in Higher Education, 44*(11), 1837–1856.

Bretag, T., Harper, R., Burton, M., Ellis, C., Newton, P., van Haeringen, K., Saddiqui, S., & Rozenberg, P. (2019b). Contract cheating and assessment design: Exploring the relationship. *Assessment & Evaluation in Higher Education, 44*(5), 676–691.

College Pulse. (2020). *COVID-19 on campus: The future of learning.* https://marketplace.collegepulse.com/img/covid19oncampus_ckf_cp_final.pdf

Conifer, D. (2016, June 14). Federal election: NBN promises past and present explained. *ABC News.* https://www.abc.net.au/news/2016-06-13/federal-election-nbn-promises-past-and-present/7506714

CQUniversity. (2020). *CQUniversity 2019 annual report.* https://www.cqu.edu.au/__data/assets/pdf_file/0017/136151/CQUniversityAustralia_2019_Annual Report.pdf

Cuskelly, E., Purnell, K., & Lawrence, G. (1995). *Student experiences of distance education at Central Queensland University: Findings from focus group research.* Central Queensland University.

Gulikers, J. T. M., Bastiaens, T. J., & Kirschner, P. A. (2004). A five-dimensional framework for authentic assessment. *Educational Technology Research and Development, 52*(3), 67–86.

Guo, P. J., Jim, J., & Rubin, R. (2014). How video production affects student engagement: An empirical study of MOOC videos. In *L@S '14: Proceedings of the first ACM Conference on Learning @ Scale* (pp. 41–50). Association for Computing Machinery.

Jones, D. (1999). Webfuse: An integrated, eclectic web authoring tool. In B. Collins & R. Oliver (Eds.), *Proceedings of ED-MEDIA '99: World Conference on Educational Multimedia, Hypermedia & Telecommunications* (pp. 1799–1801). Association for the Advancement of Computing in Education.

Köpper, M., Mayr, S., & Buchner, A. (2016). Reading from computer screen versus reading from paper: Does it still make a difference? *Ergonomics, 59*(5), 615–632.

MacAndrew, S. B. G., & Edwards, K. (2002). Essays are not the only way: A case report on the benefits of authentic assessment. *Psychology Learning & Teaching, 2*(2), 134–139.

McCarthy, K. (2020, March 16). Zoom goes boom, Teams tears at seams: Technology stumbles at the first hurdle for this homeworking malarkey. *The Register.* https://www.theregister.co.uk/2020/03/16/zoom_teams_outage/

Medina, J. (2008). *Brain rules: 12 principles for surviving and thriving at work, home, and school.* Seattle, WA: Pear Press.

Pillhofer, A. (2020, March 19). CQUni coronavirus response means shift to virtual classes. *The Morning Bulletin.* https://www.themorningbulletin.com.au/news/cquni-coronavirus-response-means-shift-to-virtual-/3975906

Rudd, K. (2009, April 7). *Media release: New National Broadband Network* [Parliament of Australia Press Release]. https://parlinfo.aph.gov.au/parlInfo/search/display/display.w3p;query=Id:"media/pressrel/PS8T6"

Walker, M., & Townley, C. (2012). Contract cheating: A new challenge for academic honesty? *Journal of Academic Ethics, 10*(1), 27–44.

CHAPTER 2

TEACHING LARGE ONLINE CLASSES

Strategies to Structure and Support Supersized Learning

Peggy Semingson
The University of Texas at Arlington

Karabi Bezboruah
The University of Texas at Arlington

ABSTRACT

This chapter examines the challenge of designing effective personalized learning for teaching large online classes while providing research-based solutions that focus on collaboration, predictive analytic tools, and the issue of cognitive load. One evidence-based solution entails reducing cognitive load through intentional design structures. The second support tool for teaching large online or blended courses includes implementation of structured collaborative learning experiences, thus building a community of inquiry (Garrison et al., 1999) where social presence, teacher presence, and cognitive presence take place in the course. A third support tool involves using predictive analytics software to create customized emails for students as virtual outreach and support. The overarching guiding question that focuses the chapter is: "What evidence-based strategies can instructors use to reduce learner cognitive overload, foster strategic virtual outreach, and support collaborative learning through both structure (course design) and teacher presence in large online and blended courses?" Although the focus of the examples and literature is on university-based online courses, the authors also draw on literature from massively open online courses (MOOCs) to provide suggestions and insight into teaching large online courses.

This chapter identifies evidence-based best practices and strategies from recent research and practice that instructors of large online and blended classrooms can utilize for increasing collaborative learning, using predictive analytics for virtual communications and outreach, and reducing learning cognitive load, while fostering externally regulated and self-regulated learning. The authors also draw on extensive experience in teaching midsize to large online courses in all online graduate programs with 50–150 or more online students. For the theoretical framework, we draw primarily on the robust and well-documented community of inquiry learning model (Garrison et al., 2001), specifically focusing on the concept of teacher presence, as well as the broader literature on cognitive load theory.

BACKGROUND AND STATEMENT OF THE PROBLEM

The authors of this chapter each have over a decade of experience teaching large classes with over 50 students, and in some cases up to 300 or more online students in Peggy's literacy master's level courses online. Both authors teach large online classes at the graduate-level only, although Peggy has had one large undergraduate class online. The first author, Peggy, has taught in a large entirely online master's degree program in literacy studies, teaching K–12 teachers in this program since 2009. The literacy studies degree focuses on advanced practitioner knowledge for a wide range of teachers (largely female) who seek to specialize in literacy and reading expertise. In addition to the knowledge gained, the program functions as a way for students to gain knowledge to be a mentor and leader (informal or formally) in specialized literacy instruction. Therefore, instruction must function beyond declarative knowledge and move towards mentoring to be an effective model of the type of leadership the graduates should take back to their workplaces.

The second author teaches in a graduate public administration program that has been offered completely online since 2013. This program, the Master of Public Administration (MPA), prepares the next generation of federal government officers, municipal and local managers, and nonprofit sector administrators. This MPA degree is accredited by the Network of Schools of Public Policy, Affairs, and Administration (NASPAA) and focuses on academic standards and core competencies that graduates need to accomplish in the program. The courses taught within this program have set objectives, competencies, and standardized learning outcomes that are assessed through various assignments. The focus of the MPA program, therefore, is to impart knowledge and instill skills and qualities to be prepared for leading public and nonprofit sector organizations, and these are done via online education. Both authors have sought out additional expert training in teaching online through research, study, mentoring, and recognition with teaching awards in distance learning.

As this chapter was being written, the entire world was navigating through a global massive shift towards sudden online instruction as a result of the COVID-19 pandemic. Therefore, recent interest and practice of online teaching is now a topic of interest, largely out of necessity. Some of these courses were likely large online courses, and the topic of ideal course size for online courses became part of the broader public discourse. One of the authors came across a post from a colleague on Facebook that stated the idea that online classes should be no more than twelve students to facilitate personal interaction (Newton, June 28, 2020). This article draws on research by Tomei and Nelson (2019) which suggests smaller classes are more effective. While this may be a theoretically ideal number for personalized interaction and feedback, this is largely not realistic due to constraints on staffing courses, in addition to other factors.

Additionally, Nagel and Kotze suggest (2009), "Research shows that the ideal size of online classes is between 25 and 30 students" (Arbaugh & Benbunan-Finch, 2005). We suggest here and in our other scholarship that it is an unrealistic way of conceiving of online courses through the lens of small as ideal as there are evidence-based emerging practices that can help to facilitate learning in large online courses. In contrast to the belief that only small online courses are ideal and personalized, Nagel and Kotze (2009) suggest, "The perception of an 'ideal size' online class lives in an unrealistic world. Education is becoming massified, and blended delivery modes are progressively containing more e-learning elements" (p. 50).

However, we are not impervious to the issues that remain with teaching large online courses. Several key problems persist such as (a) it is hard to personalize learning with large groups of students, (b) there is a need to develop community and communication with students, and (c) the issue of providing feedback and monitoring individual learners can be challenging. Even with teaching assistance or graders, automated grading, and novel emerging tools like chatbots and artificial intelligence, personalization issues and humanizing learning remain. We suggest further work into researching humanizing learning in large online courses (e.g., as explored by Prusko et al., 2020).

THEORETICAL FRAMEWORK

In this section, we describe two primary frameworks that have long informed robust instruction in teaching online and lend themselves well to conniving solutions to the challenges of teaching large online courses. First, the community of inquiry model has been useful to online researchers, practitioners, and designers since 2000 (Garrison et al., 2001). It situates the online learner in a framework of teacher presence, social presence, and cognitive presence, all of which intersect and provide a foundation for effective course design and practice. Second, we provide a brief theoretical overview of cognitive load theory, which suggests that learners must not be overwhelmed with information (Sweller, 1988). Both are crucial to the unique needs of large online courses.

The Community of Inquiry Model

The community of inquiry (CoI) conceptual framework (Garrison et al., 2001) suggests that students' educational experience in online and blended courses is a combination of cognitive presence, teaching presence, and social presence. The CoI framework is based on collaborative constructivism and meaningful approaches to learning (Garrison & Archer, 2000). This approach touts the importance of incorporating higher-order learning where learners are engaged in active learning and critical thinking activities. The overlap of the three main elements of the framework (cognitive, teaching, and social presence) demonstrate the "dynamics of deep and meaningful online learning experiences" (Garrison et al., 2010, p. 32). In the CoI framework social, teaching and cognitive presences interact with each other and can enhance engagement and interaction in the online classroom.

The cognitive aspect of the COI framework in the course is focused on the course content, learning outcomes, and philosophical inquiry. It emphasizes the learning and inquiry process that is inherent in any coursework. Cognitive presence includes problem definition, exploration for relevant information and knowledge, integration of ideas, and testing plausible solutions. It is imperative for instructors of online courses to integrate reflection and discourse, analysis, and synthesis in the course for accomplishing learning outcomes.

Teaching presence in the CoI framework is defined as "the design, facilitation and direction of cognitive and social processes for the purpose of realizing personally meaningful and educationally worthwhile learning outcomes" (Anderson et al., 2001, p. 5). This presence includes curriculum development, content design, and establishing learning activities. Teaching presence also covers monitoring of course activities and managing purposeful collaboration and reflection by which the learning objectives are accomplished through proper instruction, resources, and direction. In the online context, teaching presence involves more than instructor guidance, monitoring, and support. It also includes building online communities through the establishment and maintenance of relationships with learners to promote meaningful learning (Koseoglu & Koutropoulos, 2016).

Social presence is defined as "the ability of participants to identify with the community (e.g., course of study), communicate purposefully in a trusting environment, and develop interpersonal relationships by way of projecting their individual personalities" (Garrison et al., 2010, p. 32). Social presence, which is very much a part of physical classrooms, can be a challenge to incorporate in online classrooms without any visual cues. Yet, literature evidence strongly suggests the importance of building online communities of learners to obtain the education experience. Garrison et al. (2010) state that the social presence aspect could be a mediating variable between teaching presence and cognitive presence as it is part of the responsibility of teaching presence and a condition for creating cognitive presence through collaborative inquiry.

Teaching presence underscores the importance of the teacher in the cognitive as well as the social aspects of the class. Teachers can make their classes engaging and interesting by designing their courses to address both the cognitive and social needs of the learners. By doing so, teaching presence can be felt in how the course was designed not only to meet the curriculum but also to meet the learning objectives and accomplishing the skill sets. Previous research by Swan (2001) finds that the "clarity of design, interaction with instructors, and active discussion among course participants significantly influenced students' satisfaction and perceived learning" (p. 306). Additionally, teaching presence has been found to increase student learning and build communities of online learners. Bezboruah (2019) conducted a case study on teaching presence in both cognitive learning and social presence and found that learners in the two graduate classes were more engaged in the course activities and took a keen interest in their academic performance. Findings also showed that learners gave extra effort to perform well and attended live synchronous sessions with their peers and instructor voluntarily. Finally, the extra effort provided by the instructor through their social presence was appreciated by students as they understood that the instructor gave up part of their weekend (and family time) to assist them with the coursework.

Cognitive Load Theory

Cognitive load theory was developed by John Sweller (1988) and focuses on the constraints of working memory in terms of how information is processed and learned. Working memory plays a significant role in learning. When students must expend extra mental energy focusing on problem-solving beyond what is already known (their prior schema or background knowledge), better information acquisition takes place, according to Sweller. Cognitive load theory is especially important in large online courses as students are often left to their own devices to navigate the course layout, expectations, and to work independently on tasks while staying motivated. When students are spending an inordinate amount of time navigating a confusing course layout or reading lengthy amounts of text, for instance, they are spending less time learning content and material.

RESEARCH ON LARGE ONLINE COURSES

We summarize key recent research relating to empirical studies of large online courses. These studies include collaboration, self-regulated learning, reducing cognitive load, and the use of predictive analytics. This type of research is essential in fostering student engagement when the instructor cannot monitor or provide oversight for individual students due to the large class size.

Collaboration in Online and Large Online Courses

While physical classrooms provide the ability for socialization and community building among students and between students and instructors, online classrooms are not able to facilitate collaborations without the initiative and support of the instructor. The instructor not only provides and facilitates the cognitive aspect of the course, but also is critical for designing coursework that engages and builds communities of online students (Bezboruah, 2019; Northrup, 2001). In essence, pedagogy determines the level of interaction and student achievement of academic and learning goals. The CoI framework underscores the importance of the teaching, cognitive, and special presence in students' educational experiences in online courses.

Research on this framework has shown that the teacher facilitates both the cognitive and social presences through their pedagogy (Conrad, 2005; Nagel & Kotze, 2009). Especially in large online courses, teachers can integrate tools and techniques to foster collaboration among students and build online communities for teamwork and problem solving. Studies also suggest that provision of additional resources within the learning management system (LMS), regular constructive feedback from instructors and peers, peer evaluations, strong course design, teacher's cognitive and social presence, and advanced planning and course management (Bezboruah, 2019; Garrison et al., 2001; Nagel & Kotze, 2009; Swan et al., 2000) can result in the accomplishment of learning outcomes in large online courses.

Interventions and Instruction in Large Online Courses

Recent extant literature on teaching online suggests that (a) meeting the needs of online learners with a focus on the idea that standardization of course design can reduce the cognitive load for online learners and (b) increasing teacher presence (Garrison & Cleveland-Innes, 2005) in the course as well as external regulation (e.g., reminders, email nudges, and strong support for assignment directions) and fostering of self-regulated learners to guide large classes. The teacher has a strong role to play in supporting online learners through strategic course design as well as structuring course activities to guide collaborative learning endeavors. For example, Gašević et al. (2015) found that externally regulated scaffolding facilitated an online learner's cognitive presence in online discussions.

Self-regulated learning approaches, based on recent MOOC research, can help teachers support online learners in large classes through a specific structure such as course content, assessment, and learner control, even in a self-paced learning environment (e.g., Jung et al., 2019). They suggest that it is especially the case that older students have a stronger sense of lifelong learning and may be able to have a stronger sense of control over their learning. Wong et al. (2019) found in a meta-analysis of studies related to self-regulated learning in MOOCs that adapting instruction to diverse learner needs emerged as a finding. They suggest a multifaceted approach to meeting different learning needs, not a monolithic one-size-fits all design: "A singular approach to support SRL might not be as effective as approaches that are adapted for different needs (e.g., deploying generic or direct prompt depending on learner's level of expertise)" (p. 368).

Learning analytics also have an impact on facilitating such feedback for students in online courses. Lim et al. (2021) found that learning analytics can be used to provide targeted feedback for students, resulting in higher achievement. It also provided an opportunity to use data from the learners to structure personalized email support. The authors state:

> Data can be in the form of log data; mid-term quiz marks; attendance in face-to-face sessions, that serve as learner operations relevant to the course. *OnTask* provides an interface to transform these data into different rules for

email generation, thereby providing personalised feedback from the instructor for each student based on their own learner data. (p. 3)

Additionally, messages can include a call to action with links as part of the feedback. Research by Iraj et al. (2020) suggests this results in higher success in the course. In their research, the researchers drew on aspects of successful digital marketing and sending customized messaging to students. They examined how messaging and feedback to students using technology-based calls-to-action impacted student learning and perception of the feedback for 218 students in a large undergraduate online introductory science course. The researchers found that students who engaged with feedback messages early in the course were more successful in finishing the course indicating that early course engagement is potentially impactful.

SUGGESTIONS FOR INSTRUCTORS AND INSTRUCTIONAL DESIGNERS

In this section, we build on aspects of the research base about teaching large online classes, with the proviso that faculty can still provide opportunities for collaboration, personalized learning through structured virtual outreach, messaging, and communications, and structured learning through efforts to reduce cognitive load on the online learners. Practical suggestions for teaching large online classes focus on enhanced collaboration amongst students to foster personalized learning as well as combining both uses of synchronous and asynchronous aspects of the class. Such approaches foster student engagement.

Enhancing Collaboration Within Large Online Classes

Some strategies of how collaboration can be enhanced online are as follows:

1. Instructors' pedagogy can direct the course design. When the design is strong and clear, students feel more confident about taking the course. For online community building, instructors must push students beyond their comfort zones to work in virtual teams to problem solve in a collaborative manner. While there might be some initial reservations, most students work very well in teams. In addition, programs such as public affairs and literacy studies are largely competency-based. As such, working in virtual teams and

virtual problem solving and presenting findings are within the competencies expected of new graduates in these fields.
2. Learning objectives and outcomes must be clearly defined and courses that have a variety of activities to meet the stated objectives often have the most learning outcomes. Students learn best through hands-on experiences. Thus, having experiential projects, case studies, and simulations that are conducted in teams helps to foster collaboration and community building. The instructions for such activities must be clear and well planned for these activities to be successful.
3. Discussion boards are also a great way to build community. Having a question and answer forum and a social discussion board (i.e., "virtual water cooler") within the learning management system (LMS) encourages students to post queries either about the course or if they need help with something else related to the course. This could include help from peers in finding a resource from the library website, or peers critiquing their work prior to submission.
4. Regular communication from the instructor through weekly course announcements help to instill a sense of belonging and care for the students. Often online learning is a solitary exercise and having regular communication from the instructor helps to connect with the coursework. Most LMSs provide reminders regarding assignments and "to-dos." Additionally, a reminder from the instructor via email or announcement feature of the LMS helps with motivating the students to complete the work.
5. Having some synchronous sessions in a typically asynchronous online class helps to enhance interaction and engagement among students. While synchronous sessions could be challenging to schedule or manage in large online classes, having one at the beginning of the term helps to set the stage. Although there might be many students missing, the session could be recorded and posted for later viewing. In order to increase participation and engagement, instructors can use icebreakers, games, activities, and questions to start the session. Each session must be structured, so students do not feel that that wasted time, but received something valuable and meaningful.
6. Finally, consider having students incorporate their social media curation into the discussion board in the learning management system, as Matrix (2014) suggests as a way to integrate what students are curating professionally on their own into the more structured LMS.

Virtual Outreach for Fostering of Self-Regulated Learners

As noted earlier, recent empirical research on large online courses suggests that predictive analytics can serve as a critical resource for large scale online courses (e.g., Lim et al., 2021), "big data" sources such as predictive analytics software can be used to analyze and track student engagement in the course to see who may benefit from more focused and carefully crafted email from the instructor to help the student reach a specific customized learning outcome. Based on this data, strategic customized and personalized emails can be sent out via email using specific software systems to groups of students, such as those who are less engaged in the course to remind them to stay on track with course content and assignments. Software such as Civitas® Inspire for Faculty is a productive tool to determine student engagement with the learning management system as well as preexisting data such as GPA, and other quantitative factors which may predict student success in the course. Such data can be used to send students nudging emails to foster student responsibility for their own learning (e.g., Fritz, 2017). Examples of nudge email messaging might include targeted language such as the following for helping students to be successful in large online or blended courses:

- encouragement to the student to interact with the course materials and content to stay a self-regulated learner;
- motivation to stay part of a learning community in the course, thus fostering a Community of Inquiry (Garrison et al., 2001); and
- nudges to click on specific links and calls to action (e.g., as suggested by Iraj et al., 2020).

An example of a nudge email that was sent to a student with very low engagement with the learning management system is below. As Iraj et al. (2020) suggest, a call to action with links is included in the email. The name used is a pseudonym.

> Dear Ariel,
>
> I am glad you are in the LIST 4373 course! Can you believe it is already Week 2? How is the class going for you so far? Don't forget I am here if you have any questions about the course. I am very easy to reach via email, direct messaging in Teams, or email via Canvas! I encourage you to continue to check Canvas to interact with the materials. The more you can check out the Canvas course content, the more you will make progress. The Canvas Student mobile app is another way to check on course content and assignments.

Reminders for what is due this week (Week 2):

Review the Studymate glossary terms: [Redacted: URL link to content is here.]

Read the course readings, materials on Canvas, and view the videos and podcasts.

1. Quiz: Module 1 quiz over readings from Module 1 content. (Take Module quiz during Week 2). The quiz window is June 15, 2020 (12:01 a.m.)– June 21, 2020 (11:59 p.m.). Do the practice quiz first.

2. Application Activity #2: Begin reading mini-lesson with objective, instruction, and assessment using gradual release model. Submit post/task by Monday, June 15, 2020 (11:59 pm). Post five+ replies by Friday, June 19, 2020.

3. Video discussion: Submit post/task by Monday, June 15, 2020 (11:59 p.m.). Post five+ replies by Friday, June 19, 2020.

Continue to work in your writing notebook on your own, using the information about the writer's notebook on Canvas in Module 1. This week is brainstorming possible writing topics.

Email me if you have any questions!

Take care,

Dr. Semingson

Steps for using targeted emails based on predictive data from software such as Inspire for Faculty are outlined below:

1. Create a calendar of how often you will use predictive data to send emails to students in the large online course.
2. Decide the focus of the customized email message. For instance, some messages can be general motivational words of encouragement to make better use of the resources in the course and to generally motivate, but other messages might focus on more specific advice and tips depending on which point in the semester it is. Analytics can also track progress over time in the course in terms of engagement and grades so as the semester goes on, more data can inform the messages. Include a call to action with clickable links that will positively impact the success of the student in the course.
3. You can also look for trends in the overall class data in the aggregate (collectively) in the class such as using the heat map to determine overall class engagement. This can be used to inform the instructor's more general email ("group feedback") without naming anyone. This helps the instructor to see at-a-glance, trends in the usage of the learning management system and trends over time.

4. Be ready to respond to student replies to the targeted email to create a more personalized connection with the student.

Strategies for Reducing Cognitive Load in Large Online Courses

Cognitive load theory suggests that students should not be overwhelmed with information that adds to the amount of information they must process. The key to designing online courses, then, is to focus on standardizing the basic course design so that the module content is organized in the same way within the course across courses. Not having to navigate a new course organization that is counter to what students may expect in a course helps to reduce cognitive load. Key ways to do this are listed below:

1. If the large course is part of a bigger degree program, consider standardizing the format of the course (such as making all content modular with the same appearance, look, and location of basic materials).
2. Use step-by-step instruction to add clarity in navigating the course. Requiring students to review the instructions in the first week of the class prepares them for the rest of the term.
3. Consistency in organization and layout of course within the learning management system is important. It also helps to use templates for consistency in structure for learning tasks like the discussion board.

Caveats and Considerations

Not all these structural and instructional changes can be made at the individual course level to better support large online courses. To implement large-scale change such as a powerful predictive analytics tool requires the purchase of a significant tool and/or to make use of built-in software analytics tools in the learning management system. We encourage instructors and designers of large online and blended courses to investigate which integrated analytics tools are built into their learning management and to engage in dialogue with colleagues about how this data can be used for course improvement and also program improvement. Also, considerations for standardizing courses to reduce cognitive load could be a dialogue that takes place at the program or degree level and can involve multiple stakeholders such as instructional design specialists and multiple instructors. We encourage such dialogue and knowledge sharing to better meet the challenges of teaching large online courses.

Recommendations and Future Research

Instructors in large online classes often encounter challenges in implementing all three dimensions of the CoI framework—teaching, social, and cognitive—in their course design (Flock, 2020; Shea & Bidjerano, 2012) and knowing their role in the process. Instructors need to find a balance in their teaching pedagogy and incorporate these dimensions during the design, development, and planning phases of the course. Having an understanding of the alignment between course learning objectives and student success, instructors can prepare the course to incorporate activities that enhance social and cognitive aspects through their teaching. Social presence activities could include opportunities for students to work collaboratively in small groups, discussion boards to share students' personal interests and professional aspirations, developing icebreakers for student engagement and interaction, among others (Flock, 2020). Cognitive presence should focus on content that is delivered in small chunks in video format to provide students to better understand the materials, conduct asynchronous teaching using interactive activities, quizzes, and Easter egg hunts to keep students' focus intact. Having synchronous instruction or interactive sessions with the instructor can assist with teaching presence and student retention and success (Bezboruah, 2019). We provide additional suggestions in Table 2.1.

While the above practices can be used effectively to increase student learning outcomes, more research is needed to understand how other external factors have an impact on student success. For example, during the COVID-19 pandemic, higher education institutions globally have transitioned to online instruction to continue to meet the educational needs of their students. In this case, it is important to explore how the mental anxiety caused by the pandemic impacts instructors and students alike and how the CoI framework can be modified or revised to include the mental and emotional needs. Additionally, future research can examine what entails student success—is its academic achievement through online courses, or does it also include behavioral aspects for students in large online classes. For example, how students interact during video conferencing, participation in group activities, and engagement in the content.

FUTURE DIRECTIONS AND RESEARCH

For future research recommendations to cognitive load theory, Community of Inquiry and teaching online courses, we recommend the following suggestions. While the above practices can be used effectively to increase student learning outcomes, more studies and research are needed to understand how other external factors have an impact on student success.

TABLE 2.1 Recommendations Based on Best Practices Including Features of CoI Framework and Cognitive Load Theory

CoI Framework	Instructional Activities Examples	Incorporation by Instructors	Supportive Ideas From Cognitive Load Theory
Cognitive	• Content designed with interactive activities • Content aligned with learning objectives and deliverables • Content categorized into small manageable chunks for better absorption • Expectations for students and instructor clearly outlined in the syllabus	• Course design and development phase • Refine and revise based on student feedback and self-reflection	• Provide video-based overview tutorials to help students navigate the tasks and assignments (e.g., screen casting with instructor thinking aloud) • Chunk content into microcontent and microlearning so students can process information in shorter working memory rather than lengthy content
Teaching	• Instructor presence through regular communication using discussion boards, announcements, and emails • Response by the instructor to student queries within a specific time • Having virtual office hours to meet with students • Sending "nudge" emails prior to exams and major deliverables to assuage students' stress and anxiety.	• Planning phase of course • Weekly schedules for sending announcements and emails • Weekly virtual office hours to connect with students	• Provide an overview video from the instructor about success tips for the course • Include ways the student can seek help when feeling confused or lost in the course (e.g., email, virtual office hours, etc.) • Avoid long or lengthy videos or podcasts or use of a "wall of text"
Social	• Course activities designed to enhance collaboration among students • Discussion boards designed to facilitate and share personal interests and professional aspiration • Short videos by the instructor that covers the major points of each week's content • Small group activities for enhanced interaction and engagement among students and collaborative learning	• Course design and planning phase • Maintaining regular presence by the instructor	• Provide tips and explicit guidance of what social interaction will "look like" for live sessions (e.g., visual display of the live learning environment) • Provide tips and guidance for what effective discussion boards look like with specific examples of effective posts and replies. • Rubrics can also provide guidance to streamline student's ability to not be overwhelmed by expectations for asynchronous discussions.

Further research could also look at access and equity issues in large online classes from factors such as having access to high-speed Internet services, accessing the content to examining equitable outreach by higher education institutions, and democratization of education access through the internet.

Regarding cognitive load theory, research should be done to examine student perception of cognitive load across various learning management system platforms and across mobile learning contexts. What can be done by instructors to further reduce cognitive load across platforms and devices for students? What types of professional development are needed at a systems level to develop instructor and instructional designer knowledge about cognitive load and also the robust CoI model? What tools can be effectively used to reduce cognitive load in terms of using predictive analytics software in order to send customized nudge emails to guide and support students?

CONCLUSION

In this chapter, we draw on recent literature as well as our own experience teaching large online courses at a large urban public university. Faculty teaching large online or blended courses should not be intimidated by the challenge of providing personalized instruction and interaction with large-sized courses. The framework of the CoI provides guidance towards structuring collaborative working groups within larger courses to create a small course feel and abilities for students to partner with one another. Drawing on cognitive load theory (Sweller, 1988) and research, students in large online or blended courses will be able to navigate the course structure by drawing on salient directions and step-by-step guidance from the instructor. Indeed, cognitive load theory intersects with the notion of teacher presence from the CoI model (Garrison et al., 2000) and that the instructor's role is to support students as they navigate learning and the online course. Overall, we suggest not bombarding students with too many twists and turns with online courses. In this way, expectations for students are crystal clear, the layout is predictable, and students can spend more time in dialogue; engaging with peers, the instructor, and the content; and with learning.

REFERENCES

Anderson, T., Rourke, L., Garrison, R., & Archer, W. (2001). Assessing teaching presence in a computer conferencing context. *Journal of Asynchronous Learning Networks, 5*(2), 1–17.

Arbaugh, J. B., & Benbunan-Finch, R. (2005). Contextual factors that influence ALN effectiveness. In S. R. Hiltz & R. Goldman (Eds.), *Learning together online:*

Research on asynchronous learning networks (pp. 123–144). Lawrence Erlbaum Associates, Inc.

Bezboruah, K. C. (2019). Live sessions and accelerated online project-based courses. In J. Yoon & P. Semingson (Eds.), *Educational technology and resources for synchronous learning in higher education* (pp. 23–55). IGI Global.

Conrad, D. (2005). Building and maintaining community in cohort-based online learning. *Journal of Distance Education, 20*(1), 1–20.

Flock, H. (2020). Designing a community of inquiry in online courses. *International Review of Research in Open and Distributed Learning, 21*(1), 134–142. https://doi.org/10.19173/irrodl.v20i5.3985

Fritz, J. (2017). Using analytics to nudge student responsibility for learning. *New Directions for Higher Education, 2017*(179), 65–75. https://doi.org/10.1002/he.20244

Garrison, D. R., Anderson, T., & Archer, W. (1999). Critical inquiry in a text-based environment: Computer conferencing in higher education. *The Internet and Higher Education, 2*(2/3), 87–105.

Garrison, D. R., Anderson, T., & Archer, W. (2001). Critical thinking, cognitive presence, and computer conferencing in distance education. *American Journal of Distance Education, 15*(1), 7–23.

Garrison, D. R., & Archer, W. (2000). *A transactional perspective on teaching-learning: Framework for adult and higher education.* Pergamon.

Garrison, D. R., & Cleveland-Innes, M. (2005). Facilitating cognitive presence in online learning: Interaction is not enough. *American Journal of Distance Education, 19*(3), 133–148.

Garrison, D. R., Cleveland-Innes, M., & Fung, T. S. (2010). Exploring causal relationships among teaching, cognitive and social presence: Student perceptions of the community of inquiry framework. *The Internet and Higher Education, 13*(1/2), 31–36.

Gašević, D., Adesope, O., Joksimović, S., & Kovanović, V. (2015). Externally-facilitated regulation scaffolding and role assignment to develop cognitive presence in asynchronous online discussions. *The Internet and Higher Education, 24*, 53–65.

Iraj, H., Fudge, A., Faulkner, M., Pardo, A., & Kovanović, V. (2020,). Understanding students' engagement with personalised feedback messages. In *Proceedings of the tenth international conference on learning analytics & knowledge* (pp. 438–447). Association for Computing Machinery.

Jung, E., Kim, D., Yoon, M., Park, S., & Oakley, B. (2019). The influence of instructional design on learner control, sense of achievement, and perceived effectiveness in a supersize MOOC course. *Computers & Education, 128*(1), 377–388.

Koseoglu, S., & Koutropoulos, A. (2016, May 9–11). *Teaching presence in MOOCs: Perspectives and learning design strategies* [Paper presentation]. 10th International Conference on Networked Learning 2016, Lancaster, PA.

Lim, L.-A., Gentili, S., Pardo, A., Kovanović, V., Whitelock-Wainwright, A., Gašević, D., & Dawson, S. (2021). What changes, and for whom? A study of the impact of learning analytics-based process feedback in a large course. *Learning & Instruction, 72*. https://doi.org/10.1016/j.learninstruc.2019.04.003

Matrix, S. (2014, January 1). Using the LMS as a social network in a supersized course. *Educause.* https://er.educause.edu/blogs/2014/1/using-the-lms-as-a-social-network-in-a-supersized-course

Nagel, L., & Kotzé, T. G. (2009) Supersizing e-learning: What a CoI survey reveals about teaching presence in a large online class. *The Internet and Higher Education, 13*(1/2), 45–51. https://www.sciencedirect.com/science/article/pii/S1096751609000736

Newton, D. (2020, June 28). Online college classes should have no more than 12 students. *Forbes.* https://www.forbes.com/sites/dereknewton/2020/06/28/online-college-classes-should-have-no-more-than-12-students/#6a876a4d3179

Northrup, P. (2001). A framework for designing interactivity in web-based instruction. *Educational Technology, 41*(2), 31–39.

Prusko, P. T., Robinson, H., Kilgore, W., & Al-Freih, M. (2020). From design to impact: A phenomenological study of human MOOC participants' learning and implementation into practice. *Online Learning, 24*(2).

Shea, P., & Bidjerano, T. (2012). Learning presence as a moderator in the community of inquiry model. *Computers & Education, 59*(2), 316–326.

Swan, K., Shea, P. J., Fredericksen, E. E., Pickett, A. M., & Pelz, W. E. (2000, October 30–November 4). *Course design factors influencing the success of online learning* [Paper presentation]. WebNet 2000 World Conference on the WWW and Internet, San Antonio, TX.

Swan, K. (2001). Virtual interaction: Design factors affecting student satisfaction and perceived learning in asynchronous online courses. *Distance Education, 22*(2), 306–331.

Sweller, J. (1988). Cognitive load during problem solving: Effects on learning. *Cognitive Science, 12*, 257–285.

Tomei, L. A., & Nelson, D. (2019). The impact of online teaching on faculty load–revisited: Computing the ideal class size for traditional, online, and hybrid courses. *International Journal of Online Pedagogy and Course Design (IJOPCD), 9*(3), 1–12.

Wong, J., Baars, M., Davis, D., Van Der Zee, T., Houben, G. J., & Paas, F. (2019). Supporting self-regulated learning in online learning environments and MOOCs: A systematic review. *International Journal of Human–Computer Interaction, 35*(4/5), 356–373.

CHAPTER 3

BUILDING A BETTER LARGE BLENDED COURSE

Jami Nininger
Mount Carmel College of Nursing

Miriam R. Abbott
Mount Carmel College of Nursing

ABSTRACT

The development and successful execution of large blended courses requires adherence to best practices across a variety of course delivery systems. As a foundation, clear definitions of the expectations associated with "blended learning" are considered. Such definitions assist in the identification of appropriate contexts for the implementation of large blended courses. Successful implementation begins at the point of course design and employing evidence-based standards to design features. Appropriate integration of instructional tools and the development and disclosure of sound course policies provide support for design. Given the foundation of sound course design, successful execution depends largely on faculty preparation and training in best practices for course facilitation.

To facilitate clarity in any discussion, it is helpful to begin with an understanding of the terminology used. Certainly, this truth applies when establishing a framework for developing large blended courses. The term "large" is generally a relative term. For an instructor of a composition course, wherein learners compose multiple lengthy essays, 40 students in a section would be dauntingly "large." Then again, for a course wherein all assessments are objective multiple-choice exams, "large" might be more aptly applied when enrollment exceeds 100 students. The term "large" will be admittedly slippery in many academic contexts.

In describing learning formats, the term "blended" (or "hybrid") is broad and slippery as well. In contrast, online and face-to-face delivery formats are fairly narrowly defined. Online students can expect virtual classrooms and asynchronous activities. Face-to-face students can expect traditional classrooms and synchronous activities. A blended course integrates elements from both delivery formats. The proportion of time devoted to each delivery platform, however, can have great variance. One blended course may feature weekly class meetings, another may meet only two to three times per semester.

With this very basic understanding of terminology in hand, two questions then arise: "Why offer large blended courses?" and "How should they be developed?" As may be anticipated, the answer to the first question will shape our answer to the second question.

DESIGN ELEMENTS OF A SUCCESSFUL BLENDED COURSE

Why Offer Large Blended Courses?

Large blended courses are well-suited to address a growing number of institutional and student needs in the academic community. Approximately 70% of today's college students balance class participation with employment opportunities (St. Amour, 2019) and 25% of college students are parents with dependent children (Berman, 2017). Competing obligations from family and workplace make online coursework highly desirable for students seeking to register for courses. Flexible online offerings are therefore growing in popularity.

However, it's not clear that online delivery is the best platform across the board. Skill and lab-based content may be better-suited for traditional delivery. Guaranteeing the integrity of testing and assessment is often easier and more affordable in live classrooms. It has been proposed that online courses are associated with higher rates of failure, and in general, if not well managed by faculty, may be deficient in providing satisfying student-instructor interaction (Fain, 2019). In fact, the 90% dropout rate in MOOCs (massive open online courses) has been attributed to the lack of instructor engagement (Singh, 2019). In large courses, the task of maintaining meaningful student-faculty interaction can be insurmountable if not well-managed.

Large blended courses, then, are well-situated to offer students and faculty the best of both worlds; improved scheduling flexibility for students, while facilitating more synchronous student-instructor interaction. Successful development of a large blended course will require more than "scaling up." Facilitating student engagement in a course with high enrollment requires careful planning and consideration. What determines a large blended course's success in bridging this gap, is a matter of design, instructor preparation, and institutional support.

Evidence-Based Design Standards

Strong blended courses are built using consistent, evidence-based standards of design that facilitate active learning implementation. Faculty and administration hold accountability for leveraging evidence-based standards to guide course design and implementation and the accompanying student support structures. Design standards determine how the course is built, but must be coupled with evidence-based teaching practices or instructional styles that facilitate meaningful learning, interaction, and active learner engagement. Course design standards may be identified independently by institutions. Alternately, standards established by businesses and governmental organizations may influence design and implementation approaches.

Organizations, such as Quality Matters and the Online Learning Consortium, also provide clear guidance on the design of online courses. While standards for traditional courses may be familiar to faculty, online standards and the integration of related structures may be weak spots. As such, design and implementation standards for blended courses can serve as valuable guides for the development of blended courses that foster active learner engagement.

Institutional Definitions

Because large blended courses may take on a multitude of formats, institutions should take the lead in identifying the basic defining characteristics of the blended courses within its curriculum. Such a definition process ensures transparency for both faculty and for an evolving student population that may have obligations that create obstacles to attending traditional face-to-face courses. While not as flexible as online courses, typical blended courses host fewer synchronous activities than traditional face-to-face courses, and thus offer students more scheduling flexibility. For example, one institutional definition might read as follows:

> A blended course is a course that replaces 30% to 70% of in-class-time with teaching and learning strategies that are appropriate for facilitating learning in the context of online delivery.

Armed with such a definition, both faculty and students have an understanding of the boundaries and expectations regarding class meetings and online activities. Further, the institution may choose to dictate a number of times, frequency, or duration that a large blended course meets during a term. The institution should also identify, at the point of registration, the times that students are expected to be engaged in synchronous activities.

In identifying defining characteristics of large online, blended, and traditional seated classrooms, institutions would be well-served to establish distinctions between the characteristics of a blended classroom and characteristics of a flipped classroom. A flipped classroom is an interactive student-centered approach that can be used in any face-to-face classroom. Generally, a flipped classroom permits reading materials and lectures to be available outside of class meeting time, and the synchronous sessions are student-centered and steeped in activities that promote active learning (Devraj et al., 2010). Certainly, some aspects of the flipped classroom are well-suited for implementation in the larger blended course. The practice of making video lectures available outside of synchronous meetings permits the instructor to dedicate synchronous class time to activities that engage students in active learning events. As engagement in larger online courses is traditionally a challenging task, the flipped model creates additional time for active learning and two-way interaction with the instructor.

In blended course offerings, faculty leverage the benefits of both the online and the seated classrooms to drive active learning within the course. For example, in-class activities may include infused lecture elements amidst case studies or other problem-based formats, and online activities may include a variety of asynchronous student-led events, including group projects, discussions, and interactive lessons.

Consistency

The standards and expectations applied to large blended courses must be consistent with standards applied to both online and face-to-face courses. This establishes a predictable pattern and protocol, a characteristic valued by students, and higher education accreditors. For instructors of online courses, the importance of establishing consistency in instructional design has been an element of discussion established in the literature for some time. Faculty accustomed to teaching in traditional seated classrooms who wish to transition to blended delivery may be uncertain of both the importance of consistency in creating online presence and its foundations for student learning, as well as how to achieve it.

To achieve consistency, several paths may be pursued. At many institutions, an instructional design team is responsible for building online courses across the curriculum. While this model may operate at the expense of some level of academic freedom for faculty, the institution is assured that all courses will demonstrate consistency in vocabulary, organization, and navigation options. Alternatively, a design template such as the one illustrated (see Figure 3.1) may be distributed to faculty to guide independent course development while facilitating design consistency.

When faculty follow similar organizational patterns, students are better set for success in course navigation and resource findability. As in the illustration, instructional materials for each module are found in a consistent area. Similarly, action items would be consistently identified in the "To Do List" section within each module. A program that uses template-based independent design for online design in large blended courses can benefit from quality assurance auditing or in-house approval processes prior to course launch. Such approval processes may require:

- instructor training for blended/online design and delivery
- standards that will guide course design
- course reviews by institutionally designated auditors
- support from academic leaders and faculty

Such an approval process ensures that the course is designed to meet its objectives, and that the instructor is prepared for successful course delivery.

Figure 3.1   A design template example.

In practice, consistency within an institution means that students will know where to go to find a syllabus, policies, assignments, and deadlines in any classroom. Consistency is valuable not only in the online and blended worlds, but in face-to-face delivery as well.

Design Elements of a Large Hybrid Course

With a clear understanding of the demands for consistency in course design, a large blended course may pair its live meetings with several online features designed to support and promote student engagement. In a review of six widely used evaluation instruments for online course design, Baldwin et al. (2018) identified design characteristics that were valued across all instruments. In general, the investigated instruments all emphasize clear statements of course objectives, a foundational value for courses that use any delivery platform.

Valued characteristics that are unique to online and blended courses include intuitive navigation that facilitates resource findability. Students can be primed for successful course navigation through orientation programs, and consistent patterns of content delivery. Within a large blended course, these characteristics are manifested at the point of design. General characteristics that are also valued are:

- technology that promotes learner engagement,
- activities that build community and interaction,
- clearly stated standards for behavior and communication,
- transparency in grading practices (rubrics), and
- providing points of contact for both the professor and institutional services (Baldwin et al., 2018).

Student Orientation

To ensure a foundation for learner familiarity with the digital architecture of the course and the clarity of expectations for learning in the course, every blended course should begin with a student orientation. Differentiation of expectations and learning must be explicit as it relates to face-to-face and online learning within the course. Within the context of large courses, such orientation is especially essential: When a firm foundation for success is established for all students, this reduces the number of questions from individuals.

A course orientation is most engaging for students when provided through a video or by using voice-over-screen tools such as Screencost-O-Matic™, particularly if the student's initial encounter with the course will not be held synchronously or face-to-face. The foundation of the orientation assures that students are provided with resources that support student success and confidence in course navigation, access to support resources, course materials, and gaining familiarity with the overall expectations for learning for the course. Within the context of a large blended course, asynchronous orientation can serve two functions:

- It provides orientation at a time that meets a myriad of student scheduling needs.
- It provides an opportunity for the learner to revisit and review more than one time, thereby stemming the tide of student questions.

It is helpful for institutions to provide faculty with customizable orientation packages or templates that address these essential elements. Course orientation templates then promote consistency in orientation approaches within courses and ensure that all topics foundational to student success are addressed.

Discussion Boards versus Engagement Spaces

Most learning management systems (LMS) boast capabilities for supporting discussion forums. Online discussion boards are frequently used tools in both face-to-face and online courses. They have played a celebrated role in fostering student engagement (Ni, 2018). Although often approached as a text-based tool, discussion boards can serve as an interactive space providing large blended courses with a technology platform that builds engagement and community (Riggs & Linder, 2016). Within a large blended classroom, discussion boards with hundreds of responses can detract from the overall value of the interactive exercise. Moreover, using only a text-based approach in the discussion platform may influence instructor presence in courses with large enrollment. As such, innovation in the use of discussion platforms as engagement spaces establishes a foundation for active learning for students and effective management and presence for faculty.

Beyond the text-based interactions hosted within discussion platforms, the technology effectively supports media integration, often without the need for additional software or hardware. Faculty can leverage the range of media supported within the technology to craft learning interaction that extends beyond the traditional "discussion" approach. The rich tools contained within the discussion platform of most LMSs support use of the digital as for presentations whereby students post videos, create interactive pages, engage in small group work and even engage in reflection. In courses where large enrollments exist, active learning activities beyond all text-based interaction promote learner engagement with peers and cultivates a means by which faculty can establish a presence and facilitate learning effectively and efficiently.

Despite the chosen approach for the utilization of discussion platforms, for large enrollment blended courses faculty must strategize the management of the activity considering elements of learning facilitation, instructor presence, and outcome evaluation. Strategies for managing such activities for large enrollment courses include, but are not limited to,

1. assigning discussions to smaller subgroup discussion boards that will provide more meaningful interactions;
2. assigning groups to lead a discussion or activity for larger groups throughout the course;
3. using a combination of small group and whole class activities;
4. summarizing global concepts presented through the engagement spaces to class at the end of the activity (this permits the emphasis of key concepts and an opportunity to clarify misconception);
5. leveraging media to facilitate learning and instructor presence (using video to provide feedback or comments); and
6. remembering that not every activity needs to be graded.

An important reminder in this process of designing large blended enrollment courses is that active learning and learning engagement build knowledge through meaningful interactions. Although learning activities must have relevance and build knowledge toward outcomes achievement, it is important to remember that meaningful learning in itself can be a reward.

Formative Assessment as a Tool for Engagement

The assessment and evaluation of student learning have some broad conceptual applications that apply across learning platforms. However, to be effective, the measures used to evaluate and assess learning must align closely with the goals and outcomes for learning. Moreover, the chosen assessment and evaluation strategy must be appropriate for the platform through which learning is occurring (McDonald, 2014). Both summative and formative assessment of learning can occur in online, classroom, and simulation environments (Davies & Taras, 2016; Lam, 2013; Lock & Johnson, 2015; Oermann et al., 2016).

Formative assessment is used to evaluate student learning to inform the teaching learning process. As such, measures of learning help students and faculty identify areas of strength and weakness relating to concept mastery, which then allows for adjustments in the teaching or learning approach (McDonald, 2014; Poth, 2018). Formative assessments, therefore, do not impact student grades.

In large blended enrollment courses, formative assessments can take the form of self-check quizzes, reflections, interactive games, or case studies or small group collaborations. Course question and answer discussion boards serve as a means of formative assessment, permitting students to ask questions relating to course concepts and implementations that they are struggling with, which allows faculty an opportunity to employ strategies that facilitate student learning and success. The aim of the assessment is the same, to enhance learning through the identification of concept areas of mastery, as well as areas that still need work. Formative assessments in all learning environments can also serve as powerful tools to motivate learner engagement in the process of learning while helping faculty identify areas where student groups require enhanced learning facilitation (Davies & Taras, 2016; McDonald, 2014; Poth, 2018).

Technologies such as NearPod, SoftChalk, and Kahoots are especially useful for providing formative assessment in the large blended classroom. Building objective, self-graded assessments with these tools allows students to independently test themselves and engage in active learning on the topics of study. Feedback, scoring, and redirection on such assessments should be immediate and automated, in order to provide students with a means to learn from mistakes. Delayed feedback in formative assessment jeopardizes student engagement.

Similarly, polling software can be integrated into live lectures to provide students an opportunity for active engagement by responding through their mobile devices. Polling also offers the instructor the ability to assess student comprehension of the materials. The following prompts have been effective in eliciting student responses, and in guiding instructional approach:

- What was the most difficult concept in today's lecture?
- What was the most important concept in today's lecture?
- Pose a question about today's lecture.

Group Projects

Group projects are largely reviled by students. At the same time, group projects are highly valued by educators, and may serve to promote engagement and community in a large blended classroom. Such projects may be executed within the synchronous meetings of large blended courses. Alternately, such projects may be completed asynchronously using applications such as Google Documents. As applied to large blended courses, best practices for successful group projects include:

- identifying distinct duties and/or roles for each member of the group,
- identifying a timeline with periodic progress deadlines before the final submission, and
- identifying a path for peer accountability through progressive and structured demonstration of individual work in group processes.

Assigning presentations as a group project is a common approach. In a large blended course, development of a presentation can be an online activity. Delivery of the presentation can occur during a live class meeting. Particular duties within the project may include:

- finding appropriate sources of information
- translating the sources into a presentation
- formatting the references and citations
- editing the finished project
- presenting the finished project
- submitting individual work toward contributory to the group's project

Each member might be asked to contribute one source of information with a properly formatted reference. Alternatively, formatting might be an appropriate task for one particular member. There are many ways to divide the duties successfully, as long as they are accompanied by a schedule that promotes progress on the overall project. That is, the deadline for finding appropriate sources of information should occur well in advance of the final project deadline. Such sub-deadline scheduling promotes successful collaboration among students who may have divergent working styles as well as competing obligations.

Grading Rubrics

While the former elements of course design have centered around student engagement, within a large blended course, grading rubrics are essential tools for grading written assignments. In any course, grading rubrics promote objectivity and transparency in assessment. In large blended courses, grading rubrics also expedite what can otherwise be an incredibly time-consuming grading process.

Grading rubrics typically appear in two different formats. At the minimalist end, an assignment may issue a rubric with the point breakdown depicted in a list-format. Within the context of a large blended course, however, a more complex rubric is especially useful. Such a rubric model is typically depicted as a table that associates points directly with descriptive characteristics. Assessment then becomes a matter of checking the appropriate boxes.

While instructors may add additional comments, point values are clearly correlated with extended feedback to support student growth and achievement. Such a tool expedites grading, while promoting objectivity in the grader.

Testing

As testing technology evolves, testing itself is changing rapidly at institutions of higher education. Most online learning management systems have embedded applications in which exams may be written, administered, and automatically graded. Additionally, software vendors such as ExamSoft and Examplify provide educators with secure mediums to administer and collect examinations that are completed on students' personal computers and mobile devices. Many institutions host testing centers that facilitate the administration of exams for online and face-to-face students.

Large courses, in all formats, have traditionally relied heavily on objective, multiple choice assessments, accompanied by automated grading. By definition, this format achieves objectivity in grading. Additionally, automation provides students with timely results.

A newer approach in testing has promising applications in large blended courses: two-stage testing. Within the context of a live course meeting, students complete an objective test individually, then break into small groups and complete the test for a second grade, collaboratively (Berrett, 2018). Such an approach not only builds community, it also provides built-in robust feedback in the form of peer review and has been demonstrated to improve student learning.

Course Communication

The success of the aforementioned design features will, in no small part, depend upon the instructor's communication style adopted for the online segments of a blended course. Instructional writing is different from lecturing, it is also distinct from academic writing. It is also critical to communication within the online classroom. Instructional writing is most effective when clear communication is its objective. To that end, those taking on the task of composing online elements should keep the following directives in mind:

- Avoid jargon and complicated sentence structure.
- Write in shorter paragraphs optimized for online reading.
- Create clear distinctions between action items and reading material.
- Use headings and white space to organize text.

A clear plan for communication is essential to the management of large enrollment blended courses; for both students and faculty. To facilitate communication and establish presence and availability to students, it is important to communicate to students the preferred method of communication for the course. In addition to an awareness of the mode of communication, specifying to students the time frames in which they can expect a response to communication and feedback on assignments establishes standards around the flow of communication. Importantly, faculty communication plans must incorporate structures that model what is expected of students and provide students with information through various modalities to ensure the clarity and delivery of information and expectation.

INSTRUCTOR PREPARATION

The success of a large blended course is determined not only by its design, but also by its execution. Preparation for success leading a large blended course will require instructional skills specific to online and face-to-face classrooms. It will also require skills in managing high-enrollment environments.

Consistency, Revisited

Consistency in course design has been highlighted as a desirable quality. Consistency in instructional approach should also be emphasized. Within a large blended course, familiarity with and adherence to classroom and institutional policies becomes paramount, as the consequences of inconsistent compliance may grow well beyond manageability. A lapse in judgement that affects a handful of students is easily addressed. A lapse in judgement that requires correction for 150 individually mismanaged students is a different matter entirely.

Constancy

It is generally recommended practice that instructors check online classrooms and email daily. Even in the context of a course that features live meetings, online instructional presence is valued by students. Such presence does not require hourly vigilance or replies on every discussion post. In a large blended course, such a task would be impossible. What is advised, however, is a strategic approach. For example, the instructor may choose to participate on the discussion board in its initial stages, and then shift to monitoring-facilitating responsibilities as the student community grows more active closer to the deadline.

Feedback and Communication

Providing timely, quality feedback for students enrolled in a large blended course would be a challenging task for any instructor. Time-management skills play a critical role in instructional success. While writing comments on student work is time-consuming, it is also much more engaging than numerical scores alone. Copy–paste comments may save time; however, this approach should be used sparingly and with caution, as students are aware of keyboard functions and their applications which can convey a lack of personalization and engagement.

A template that blends copy–paste and personalization strikes a helpful middle ground. Consider this foundation, using the popular "sandwich" approach:

> You've got a good start on this essay. I like <Insert areas of strength>. You may want to look at <Insert area of weakness>. Once you've mastered that task, we'll be on our way to success.

Alternately, this foundation uses a BLUF (Bottom Line Up Front) approach

> Your <area of weakness> is holding you back here. You demonstrate strengths in <areas of strengths>. I think you can use this feedback to help your strengths shine.

To be sure, a solid grasp on the power of word choice and communication style is an essential skill for an instructor of a large blended course. Every communication is an opportunity to build community, demonstrate instructor engagement, and foster student engagement in a classroom context in which such attributes are not default settings. Guidelines from behavior science suggest that adoption of the following rhetorical devices is helpful:

- use of inclusive first-person plural (we, our);
- use of student names;
- use of positive peer pressure ("87% of our students have already submitted a post");
- direct calls for community action ("Join us as we explore..."); and
- remember the power of video (most learning management systems host video recording which permits time efficiency in providing detailed feedback on assignments).

Grading rubrics, as noted earlier, not only promote objectivity in assessment, they also expedite the grading process. Other recommended approaches may include:

- setting due dates that allow for sufficient time between labor-intensive grading activities; and
- dividing student populations (assign groups), and setting different activity deadlines for each population.

Lifestyle choices, generally, will affect an instructor's success in providing feedback in a timely fashion. Common technology-based detractors such as instant messaging can undermine even the most focused grader. To that end, a successful instructor of a large blended course is an instructor who has access to ample institutional education and support.

INSTITUTIONAL SUPPORT

Institutional support plays a prominent role in the implementation of large blended courses. To support students and instructors in the context of a large blended course, institutions themselves may pursue a variety of paths which include training, peer auditors, and instructional support staff. These supportive structures provide a foundation that bolsters student and instructor success.

Training

Blended instruction requires instructional aptitudes that are not necessarily acquired in face-to-face instruction. Traditional classroom course delivery typically provides some flexibility in how objectives are met: The content of a live class meeting may be fluid, as long as course or unit objectives are met. Because the blended classroom blends traditional and online delivery systems, flexibility is diminished. To ensure consistency and alignment, faculty must plan and organize blended coursework in advance of launching the course. In terms of course preparation, standards for the blended course align closely to standards for online courses. Faculty who transition from traditional teaching environments will therefore require some support during adjustment.

A robust training program that fosters mastery in online pedagogy, as well as familiarity with institutional policies regarding course design and best practices, provides the foundation of support for faculty who wish to use a blended format for course delivery. Keeping in mind the aforementioned discussion regarding consistency, an instructor's mistake in a small classroom may be easily addressed. Inconsistencies and failure to comply with college policy in a larger blended classroom context creates exponentially more problems for both the instructor and the institution itself.

In terms of developing such a training program for faculty, certainly it should include online learning opportunities. Such opportunities provide role modeling for course design and execution. Further, effective training programs will provide faculty opportunities for hands-on engagement in practicing activities such as developing, deploying, and evaluating within a large blended course.

Peer Auditors and Mentors

Having one's work assessed in performance evaluations can be stressful. Peer auditors are well-positioned to identify strengths and areas for development in a less intimidating context. A peer auditing team typically consists of faculty who possess both analytical and interpersonal skills. Given a quality assurance checklist, an auditor can efficiently assess whether a large blended classroom and its respective instructional team are equipped to meet course and institutional objectives. Interpersonal skills guide the auditor to conduct the assessment in a collegial way, while identifying areas for improvement with productive suggestions.

Mentors work much like auditors, in terms of course evaluation and suggestions. Mentors, however, may be empowered to make changes and additions to courses under review. These collegial interventions and assurances can provide faculty with additional support that is sometimes needed.

Instructional Support Team

Most institutions retain technology specialists to assist faculty and students in navigating software applications. Beyond problem-solving, an instructional support team can identify areas for faculty development and help lead innovation in course delivery. Faculty engagement in formal developmental workshops may suffer because of perceived lack of time and energy. Instructional support teams have, in recent years, found alternative modes to foster continuing education, including the production of brief video tutorials for independent viewing. Additionally, short development activities may enhance regular faculty meetings. Consider the following 5-minute additions that add value to faculty meetings:

- a new course tool, demonstrated by a technology specialist;
- a new article about pedagogy, for community reflection; and
- a new grading approach, shared by a faculty member.

Continuous Quality Improvement

The final step in the launch of any project is evaluation and the use of outcome data as a foundation for improvement. Instructors themselves often have a sense of successes and failures as a new course evolves. Students also have a perspective to share about any course. Formative assessments serve as valuable tools to check the pulse of the course as it progresses. Feedback elicited through such assessments allows faculty an opportunity to adjust teaching and learning strategies and clarify concepts or instructions to promote the foundation for student success. Student outcomes and end of course surveys also serve as valuable data sources for evaluating course and teaching effectiveness and for informing refinements for improvement. While the veracity of student evaluations is subject to passionate debate, the perspectives of students should be investigated by faculty when the following observations are frequently noted:

- instructions are unclear
- feedback was missing, not constructive or not timely
- course is disorganized
- faculty was not available

Such concerns directly impact student satisfaction, engagement, and motivation in learning and success in the course. Often these concerns can be directly addressed by revisiting online course design, assignment instructions, and teaching practices.

Although blending traditional and online classrooms can be challenging, faculty who leverage the best of both platforms stand to drive learning that is perceived as meaningful and fulfilling by learners. Certainly, there are more variables for which institutions must account when offering blended courses; particularly when course enrollments are large. At the same time, a blended format can meet student learning needs in ways in which other formats cannot. Used appropriately, live class meetings can support online learning, and online learning can support live class meetings cultivating a true foundation of active learning engagement that drives student success through the motivation for learning.

FUTURE DIRECTIONS AND RESEARCH

While many instructional guidelines for college courses are consistent across the curriculum, the classroom subject will profoundly influence the best practices in delivery of large hybrid courses. Humanities courses are different from engineering courses, and engineering courses are different from nursing courses. Activities such as online discussion may seem valuable in an ethics course, and they may seem less valuable in a trigonometry course. Even within the context of a single-purpose nursing institution, course development practices are adapted to the subject matter. Within the field, new software has emerged to permit students to work with virtual patients in virtual labs. This software creates an opportunity for students in courses with large enrollment to have identical, active learning experiences.

Several recent developments have blurred the lines between online, blended, and traditional classrooms. Colleges increasingly depend upon online LMSs in the delivery of traditional coursework. Many instructors, regardless of course delivery mode, collect, grade, and record student assignments online. Textbooks are available online. Policies and syllabi are widely posted online. Online tools facilitate institutional transparency and communications, and these features are valuable across delivery formats. Further, the recent pandemic has facilitated rapid deployment of both online and blended courses in contexts that had, heretofore, seemed impossible. Lecture halls have moved to internet meeting spaces. There is more emphasis on the written word. There is more emphasis on creating engagement in new spaces with new tools.

The sciences, in particular, have embraced the blended format as a means to team online lectures and materials, with traditional in-person lab opportunities. The disruption associated with the crisis has given rise to a tidal wave of new technologies for enhanced course delivery. Despite these advancements, students continue to articulate a general preference for the humanity of the traditional classroom, and for the level of engagement associated with smaller class sizes. Preferences in delivery formats may change, as technology continues to advance, and faculty and students become more familiar with online learning. The internet has changed the human brain, both in terms of attention span, as well as in terms of social interaction. The student preference for engaged faculty, however, seems unlikely to change. Successful deployment of large, blended courses requires sound design principles, and it requires faculty willingness to be fully present and recognize the humanity in their students. Future research efforts must focus on evolving student learning needs, and tools that can facilitate meaningful instructor engagement with each member of the large blended classroom.

REFERENCES

Baldwin, S., Ching, Y., & Hsu, Y. (2018). Online course design in higher education: A review of national and statewide evaluation instruments. *TechTrends, 62,* 46–57. https://link.springer.com/article/10.1007/s11528-017-0215-z

Berman, J. (2017, August 17). This is what today's college students really look like. *MarketWatch.* https://www.marketwatch.com/story/this-is-what-todays-college-students-really-look-like-2017-08-16

Berrett, D. (2018, April 19). How to turn your exams into learning opportunities. *Chronicle of Higher Education.* https://www.chronicle.com/article/How-to-Turn-Your-Exams-Into/243164

Davies, M. S., & Taras, M. (2016). A comparison of assessment beliefs of science and education lecturers in a university. *Multidisciplinary Journal of Educational Research, 6*(1), 77–99. https://doi.org/10.17583/remie.2016.1766

Devraj, R., Lakesha, B., Gupchup, G., & Poirier, R. Active-learning strategies to develop health literacy knowledge and skills. *American Journal of Pharmaceutical Education, 74*(8), 137. https://doi.org/10.5688/aj7408137

Fain, P. (2019, January 16). Takedown of online education. *Inside Higher Ed.* https://www.insidehighered.com/digital-learning/article/2019/01/16/online-learning-fails-deliver-finds-report-aimed-discouraging

Lam, R. (2013). Formative use of summative tests: Using test preparation to promote performance and self-regulation. *Asia-Pacific Education Research, 22,* 69–78. https://doi.org/10.1007/s40299-012-0026-0

Lock, J., & Johnson, C. (2015). Triangulating assessment of online collaborative learning. *The Quarterly Review of Distance Education, 16*(4), 61–70.

McDonald, M. E. (2014). *The nurse educator's guide to assessing learning outcomes.* Jones & Bartlett Learning.

Ni, A. (2018). Comparing the effectiveness of classroom and online learning: Teaching research methods. *Journal of Public Affairs Education, 19*(2), 199–215. https://www.tandfonline.com/doi/abs/10.1080/15236803.2013.12001730

Oermann, M. H., Edgren, S. K., & Rizzolo, M. A. (2016). Summative simulated-based assessment in nursing programs. *Journal of Nursing Education, 55*(6), 323–328. https://doi.org/10.3928/01484834-20160516-04

Poth, C. (2018). The contributions of mixed insights to advancing technology-enhanced formative assessment within higher education learning environments: An illustrative example. *International Journal of Educational Technology in Higher Education, 15,* Article 9. https://link.springer.com/article/10.1186/s41239-018-0090-5

Riggs, S., & Linder, K. (2016). *Actively engaging students in asynchronous online classes.* IDEA. https://files.eric.ed.gov/fulltext/ED573672.pdf

Singh, H. (2014). What's wrong with MOOCs and why aren't they changing the game in education. *Wired.* https://www.wired.com/insights/2014/08/whats-wrong-moocs-arent-changing-game-education

St. Amour, M. (2019, November 18). Working college students. *Inside Higher Ed.* https://www.insidehighered.com/news/2019/11/18/most-college-students-work-and-thats-both-good-and-bad

CHAPTER 4

USING A BLENDED LEARNING APPROACH IN A LARGE COMMUNITY ENGAGEMENT COURSE

Martina Jordaan
University of Pretoria

Dolf Jordaan
University of Pretoria

ABSTRACT

Teaching a large class requires a lecturer to develop new skills in presenting a blended learning course and to have a physical and a virtual presence for the course outcomes to be achieved. This chapter describes how a community-based course with an annual enrollment of between 1,600 to 1,900 students is facilitated by only one lecturer and one administrative staff member using the university's learning management system, among other forms of educational technology.

Teaching Large Online and Blended Classes, pages 51–70
Copyright © 2022 by Information Age Publishing
www.infoagepub.com
All rights of reproduction in any form reserved.

The community-based project (code: JCP) course of the University of Pretoria (UP), South Africa, is a compulsory undergraduate course of the faculty of Engineering, Built Environment, and Information Technology (EBIT). The main objective of the course is that the community project must have a beneficial impact on a chosen section of society, which must be different from the students' own social background. Through the execution of a project, students must develop an awareness of their personal, social and cultural values, and an attitude that shows that they are willing to serve. The outcomes of the course allow students to gain experience in dealing with a range of social issues associated with community-based projects, to develop skills to communicate effectively, and to work in a multidisciplinary environment to perform critical social upliftment functions. It entails students working for at least 40 hours in the community.

The course was an innovative new endeavour for the faculty in 2005 and was the first of its kind for EBIT students in South Africa. Since community-based learning was not included in existing courses at the time, the establishment of a new, separate, free-standing course was necessary.

Some of the complicating factors were not only to design and develop such a course, taking cognisance of the demanding time schedules of EBIT students, but also to implement a unique learning design by considering the importance of the presence of the lecturer in facilitating the course. To warrant proper assessment and the completion of students' projects, a variety of educational tools are used. Fundamental to these tools is the learning management system (LMS), Blackboard, which facilitates the activities, updates community information, administers group management, and assists with communication and the coordination of projects.

The course begins with an orientation lecture at the University's auditorium. After that, the students book a session on the LMS for their project proposals. During this session, a possible project is discussed in terms of how it will be executed, the community partner to be contacted and the submission of the students' allocated funding. Students then perform various reflective assignments on the LMS, submit their project summaries, final reports and reflection assignments on the LMS, and reflect on their learning experiences via a presentation and a YouTube video.

The learning design of the course includes assessments, experiential learning, and the students' production of learning artifacts. Online assessments such as an assignment on professional etiquette, the concepts of community engagement, gender issues and HIV/Aids in the workplace, and understanding the sustainable development goals are included in the assessment strategy. In addition to authentic learning experiences, the course extends its reach to include alumni who are appointed as mentors or project leaders to monitor projects in the community. While learning analytics is often associated with student success, this chapter exposes through descriptive data from the LMS, the level of teaching presence required to facilitate the course and to manage the logistical administration. Also, the data show that the large community engagement course success requires a level of teaching presence that is not required in pure academic courses.

This chapter provides an overview of the unique learning design and will highlight how the lecturer facilitates a course based on transactional learning analytics data. The success of the course and its blended learning design has been recognized through its receipt of several national and international awards. The course also has a high success rate with respect to student achievement.

Scholarly publications describe blended learning, with its different nuances, as focusing on the integration of contact and noncontact forms of teaching. A common trend in the literature is the variety of definitions of blended learning. For example, the simplistic view of Picciano (2009) suggests that "blended" learning is a contextual combination of teaching modes. Other definitions of blended learning include "the thoughtful combination of instruction from two historically separate models of teaching and learning: traditional face-to-face learning and distributed learning systems" and where learning in a face-to-face mode and online learning are optimally integrated to benefit students (Dziuban et al., 2018; Garrison & Kanuka, 2004; Graham, 2006; Rasheed et al., 2020; Vaughan, 2010).

Subsequently, learners in undergraduate courses seem to benefit more from blended learning than graduate students. Blended learning can be defined according to the relative time spent online and on face-to-face instruction in courses (Means et al., 2013). Thus, where at least 50% of the total course time should be dedicated to face-to-face instruction, this appears to be in the lower limits of in-class modes in the blended learning format. In this case, online learning outside the class (combined with face-to-face) does not exceed 50% of the course time. Face-to-face classroom time can, therefore, be greater than 50% (Bernard et al., 2014).

Garrison and Kanuka (2004) describe a blended learning model as one that requires reconsideration and restructuring of teaching and learning relationships between stakeholders, as evidence shows its positive impact on traditional campus-based institutions of higher education. It can also combine essential reflective elements of teaching with various forms of communication that meet specific learning requirements.

Any blended learning course must focus on the engagement of students through critical discourse and reflection (Vaughan, 2010). Research has shown that blended learning has proved to be efficient for meaningful learning experiences (Garrison & Kanuka, 2004) and to advance students' success and satisfaction (Dziuban et al., 2018). However, the success of a blended learning initiative is linked to institutional support for course design (Dziuban et al., 2018) and the institutional ability to apply actionable insight from the numerous data sources embedded in blended learning applications (Siemens & Long, 2011).

The uptake of data to measure students' activity in online educational technologies, and to report on it to improve the environment and optimize student learning and success, is referred to as learning analytics (Siemens & Long, 2011). Transactional data from the LMS is used to support the blended approach of the macro community-based course as it provides visual evidence of the value of the learning design applied, and the importance of the lecturer's presence to ensure that students achieve the set outcomes of the course.

COMMUNITY ENGAGEMENT AT THE UNIVERSITY OF PRETORIA

South Africa's higher education policy frameworks include several documents that address the role of higher education in the development of social responsibility and economic development in students. "The Education White Paper 3: A Programme for the Transformation of Higher Education" (Department of Education, 1997) laid the foundation for integrating community engagement into teaching, learning, and research in higher education (Erasmus & Van Schalkwyk, 2011). "The White Paper for Post-school Education and Training in South Africa" integrated community engagement into the core domain of higher education (Department of Higher Education and Training, 2013). In answer to the white paper, the Engineering Council of South Africa (ECSA) adhered to the national guidelines by including community engagement as the Exit Level 10 outcome of engineering curricula: engineers function within local, national and global communities, which requires them to act professionally and ethically as responsible citizens (Engineering Council of South Africa, 2014).

The University of Pretoria supports curricular community engagement, and more than 90% of its undergraduate and honors programs have compulsory curricular community engagement embedded in their curricula, for which students earn credits. As a result, graduates develop a sense of social responsibility, respect for human rights and dignity, and exhibit informed civic, cultural, and environmental awareness (University of Pretoria, 2020a).

The Community-Based Project Course

The University of Pretoria developed an undergraduate course, community-based project module (code: JCP) for all undergraduate students in the faculty EBIT. The main objective of the course is that the community project must have a beneficial impact on a chosen section of society, which must be different from the students' own social background. Through the execution of a project, students must develop an awareness of their personal, social, and cultural values and an attitude that shows that they are willing to serve. By implementing these projects, students develop an understanding of the range of social problems in South Africa and globally. Above all, they need to develop vital multidisciplinary life skills such as communication, interpersonal, and leadership skills (Jordaan, 2014).

A critical factor that complicated the initial design and development of the course was the students' demanding academic schedules. Many students are enrolled annually (2019: 1,598 students; 2020: 1,911 students),[1] which necessitates specific logistical, teaching and learning processes. The course enrollment categorizes the course as a large-class course. Large classes and high student–staff ratio are acknowledged challenges facing universities in South-Africa (Tewari & Ilesanmi, 2020). The course is one of eight undergraduate academic courses in the faculty with an enrollment of more than 1,000 students. The one lecturer responsible for the course must manage the students, the community partners, and the projects. The student–staff ratio compelled the faculty to adopt a blended learning model, whereby the students and the lecturer rely on the continuous use of the LMS. Unique to the course's model is the fact that the students have some control over time management, their pace of learning, and the path they follow to achieve the learning outcomes (Jordaan, 2013).

The course is an eight-credit module, where one credit equals 10 notional hours. This implies that students must work in the community for at least 40 hours and be actively engaged in the LMS. They must also be prepared to complete various assignments during the other 40 hours. These assessments include a final presentation, a group report, and a reflective vlog (a YouTube video; Jordaan, 2014).

Students have the option to choose their projects within course-specific criteria, or they may identify a project from the proposed projects identified by the JCP office. The criteria include that the project may not be associated with a specific religion or political party and that students may not earn money while doing the project (Jordaan et al., 2012). Typical projects include building jungle gyms, teaching community members basic computer skills, various renovation and building projects at pre-schools, primary school, secondary school, zoos, and nonsubsidized museums.

Various community partners identify possible projects, which the lecturer approves before sharing them with students in the LMS. The students also have the option to identify their own projects. An on-site supervisor checks the students' hours, signs off on the completion of the project, and assesses the students according to the module outcomes. Where there is no community supervisor available, a student mentor or a student project leader is appointed to fulfill these duties. Former JCP students can become mentors or project leaders. These students or alumni assist with the assessment of the students and check the students' log hours. Examples of such projects are the development of a local public community park or computer training for the community (Jordaan & Mennega, 2019).

Blended Learning at the University of Pretoria

The success of a blended learning strategy relies on its alignment with the goals and outcomes of the institution's teaching and learning strategy (Moskal et al., 2013) and how it relates to the institution's graduate attributes. The University of Pretoria has followed a blended learning model since 1998, in which the Blackboard Learn LMS (branded as clickUP) is core to an integrated educational technology ecosystem. The ecosystem includes Blackboard Mobile applications, Blackboard Collaborate, and data technologies to support the students' learning experience. The University's blended learning model provides lecturers with the opportunity to combine the best of contact and online delivery modes for teaching purposes. Therefore, it converges learning environments to engage students actively in different authentic learning environments, such as curriculum-orientated community engagement projects. With more than 2 decades of blended learning at UP, the instructional model and ownership of the learning process have shifted to include students taking ownership of their learning and success. This implies an education philosophy of inclusive education where both affluent students and first-generation students are granted opportunities to achieve similar institutional student graduate attributes, which includes service to their community (University of Pretoria, 2020d).

The Facilitation Role of the Lecturer

The community of inquiry (CoI) framework offers an acknowledged collaborative constructivist foundation to analyze the contribution of lecturers through their teaching presence. It aims to show the integration of teaching presence with social presence and cognitive presence to support the students in their learning experience (Vaughan, 2010; Shea & Bidjerano, 2010). The CoI framework emphasizes the role of presences as building blocks for knowledge construction through collaborative engagement between the teacher, the students, and the domain-specific knowledge sources. The teaching presence highlights the importance of the organization and the design and development of the course, discourse, and course facilitation, and direct facilitation to support social and cognitive presence (Rourke et al., 1999;

Shea & Bidjerano, 2010). Subsequently, the CoI framework is viewed as a concise and descriptive model to understand the value of online learning (Shea & Bidjerano, 2010). While there is enough evidence of scholarly acceptance in the literature, the CoI framework's teaching presence value is not often applied to online learning in the field of community engagement. The focus of this chapter is on the instructional elements embedded through the teaching presence in implementing a unique blended learning model for a macro community project-based course in a hard science domain.

Teaching presence can be measured through the different data sources available to lecturers at UP. Students and instructors' LMS activity data is embedded in a data warehouse and provides a descriptive, aggregated overview at course, departmental, faculty, and institutional level of the use of the LMS. The data presented in this chapter provides insight into the use of the LMS, including user time spent, tool usage, and course classification based on course archetype categories (Whitmer et al., 2016).

The Blended Model of the Community-Based Project Course

The blended model of the course includes face-to-face, online, and community interaction modes of delivery. The blended model and the learning design of the course is frequently changed based on lessons learned. For example, the development of YouTube videos was introduced when the lecturer was unable to verify the outcomes of each project. At the same time, it still requires evidence of the successful completion of the project.

The students attend a compulsory orientation lecture, presented in the university's auditorium, to accommodate the large number of students enrolled in the course. The introductory lecture contains a vital session about students' safety, presented by a campus security officer. Students also receive course-specific organizational and academic information. This includes the expected course outcomes, possible projects, course-specific timelines, and the processes involved. The face-to-face session ensures that the students understand the course's expectations.

The primary stakeholders of the course include the students and the lecturer, but also the community partners as a vital element to support the students' learning process (Jordaan, 2012; Jordaan, 2013). Figure 4.1 illustrates the three blending modes and the importance of the community partners in the management of the course cycle.

Using advanced course classification algorithms developed by Blackboard data scientists, the course level of LMS use is classified as holistic. Blackboard data science research of 3,374,462 unique learners in 70,000 courses at 927 international institutions resulted in course classifications

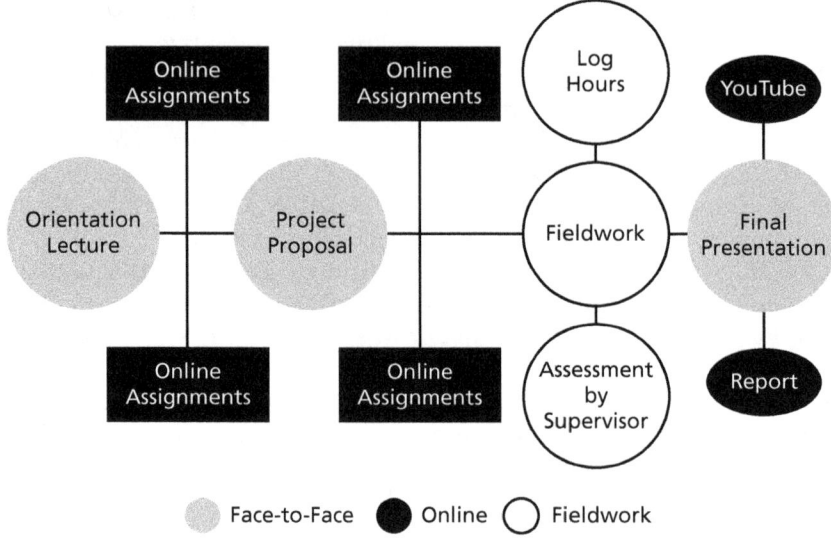

Figure 4.1 Blended model of the course.

or archetypes to demonstrate contextual diversity in the ways in which the Blackboard LMS was used at these international universities (Whitmer et al., 2016). The course archetypes are the following:

- *supplemental:* courses using predominantly content with limited student interaction;
- *complementary:* courses used primarily for teacher-to-student communication;
- *social:* courses with significant peer-to-peer interaction through discussion boards;
- *evaluative:* courses relying on the use of assessments to facilitate learning; and
- *holistic:* courses with high levels of activity from both students and instructors with a balanced use of assessments, content, interactive tools, and synchronous or asynchronous discussions (Whitmer et al., 2016).

The classification of the course as a holistic course is evident in Figure 4.2 and Figure 4.3. The data was extracted from the descriptive data analytics for the learning system. The analytics system includes user LMS and student information system data. Using the data reports are developed at different levels including, institutional, faculty, departmental, and course level.

Using a Blended Learning Approach in a Large Community Engagement Course ■ 59

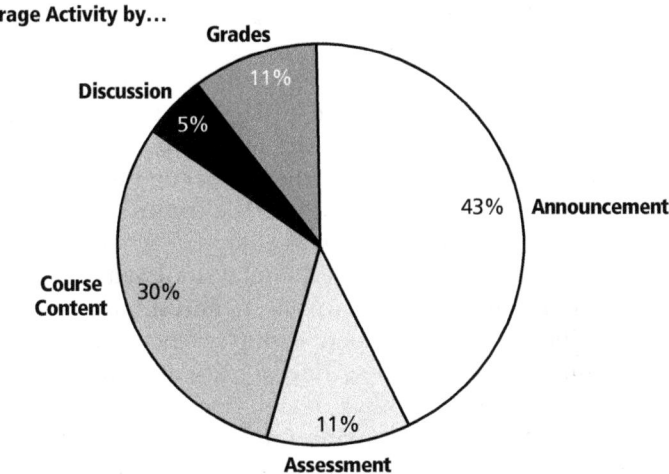

Figure 4.2 Average percentage of total student course activity by course item type.

The course design requires the students to engage in course activity, including assessments and course content. The unique model of the course with the limited traditional face-to-face lecture interaction requires the lecturer to communicate frequently with the students using announcements. Announcements, therefore, are a vital component of the course design that contribute to the success of the course. An acknowledged gap in the course design data is the absence of the measurable time students allocate to the

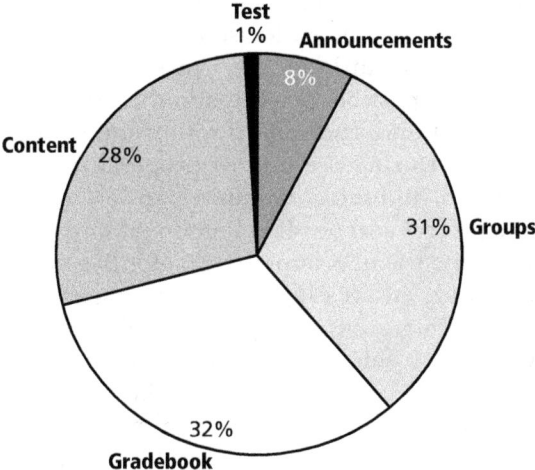

Figure 4.3 Percentage of instructor interactions per course item type.

development of the YouTube video as part of their reflection on their completed project.

Figure 4.2 shows a consistent trend in student activity within the context of the course in comparison to lecturer interaction, as indicated in Figure 4.3. Students' average activity in reading announcements is nearly 50% of their total course activity. The role of communication is vital to manage a macro community course where the lecturer has limited face-to-face contact time with students. The percentage of activity spent on grades and assessments is nearly a quarter of the total student activity. Assessments and activity by grades include both formative and summative assessments. The group activities include the use of group project proposal sessions, the use of the group tool wherein the group of students can upload their final presentation. It also includes other related documents such as the community assessment as well as the booking for the final project evaluation session Figure 4.3 provides a graphic illustration of the distribution of instructor interactions in course design and facilitation.

The percentage of the instructor's interactions in tests, the grade book, and in groups relate to the development and marking of formative and summative assessments. Nearly a third (28%) of the interactions include the development of content. Content includes the sharing of project-related information, as well as the sharing of group-related results through videos and images to share group outcomes with other students. It is essential to create a sense of community of practice by sharing achievements not only in the LMS but also on social media via Facebook and on the course's website.

Due to the unique context of the course in comparison to other academic courses, the course timeline is explained visually in the form of a roadmap to assist the students in completing tasks on the due dates. After the lecture, students organize themselves into groups of five members. The leader of the group can book for a project proposal session, where the lecturer discusses a possible project, and the group members agree to complete their project and assessments within the course criteria and by the completion date. During the project proposal session, the allocation of funding is finalized, and the community partners are contacted and informed about the project and possible timelines (Jordaan, 2013).

Group work and the use of groups are vital for the lecturer and students to manage the logistics of creating groups, managing the group project proposal, and scheduling group presentations. The group function in the LMS enables students to submit a reflective written and visual report for summative assessment purposes. Table 4.1 indicates the use of groups in the course in 2019. In total, 1633 groups were created in three categories.

Table 4.1 shows the time the students and lecturer spent in 2019 in the group sets allocated for group management (project proposals and project presentations) and group summative assessment purposes. The average

TABLE 4.1 Group Time Activity Measurements: 2019

Groups	Average Item Minutes	Average Item Accesses	Average Item Minutes per Access	Average Item Minutes per Item
Project proposals	8.3	1.5	5.7	1,464.5
Project presentations	8.5	1.4	5.6	1,313.0
Group summative assessment	94.6	70.9	1.2	151.1

item minutes measurement is a calculated measure to indicate, on average, how many minutes each user interacts with each course item (group).

The summative assessment groups, on average, show the highest average item minutes and average item accesses, yet a significantly lower average item minute per item (group). The higher average item minutes per item per group set used for group management indicates that users, on average, spend more item minutes per access in the group management group sets than they spend on the summative assessment groups. Consequently, it takes students more time per access to find a suitable time slot for group presentations or project proposals. In contrast, the summative assessment groups show a shorter engagement period. One group member must upload a pre-prepared group report and the link to the group's project video in the summative assessment group. The management of the macro community-based course would not be possible without the use of the group function in the LMS.

The lecturer uses the LMS to facilitate both summative and formative assessments. The formative assessment includes an online test, which focuses on community engagement, gender awareness, HIV/Aids in the workplace, and professional etiquette. Students also complete an online test after the face-to-face lecture. Table 4.2 provides aggregated descriptive data on users'

TABLE 4.2 Students' Assessment Time Activity Measurements: 2019

Assessments	Average Item Minutes	Average Item Accesses	Average Item Minutes per Access	Average Item Minutes per Item
Assignment on lecture	13.3	1.5	9.2	18,411.7
Community engagement	20.2	1.3	15.0	27,243.4
Gender assignment 2019	11.9	1.1	10.4	15,210.9
HIV/Aids in the workplace	12.9	1.1	11.5	16,417.5
JCP Guidelines	5.1	1.4	3.7	6,982.4
Total	12.7	1.3	10.0	16,853.2

activity as measured in minutes and the number of accesses in the formative online assessments.

The assessments allowed students two attempts to complete each assessment as it is crucial to ensure that all the students can complete the assessments, even if they experience connection problems. Each assessment includes between five and eight questions. Students spend, on average, 12.7 minutes per assessment and, on average, 10 minutes per access to complete the assessment. In total, all the students spent about 280 hours to complete all the assessments.

Forms of Communication in the Course

The scale and context of the course require frequent communication. Therefore, communication channels must be efficient, not only to manage the large number of groups working in diverse communities but also to ensure—for safety reasons—that the students and the lecturer are within easy reach. Students must be aware of any possible safety risks in the community at any given time, for example, strikes or riots. The students receive a notification of such risks on their mobile devices, as well as via email. The lecturer also uses social media platforms, such as WhatsApp, and SMSs to communicate with community partners and students. The JCP course has an allocated cellphone that students can contact in case of an emergency. The university's emergency security number is also available on the students' student cards.

Figure 4.2 and Figure 4.3 confirm students' average percentage activity spent reading the numerous announcements and the percentage of interactions by the lecturer in sharing the announcements. Detailed interaction data shows a total of 222,835 student interactions (clicks) and 1,790 instructor interactions in the announcement tool for 2019. The lecturer manages the sharing of announcements by using features such as the date function to display an announcement for a limited period of time or to a specific group of students.

Self-Evaluation of Blended Learning

The University of Pretoria developed a blended learning self-evaluation application and field guide to allow lecturers to improve their course design. The blended learning self-evaluation application uses eight dimensions as a structure for academics to reflect upon their existing practices, to self-identify their levels within the eight categories, and to record these results as benchmarks for future reference. The application identifies education practices

Using a Blended Learning Approach in a Large Community Engagement Course ▪ **63**

commonly found in tertiary blended learning environments. After working through the application and the eight elements, the lecturer receives a snapshot of the depth of the adoption (University of Pretoria, 2020b).

Figure 4.4 shows the results of a qualitative self-evaluation. This self-evaluation was developed by the University of Pretoria's Department of Education Innovation (University of Pretoria, 2020c) for a lecturer to evaluate the development of his/her course. A critical self-evaluation of the JCP course indicated that its outcomes and the blended approach followed address all eight categories of a blended learning course. The eight categories include:

- *Assessment:* An approach that monitors the process that allows students to monitor their progress.
- *Teaching and learning strategies:* Develop a place where the students can practice actively, enquiry, and authentic types of learning.
- *Learning activities:* To scale and structure participatory learning activities.
- *Content:* To introduce students to readily available resources and tools.
- *Communication:* To encourage regular communication and participation among all students.

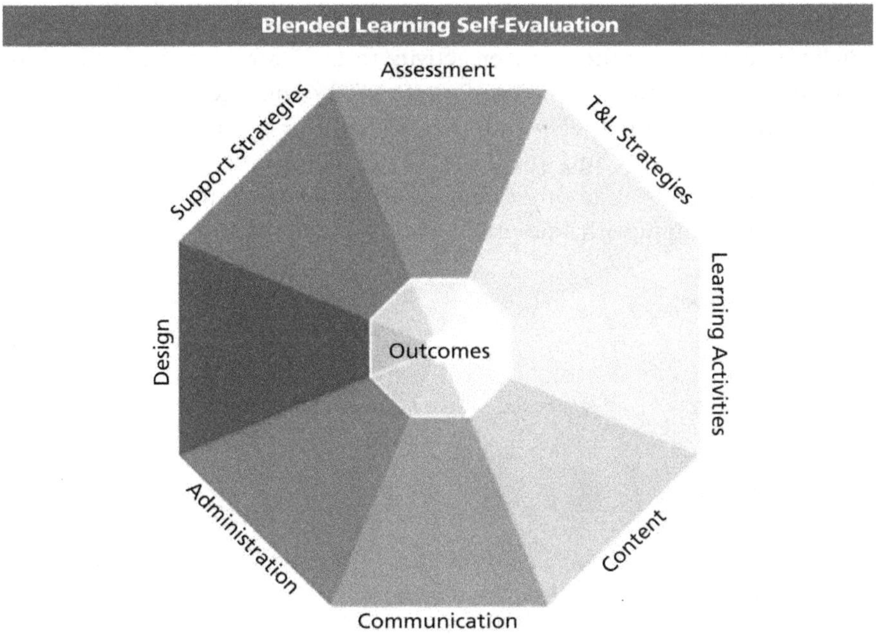

Figure 4.4 Self-evaluation of the JCP course as a blended learning course. All eight categories are fully implemented in the JCP module.

- *Administration:* For students to use technology in a way that mitigates risks.
- *Design:* For all students to be able to view and access key digital elements used within the course.
- *Support:* For the appropriate direction that can address the diversity of academic and social needs of students in a timely manner.

Figure 4.4 shows that all the eight categories of a blended course are fully implemented in the JCP module.

The successful use of the LMS to facilitate the course and the applied course design would not have been possible without the dedicated involvement of the lecturer through her teaching presence in the whole cycle of the course. The scatter chart in Figure 4.5 gives aggregated data of all the active undergraduate course instructors' interactions and their average logins for 2019 at UP. The data for the lecturer is as follows:

- Logins per user: 736
- Active average minutes per user indicated in size: 98,726 minutes
- Average interactions per user: 39,795

Figure 4.5 demonstrates the dependency of the lecture on the LMS visually by comparing the lecturer activity to facilitate all the teaching and learning and administrative components of the module with all the other undergraduate courses. The number of lecturer interactions and logins indicate that the teaching presence of the lecturer required much more online engagement than other courses where lecturers have frequent face-to-face engagement with students.

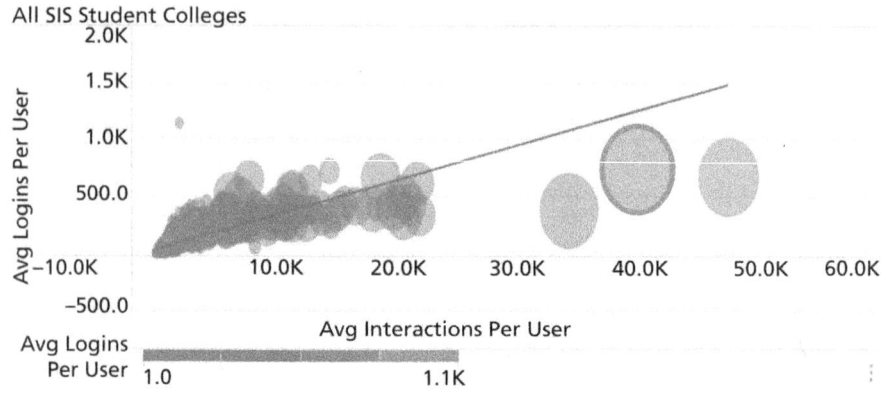

Figure 4.5 Lecturer session activity.

Using a Blended Learning Approach in a Large Community Engagement Course ▪ 65

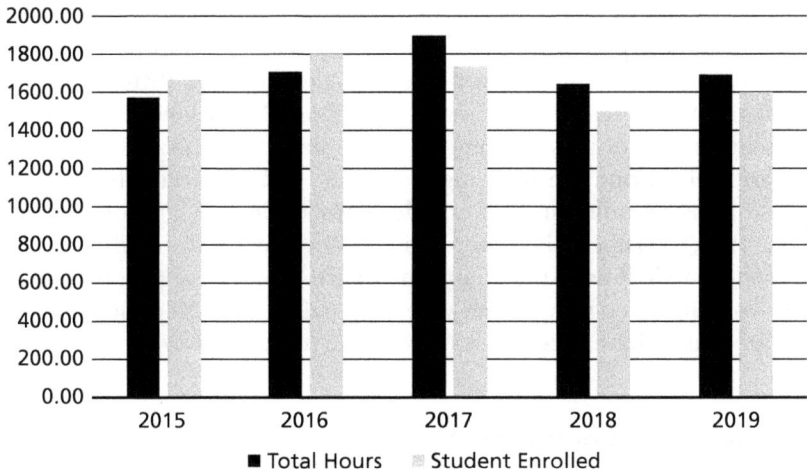

Figure 4.6 Lecturer LMS activity hours in relation to student enrollment.

The course has required a similar teaching presence since its inception due to the number of students enrolled in the course. Figure 4.6 shows an interesting trend in the relationship between the number of students enrolled in the course and the number of lecturer activity hours in the LMS.

Figure 4.6 shows nearly a one-to-one ratio between the number of hours the lecturer is active in the LMS and the number of students enrolled in the course. The 80 notional hours required by the module implies that the lecturer needs to be actively involved in the progress of each group in the module. The lecturer's active LMS hours exclude the additional academic and logistical arrangements involved to ensure that students achieve the learning outcomes of the course, including the management of the community partners. Figure 4.6 also demonstrates the commitment of the lecturer to ensure the high students' success rate in completing the module.

Fieldwork

Students must allocate at least 40 hours to work in the communities. During the fieldwork, students must take photographs and videos throughout the execution of their projects. The role of the community partner is very crucial during the fieldwork as the community verifies the students' hours, does quality control, and assesses the students' projects.

Final Student Reports and Presentations

A critical assessment of any community engagement course allows students to reflect on their experiences. The experience only becomes educational if critical reflective thought creates new meaning. The evaluation of the summative group assessment is based on a rubric to enable transparency for students to understand the assessment criteria (Hatcher & Bringle, 1997). As part of the final presentation, the students develop a PowerPoint or Prezi presentation, where they discuss the outcomes of the project with the lecturer and reflect on their learning experiences. Each group also develops a report, uploads it onto the LMS and develops a video (vlog). The video is uploaded onto YouTube to be shared on the World Wide Web for others to see and made public if both the community partners and the group approve it. Otherwise, the video is uploaded with the final report, where only the group and the lecturer have access to it (Jordaan & Jordaan, 2017).

The Role of the Community Partners

The community partners play a crucial role in the course. They identify possible projects that students can do at their sites. The most popular community partners are preschools, primary schools, secondary schools, nonprofit organizations, museums, animal shelters, and zoos. More than 350 sustainable community partners are involved in the course. The community partner may forward possible projects to the JCP office via email or on a Google form. Otherwise, possible suggestions may be made via WhatsApp or telephonically. The students and community partners agree on the outcomes that must be reached within 40 hours. The community partner also approves the final YouTube video and gives permission (if approved) for the video to be made public. Some community partners do not grant approval for this; for example, where students work at a rhinoceros sanctuary as a public, YouTube may compromise the safety of the animals (Jordaan & Jordaan, 2017).

Impact of the Course

Annually, nearly 10,000 people, including preschool, primary school, and secondary school learners and community members, are reached through the JCP course. Students have also impacted the lives of more than 1,900 animals, including rhinoceroses, leopards, lions, cats, and dogs. In 2019, 113 volunteers joined the course and students managed to find sponsorship worth R190,000 ($10,700)[2] above the R7000,00 ($39,424) in funding provided by the university. In addition, the course has received various acknowledgements institutionally, nationally, and internationally. After completing the course, students indicated that they had learned various skills, including teamwork, time management, and communication skills (Jordaan & Mennega, 2019).

FUTURE DIRECTIONS AND RESEARCH

The JCP module is a large community engagement module with more than 1,600 students enrolled yearly. The blended learning model allows the lecturer to interact with all the students and monitor their interactions. This model can be used for other large class community engagement courses, yet it requires higher levels of teaching presence and commitment from the academic staff involved

The module had to be adapted to address the challenges of the COVID-19 epidemic. With the COVID-19 epidemic, the course model changed from a blended to a fully online model relying on synchronous online meetings. This entailed that the project discussions with the students as well as the final presentations were done through Blackboard Collaborate. The lecturer and students' dependency on the functionalities in the LMS increased significantly. The types of projects also had to be adapted so that students could continue with their projects during Lockdown Level 4 and 5. Students focused more on online mathematics and science assistance for schools and creating educational resources for preschools. With the lesson learned during COVID-19, the option to use more of the functionalities of the LMS will be investigated.

More online assignments, as well as short instructional video clips, must be developed. The current cohort of undergraduate students is comfortable with using all the different resources on the learning management system after a year of online teaching. Yet, students have the same questions, and the "Frequently Asked Questions" sections must be redeveloped into an interactive question and answer section. The development of an interactive bot can be considered.

Community engagement courses require interaction from different external stakeholders, such as various stakeholders in the communities. It is important that they understand their role and responsibilities within these courses. Research on how community partners see their role in this blended learning module will add value to the outcomes of the module.

CONCLUSION

The unique context of the course does not only challenge the lecturer to coordinate such an extensive community engagement course but also requires high levels of teaching presence. Applying a unique blended model and integrating different educational technologies contribute to the success of the course. This is evident from its high throughput rate since its inception.

What makes it more challenging is the various community partners with different needs and expectations, as well as students from different study fields. The success of the course depends on good interaction and communication between the lecturer, the students, and the community. The data shows how both the students and the lecturer engage in the LMS to manage the academic and logistical cycle of the course. The immense effort or teaching presence required from the lecturer, as well as commitment from community partners and alumni, contributes to the success of the course. The students' summative feedback indicates their realization of their responsibility to deliver a project with high standards that will positively reflect the brand of the University of Pretoria. Their commitment to achieving outstanding results and their dedication to their studies ensure projects of a high standard. The context and scale of the course are still unique in South Africa, and an innovative blended learning model informs its success. However, the hourly teaching presence in the LMS remains in balance with the number of enrollments.

NOTES

1. The university does not have a criterion for large classes.
2. $1 = R17.71 as on March 23, 2020.

REFERENCES

Bernard, R. M., Borokhovski, E., Schmid, R. F., Tamim, R. M., & Abrami, P. C. (2014). A meta-analysis of blended learning and technology use in higher education: From the general to the applied. *Journal of Computing in Higher Education, 26*(1), 87–122.

Department of Education. (1997). *Education White Paper 3: A programme for the transformation of higher education.*

Department of Higher Education and Training. (2013). *National White Paper for post-school education and training in South Africa: Building an expanded, effective and integrated post-school system.* Government Printer.

Dziuban, C., Graham, C. R., Moskal, P. D., Norberg, A., & Sicilia, N. (2018). Blended learning: The new normal and emerging technologies. *International Journal of Educational Technology in Higher Education, 15*(1), Article 3.

Engineering Council of South Africa. (2014). *Whole qualification standard for bachelor of science in engineering (BSc (Eng))/Bachelor of Engineering (BEng): NQF Level 7.* https://www.ecsa.co.za/RegisterDocuments/FileNames/(BSc(Eng))%20%20Bachelors%20Of%20Engineering%20(BEng)%20Programmes.pdf

Erasmus, M., & Van Schalkwyk, F. (2011). Community participation in higher education service learning. *Acta Academica, 43*(3), 57–82.

Garrison, D. R., & Kanuka, H. (2004). Blended learning: Uncovering its transformative potential in higher education. *The Internet and Higher Education, 7*(2), 95–105.

Graham, C. R. (2006). Blended learning systems. In C. J. Bonk & C. R. Graham (Eds.), *The handbook of blended learning: Global perspectives, local designs* (pp. 3–21). John Wiley & Sons.

Hatcher, J. A., & Bringle, R.G. (1997). Reflection: Bridging the gap between service and learning. *College Teaching, 45*(4), 153–158.

Jordaan, M. (2012). Sustainability of a community-based project module. *Acta Academica, 44*(1), 224–246.

Jordaan, M. (2013). A blended approach to service learning: The faculty engineering, built environment and information technology at the University of Pretoria. In R. N. P. Osman (Ed.), *Service learning in South Africa* (pp. 206–229). Oxford University Press.

Jordaan, M. (2014). Community-based project module: A service-learning module for the faculty of engineering, built environment and information technology at the University of Pretoria. *International Journal for Service Learning in Engineering Special Edition, Fall*, 269–282. https://doi.org/10.24908/ijsle.v0i0.5553

Jordaan, M., Belino, M. C., & Paredes, C. R. (2012). International perspectives on service-learning. In T. H. Collegde (Ed.), *Convergence: Philosophies and pedagogies for developing the next generation of humanitarian engineers and social entrepreneurs* (pp. 178–203). International Journal for Service Learning in Engineering.

Jordaan, M., & Jordaan, A. J. J. (2017, June 14–15). *Using YouTube as a reflection tool for a service-learning module* [Paper presentation]. Fourth Biennial Conference South African Society for Engineering Education (SASEE), Cape Town, South Africa.

Jordaan, M., & Mennega, N. (2019). Engineering graduate attributes: Skills gained during a service-learning module. *The International Journal of Adult, Community and Professional Learning, 26*(1), 21–34. https://doi.org/10.18848/2328-6318/CGP/v26i01/21-34

Means, B., Toyama, Y., Murphy, R., & Baki, M. (2013). The effectiveness of online and blended learning: A meta-analysis of the empirical literature. *Teachers College Record, 115*(3), 1–47.

Moskal, P., Dziuban, C., & Hartman, J. (2013). Blended learning: A dangerous idea? *The Internet and Higher Education, 18*, 15–23.

Picciano, A. G. (2009). Blending with purpose: The multimodal model. *Journal of Asynchronous Learning Networks, 13*(1), 7–18.

Rasheed, R. A., Kamsin, A., & Abdullah, N. A. (2020). Challenges in the online component of blended learning: A systematic review. *Computers and Education, 144*, 103701. https://doi.org/10.1016/j.compedu.2019.103701

Rourke, L., Anderson, T., Garrison, D. R., & Archer, W. (1999). *Assessing social presence in asynchronous text-based computer conferencing.* https://auspace.athabascau.ca/handle/2149/732

Siemens, G., & Long, P. (2011). Penetrating the fog: Analytics in learning and education. *EDUCAUSE Review, 46*(5), 30–40.

Shea, P., & Bidjerano, T. (2010). Learning presence: Towards a theory of self-efficacy, self-regulation, and the development of a communities of inquiry in online and blended learning environments. *Computers and Education, 55*(4), 1721–1731.

Tewari, D. D., & Ilesanmi, K. D. (2020). Teaching and learning interaction in South Africa's higher education: Some weak links. *Cogent Social Sciences, 6*(1), 1740519. https://doi.org/10.1080/23311886.2020.1740519

University of Pretoria. (2020a). *Community-based learning.* https://www.up.ac.za/teaching-and-learning/article/2017087/gemeenskapsgebaseerde-leer

University of Pretoria. (2020b). *Impact of the use of hybrid/blended learning during #FeesMustFall2016.* https://eduvation.up.ac.za/hybridproject/

University of Pretoria. (2020c). *Hybrid learning field guide.* https://eduvation.up.ac.za/apps/open/docs/UPEISelfAssessmentFieldGuidev8.pdf

University of Pretoria. (2020d). *Teach & learn the UP way.* https://www.up.ac.za/media/shared/391/pdfs/teach-learn-up-way-2020.zp184675.pdf.

Vaughan, N. D. (2010). A blended community of inquiry approach: Linking student engagement and course redesign. *The Internet and Higher Education, 13*(1/2), 60–65.

Whitmer, J., Nuñez, N., Harfield, T., & Forteza, D. (2016). *Patterns in Blackboard Learn tool use: Five course design archetypes.* Blackboard Research Report. https://www.blackboard.com/sites/default/files/resource/pdf/Bb_Patterns_LMS_Course_Design_r5_tcm136-42998.pdf

CHAPTER 5

PHYSICALLY DISTANT BUT SOCIALLY CONNECTED

Building Community in Large Online or Blended Courses

Michael Porterfield
University of Missouri–St. Louis

Jennifer McKanry
University of Missouri–St. Louis

ABSTRACT

Having a sense of community and connectedness to others is key to a learner's success and resilience in any course. This becomes particularly critical in large online courses where it is very easy to feel a sense of isolation from your peers and instructor due to the nature of the modality and the instructor's time and effort demands when handling a larger number of students. In this chapter, we utilize the frameworks of community of inquiry (Garrison et al., 2000) and community of trust (Palmer, 2005) to break down the idea of community into its key components. Further, we provide practical, evidence-based examples that can help faculty build a learning community in their large online classes.

One of the biggest challenges of online learning can be students' sense of isolation from peers and the instructor. This is particularly so in large courses. However, we know social interaction is critical to learning. According to the theory of social constructivism, learning occurs through active participation in a group and involves a process of collaborative creation of meaning (Dewey, 1938; Vygotsky, 1978). To know something, we must both develop our own interpretation of the material and build upon it through observation of the reactions and responses of others (Anshu et al., 2010).

An important component in building any learning environment is support for that collaborative learning to exist. For the remainder of this chapter, we will refer to this as community. This can be particularly challenging online but doable, particularly thanks to the many technologies available to us today. This chapter will focus on how that community building can be accomplished in an online environment. Further, it will provide specific strategies to accomplish this in large online classes. There are various models addressing this, but the essential element is community. Common models include community of inquiry (Garrison et al., 2000); community of truth (Palmer, 2005); communities of practice (Wenger, 1998); community-of-learners (Rogoff, 1994); the learning community in online learning (Palloff & Pratt, 2007); and wisdom community (Porterfield & Isaac-Savage, 2013).

For this chapter, we look specifically at two frameworks: community of inquiry (Garrison et al., 2000) and community of trust (Palmer, 2005). The foundation of both frameworks comes from the work of a panel convened in 1989 by the divisions of independent study and educational telecommunications of the National University Continuing Educational Association (Moore, 1989). The primary outcome of this panel's work was to define three critical types of online learning interaction: learner–content interaction, learner–instructor interaction, and learner–learner interaction. This differentiation has become an industry-standard in defining and evaluating online learning.

More recently, Garrison (2017) adapted these concepts specifically to online learning in the community of inquiry model. They define the online community as a "group of individuals who collaboratively engage in purposeful critical discourse and reflection to construct personal meaning and confirm mutual understanding" (CoI Framework, n.d.). This framework builds on those social constructivist ideas by proposing that learning occurs through mutually created experiences. It includes three interdependent elements, or presences: teaching presence, cognitive presence, and social presence. Teaching presence is the design and delivery of the course including the instructor's active engagement with students in a personal and approachable manner. Cognitive presence is the interaction of the individual with the content through social engagement which helps them move through four phases of learning: triggering event, exploration, integration, and resolution. Social presence is the students' engagement with each other including opportunities to project their personality, culture, and experience into the course.

While each of these key elements has been found to be critical to student success online, teaching presence is often cited as the most significant predictor of learning, satisfaction, and sense of community in a course (Gorsky & Blau, 2009). Originally just encompassing the design and delivery of the course, the concept of teaching presence has more recently expanded to include the instructor presenting themselves as a real person (Richardson et al., 2016). Examples of how an instructor might do this include providing pictures and videos throughout the course, providing information about their background, experiences, teaching philosophy, and where appropriate sharing personal details. The instructor or teaching assistant typically is responsible for creating teaching presence. However, it can also be any member of the community. Regardless of who provides this leadership, teaching presence holds the important role of supporting the other two presences, social and cognitive.

To further delve into this idea of identity and teaching presence, we look to Parker Palmer's (2017) community of truth model. This model also includes the instructor's presentation as a real person in the course (Richardson et al., 2016). However, Palmer goes further to examine the inner life of the instructor. He notes in his classic work, this inner life is "about cultivating the inner grounds from which community grows" and "growing community from that inner ground into the classroom and the larger world" (p. 92). He further notes if an instructor is to help form community, the instructor should find holiness first. "Community is an outward and visible sign of an inward and invisible grace, the flowing of personal identity and integrity into the world of relationships" (p. 92).

The community of truth model helps all participants including instructors and learners be present and utilize active listening techniques including asking open questions to open up discussions without bias (Palmer, 2005). Palmer argues the process of finding truth is one of constant learning, only practiced through never-ending complex conversations. This social constructivist theory posits that truth is never finite but rather an always-changing concept which each learner should embrace. In the end, the "hallmark of the community of truth is in its claim that reality is a web of communal relationships, and we can know reality only by being in community with it" (Palmer, 2017, p. 97).

Building of community needs to be intentional, especially online. "Community is built upon what activities people do together instead of being based on geographical location" (Wellman, as cited in Rovai, 2002, p. 199). Learners rarely form a community on their own. Hence, online learning and community building needs facilitation and structure. The key to this is the instructor (Collison et al., 2000). According to Collison et al. (2000), the instructor must endeavor to keep students moving forward in the dialogue and the instructor's voice cannot be the central voice in the conversation. The following sections of this chapter provide examples of how to incorporate each presence in your large online course. These examples move from basic strategies to more innovative ways to build community. All examples provided from specific courses are used with the permission of the faculty credited.

COI: TEACHING, SOCIAL, AND COGNITIVE PRESENCE

Ways to Incorporate Teaching Presence

In this section, we will provide specific examples of how you can assure you are building teaching presence into your course. Teaching presence is the design and delivery of the course including the instructor's active engagement with students in a personal and approachable manner (Garrison et al., 2000). We will start with commonly used strategies then move to more innovative examples.

I. Provide a Personalized Welcome Video to Introduce the Course and Modules

One of the simplest and easiest things you can do to immediately help your students feel comfortable and at home in your course is provide a video walk-through of the course, covering material similar to what you would on the first day of a face-to-face course. Further, I find it helps students start to get a sense of who I am and my expectations as well as reducing the number of questions I get compared to just reading instructions. Be sure to include information such as how your due dates work, if you accept late submissions, where to find materials in your course, and how you expect assignments submitted.

As with your introductory video, a short welcome video at the beginning of each module or week helps students feel connected to you similar to how they would when seeing you each week in the classroom. It is also a great opportunity for you to share your personal experiences as they relate to the material and pass along your passion for the topic. It will be infectious and help students feel connected. Consider keeping your videos as generic as possible regarding time of year or current events. This allows you to reuse these videos each semester.

There are many software available that can capture your computer screen and webcam images at the same time and display them side-by-side or with a picture-in-picture framing. This helps give students your nonverbal as well as verbal cues as you walk through your priorities, expectations, and navigation advice. It is always advisable to keep videos shorter than 6 minutes. If necessary, break your recording into two. Contact your educational technology or instructional design support for information about what recording tools they recommend on your campus. Consider posting your video in an ungraded discussion board or utilizing an annotation tool (e.g., VoiceThread, Perusall) that encourages students to ask questions.

II. Provide a Welcome Message for Initial Connections

Collison et al. (2000) remind us online learning and community building needs facilitation, and the key to this is the tone set by the instructor. This makes the first welcome message or email important; this is the first step in setting the tone for the community. To help with this, I make sure my first email to my students is addressed to them personally. In my large online courses, I have found using an email merge to be the easiest and fastest way of creating a generic welcome email, personalized during the merging process. The email the student receives is individually addressed instead of one addressed to the entire class. This is the start of my developing a teaching presence in this online course. Furthermore, after the students participate in the initial discussion board, I will again send a personalized email. This response, usually through the learning management system (LMS), consists of generic language which I copy and paste with text from the student's discussion board post. Again, this simple step lets the students know I have read and felt their post was important enough to make a reply. While this takes extra time initially, especially for larger classes, building these relationships early will be a tremendous time savings in the long run. Finally, towards midterm, I will again send students an email using mail merge asking them to check in with me to let me know how they are doing. Most of the students are shocked I ask. They reply they have never had an instructor ask how they are doing. Again, this is one more step in developing teaching presence.

III. Provide Very Clear, Specific Instructions for Assignments

Another important component of teaching presence is providing clear instructions for students that minimize the guessing game. Students should be expending their limited effort on providing the best quality work and not trying to determine what an instructor wants. When teaching large classes this becomes all the more critical since faculty have limited time and ability to interact individually with students who are lost or confused. Clear instructions save you time in responding to students and save students time, frustration, and anxiety as well.

However, writing clear instructions is not as easy a task as it sounds. Do you find no matter how clear you feel your instructions are students often still struggle with key points? One model with evidence-based research showing improved student success is the transparency in learning and teaching (TILT) assignment structure (Winkelmes et al., 2019). The goal of this structure is to remove ambiguity from assignments by making their purpose, task, and criteria for success transparent. This model is particularly helpful in clarifying connections between coursework and learning outcomes. TILT implementation involves defining three elements for an assignment, the purpose, task, and criteria.

First, the purpose defines how an assignment ties back to the course learning objectives. The purpose should also incorporate plain language to explain how the assignment will be important to students' lives beyond just this course. Articulating this from the start using student-centered language helps motivate students to do well in the assignment.

Second, the task clarifies what steps should be completed and might include a recommended order for those steps. Additionally, offer suggestions upfront on how students might avoid potential roadblocks or mistakes. In some circumstances, you might want to give students creative license or have firm pedagogical reasons for wanting them to struggle with an assignment. If that is the case, be clear and intentional about where and when that is. If you desire ambiguity in the assignment, be sure to specify that here and explain why that struggle is important to the student's learning process. In all other cases, do not assume students know what you want or that they are familiar with the requirements for a specific type of assignment. Consider providing links to additional resources and materials. Students often turn to resources such as Google for ideas or suggestions. As we know, this can result in an overwhelming and often confusing or misdirecting set of information for students. Proactively providing links helps direct them to your curated results that will be more helpful and keep them on track.

Lastly, the criteria for success should define the characteristics of the finished product. Consider providing multiple examples of previous student work, which can help further clarify for students your expectations as well as providing an example of how they can achieve the desired outcome. Promote critical analysis skills by walking students through how to analyze multiple examples before beginning their own work. This analysis is further supported by including discussion of how excellent work differs from adequate work. Consider providing a rubric or other guidance for students on the evaluation criteria.

Winkelmes et al. (2019) demonstrated that by incorporating just two assignments using this transparent structure into a course increased student success, and a sense of belonging in a statistically significant fashion for all students but especially for underrepresented minorities and first-generation students. You might find it overwhelming to incorporate the full TILT model for all assignments. However, this research shows just how powerful it can be when built into even just a few assignments. Consider modifying a few assignments each semester to this format.

Finally, consider centralizing everything related to the assignment in one place by taking advantage of your institution's LMS such as Canvas, Blackboard, and so on. Most LMSs allow for instructions, and relevant resources to be embedded directly in the assignment submission area itself thus preventing students from missing critical information. Utilize the LMSs due date feature, which is also often tied to system calendars and to-do lists that will provide reminders to students about upcoming assignments. Further, having students submit materials via the LMS can also help keep you organized, which is especially critical with large courses. You will easily see who has submitted an assignment with no need to worry about lost emails, papers, or links. This is typically also tied directly to the LMS gradebook allowing for a clear and consistent place in which you can provide your feedback to students. LMS messaging tools and grade book filtering features will also allow you easily to reach out individually to struggling students.

Ways to Incorporate Cognitive Presence

Next, we will look at examples of ways you can incorporate cognitive presence into your large online course. Cognitive presence is the interaction of the individual and the content through social engagement, which helps them move through four phases of learning: triggering events, exploration, integration, and resolution (Garrison et al., 2000).

I. Use Small Group Discussions

Group discussion is well known as an important part of the engagement with content through social interaction. However, these discussions can often be overwhelming with large groups of participants. One of the easiest solutions to address this, and help build community, is to break discussions into small groups of 3 to 6 students each. Most LMSs will do this fairly easily. This helps keep the number of posts manageable and helps the group build a rapport. It can also promote a sense of responsibility to peers when students' realize their participation will be noticed and missed if not present. How you structure and engage in the discussion can be key to the successful outcome. The following are suggestions to help students be successful in group discussions.

- Assign the group members roles (e.g., manager, spokesperson, reporter, reflector or summarizer, encourager, questioner). These may rotate from week to week, so each member has a turn in each role. Alternatively assign one group leader each week responsible for making sure the group conversation is successful.
- Be intentional in your group selection to assure a diverse set of skills and experience in each group.
- Keep discussion groupings consistent throughout the semester to encourage building of relationships thus eliminating the sense of a large isolating class.
- Give the groups specific tasks each week, such as coming to a consensus on answers to discussion prompts or creating a summary of a topic they share back with the larger class.
- Provide a variety of different types of challenges each week to reach different students' strengths. For example, consider varying written assignments with visual ones such as a building a concept map, infographic, or postcard.
- Consider having students collaborate outside the traditional discussion board by using virtual meetings, Google Jam Boards, Padlet, social annotation tools such as Perusall or Hypothes.is, or video-based discussion tools such as VoiceThread, Panopto, or Flipgrid.
- Incorporate elements of reflection and opportunities to apply existing content to previous knowledge. Be transparent about the purpose of these reflections by providing materials to students to help them understand the power of reflection in their learning.
- Build relationships by pointing out commonalities and connections in students' posts.
- Be sure you read all posts and respond intermittently with encouraging prompts, so students know you are paying attention. Also, watch for cues of marginalization. This may be a student's only regular connection to others, and if a sensitive personal disclosure goes unresponded to, this can result in the student withdrawing and disconnecting from the course (Plotts, 2021). For example, if an LGBTQ student comes out in a class discussion, they would continue to revisit that discussion to see if anyone responded. If no one comments, the student may slowly withdraw, participating increasingly infrequently as their sense of disconnection increases.

II. Have Students Build Concept Maps

Concept maps are graphical tools for organizing and representing students' understanding of the material (Novak & Cañas, 2008). Circles or boxes represent the concepts. These concepts are linked together with lines and words referred to as linking words or linking phrases, which indicate the relationship between the two concepts. The strength of this tool lies in its ability to represent understanding graphically rather than verbally which is often much easier for students to process and comprehend. This can be particularly helpful in large online classes to build that important connection of the individual to the content further growing their cognitive presence.

Dr. Ann M. Steffen from the University of Missouri–St. Louis (UMSL) utilizes concept maps with her business classes of 40 or more students. She employs a free tool called CMap which was developed by the Florida Institute for Human and Machine Cognition. She found this tool helped balance out the writing intensive assignments in the class, as there were no quizzes or exams in this course. She chose to spread the points for the assignment throughout the semester in the following way: register for CMap cloud, add instructor as a CMapper (for future collaboration), create a folder named with student's last name that is shared with instructor, and create three different CMap assignments over the semester, of increasing points and complexity. She also utilized a rubric with three main areas of content: followed instructions for the concepts to be conveyed in the CMap, provided a clear organization, and used proper linking of terms.

Dr. Steffen shared her goals for this type of assignment:

> I want students to appreciate the importance of dual coding as a learning strategy. They are better able to appreciate and pay attention to visual depictions of conceptual models used in the course once they have tried to develop their own visual models of some content. And, understanding via visual models is important for older adults.

She further elaborated on the process, "Students create their CMap in CMap Cloud, then drag the CMap file into the folder that is shared with me. I have my own CMap cloud account, so in my account I can see all of the student folders" (A. Steffen, personal communication, February 25, 2020). Students were overall successful with only a few needing extra time and hand holding to manage the technology.

Another learning strategy is to incorporate concept maps into large online and blended course discussion boards. Using concept maps instead of textual responses helps students demonstrate their understanding (Bloom's Revised Taxonomy Level 2) and relationship of course materials. "With each student posting their individual mind map on the discussion board as their initial response, fellow students in the class can see how their peers are thinking about the course concepts, reflect on it, and develop a different understanding of how the concepts relate to each other" (Smith Budhai, 2021, para. 3) which helps to keep the dialogue moving forward in the quest for community.

III. Peer Teaching

Another important way to help students engage both with the content and their peers is through engaging them in development and delivery of the course itself. Early on consider having students involved in developing the expected norms for participation in the course. Also engage them in the delivery of the material. This can be done through group or individual presentations or through leading weekly discussions. Creating and providing discussion summaries back to the class is another powerful way to incorporate peer teaching into the course. Through organization of the material, they gain a deeper understanding as well as practice tying it to their previous knowledge. The presentation should also include the opportunity for feedback from peers through follow-up questions (synchronously in a live presentation via web conference, or asynchronously through a discussion board or other chat tool). This further helps the student think through the material from the different perspectives of their peers.

IV. Synchronous Problem-Based Learning

Problem-based learning (PBL) has been used in medical schools for many years. Beginning medical students were given a problem to solve before the instructor lectured on the problem topic. Dr. Daniel Federman (1999), former dean of medical education at Harvard Medical School, stated, "In small groups, guided by a tutor or facilitator, the students generate hypotheses—often ingenious and sometimes outrageous—and then go to resources including primary and secondary literature to learn the basic science required to account for the case material" (p. 93). Since this model works, it is now incorporated into the UMSL Child Advocacy Studies (CAST) courses in a blended format with the student facilitation taking place synchronously using Zoom and the rest of the course done asynchronously.

The CAST courses prepare students from various disciplines to be trained to recognize and learn to be trauma-informed professionals. Dr. Jerry H. Dunn, executive director of the Kathy J. Weinman Children's Advocacy Center, states, "PBL assists with developing several core skills we want our graduates to master: Critical thinking, collaboration and communication. PBL allows the students, at an early juncture in their education, to slow down and really think about how they are learning to think about the complexities of these cases (i.e., child abuse and neglect cases)" (personal communication, March 30, 2020).

Furthermore, Dr. Dunn states,

> The PBL exercises go a long way in building empathy for family members and other professionals. By taking on various roles associated with cases, students learn to respect both the breadth and depth of the challenges faced by everyone involved in these complex cases. PBL simulations allow for as "real life"

an experience as possible before entering the field. (personal communication, March 30, 2020)

What is novel about this blended program, the synchronous role-playing takes place via Zoom. The students meet with actors who take on the roles in the cases online, not face-to-face. This makes the blended program available to more students trained to help maltreated children and adolescents. This is successful because there is a dedicated facilitator to handle the Zoom meeting controls; this way, the instructor can focus on the instruction instead of the intrinsic aspects of Zoom. The facilitator instructs the students how to conduct their interviews in the Zoom session. According to Dr. Dunn, as the instructor, the Zoom platform made this event successful. Regarding facilitation, "The students were successfully oriented to the process by the moderator and they appeared to move seamlessly into and out of the Zoom break out rooms. Both the actors who portrayed the standardized clients and the students reported feeling comfortable with the format (personal communication, March 30, 2020).

Ways to Incorporate Social Presence

Lastly, we look at ways to incorporate social presence into a large online course. Social presence is the student's ability to be themselves in the online environment including opportunities to project their personality into the course (Garrison et al., 2000). Building social presence can be particularly helpful in breaking down barriers and increasing inclusivity.

I. Icebreaker Activity That Promotes Connections
In any class, it is important to provide students a way to get to know each other and make connections that will help support them throughout the semester. However, in an online course, it is all the more important that you make this an intentional part of your design. This can easily be done by creating a low stakes introduction or icebreaker assignment in which students introduce themselves, share something about their background and encourage them to make connections to others in the course they have things in common with. This helps build a sense of community through making connections with the others in the course.

Incorporation of video further promotes a warmer, more personable environment. Keep in mind however that not all students might have a video camera or feel comfortable or safe showing themselves and/or their environment on video. Providing an alternative, such as uploading favorite pictures can be a great way for all students to feel comfortable and included. Providing your own response to the prompt also helps by providing an exemplar and modeling the behavior of being vulnerable for your students. If you have teaching assistants or supplemental instructors in the course, encourage them to do the same.

Examples of possible prompts for icebreakers are included below. Consider tying in something related to the topic you are teaching to help them connect that topic to their lives.

- *Food.* What is your favorite restaurant and why? Share a link to their menu. Find the post of two of your peers and identify what item on their menu you would be most excited about testing and why.
- *Industry.* Which company would you be most interested in working for and why (provide a list relevant to your industry as well as links to their home pages)? Review the posts of your peers and comment on at least two of those who selected the company most different from yours.
- *Relevance of topic.* Review the following video introduction to our course topic. Post one reason why this topic might be relevant to your daily life even if you are not going into this field as a major. Share a past experience which is related in some way to this topic. How do you think having studied this topic might have changed your reaction or perspective on that experience? Comment on the examples shared by at least two of your peers.

II. Peer Review

Building peer review into a course is a great way to encourage peer-to-peer engagement. It can also be a great time saver in grading feedback for an instructor if students have already received preliminary feedback on their work prior to their final submission. This is most often used with writing assignments but could be applied to other types of assignments as well. Students not only learn from the feedback they receive, but they also learn from being able to see examples of other students' work.

The challenge in building peer review into a course is many students do not know how to give feedback. Therefore, it is important to also build in clear guidelines for students to follow that include specific prompts for them to respond to in their feedback. Using rubrics can also be helpful in communicating expectations for a peer review assignment. Figure 5.1 is an example from Dr. Deborah Cohen's UMSL history course on war and violence in modern times.

Dr. Cohen has found it important to build students' peer review skills throughout the semester: Start small so they don't panic. Do not put too much weight on one assignment. Have lots of opportunities for students to learn the process. Start with a discussion board assignment and an exemplar to practice giving feedback as a group (personal communication, February 20, 2020).

> We will be using peer reviewing to help strengthen your papers and assignments. As such, here you'll learn how to peer review (critique) a classmate's work. You will also learn to integrate the feedback into a subsequent revision of your work (see video below to help you if you don't know how).
>
> **Step 1:** You will receive a classmate's journal to peer review. Download it.
>
> **Step 2:** Read it.
>
> **Step 3:** In Word, click on "Review" tab in ribbon at the top of the page. Once there, turn on "track changes." This way you can edit and the changes will appear in a different color. Also, use "New Comment" to react to the text or make other kinds of suggestions for which you need more space.
>
> **Step 4:** Use the checklist inserted here to help you offer feedback. Remember, your goal is to offer help so that the author can strengthen the journal. Saying you liked something doesn't provide advice to improve the journal.
>
>> a) Does the journal have an argument? If "Yes," does the argument make sense? If "No," point out the need for an argument.
>>
>> b) Does the journal provide evidence/examples to support its stated argument? If you can offer additional evidence, please do so. A well-supported argument will use at least three examples/pieces of evidence.
>>
>> c) Is the journal well organized and coherently written? If not, provide examples of why it's not well organized and how to organize it in a way to strengthen the argument.
>
> Please offer other articles/videos that can work as evidence/examples of the point the author is trying to make. Also, suggest organizational changes to strengthen the journal.
>
> **Step 5:** While you can edit for grammar and punctuation, and I'm sure it'll be much appreciated by the author, you won't get credit for doing so. The goal of PEER REVIEW is to engage with your classmate's ideas, to aid them in developing and supporting the argument more strongly, and to tie evidence/examples more fully back to the argument.
>
> **Step 6:** Upload ON ORIGINAL ASSIGNMENT (link) BY SUNDAY @ 11:59 PM. On the right-hand side, you'll see a comments box. There's a link where you can attach a new file. If you are having trouble figuring out how to find the review document or upload your review see these (link) instructions.

Figure 5.1 Peer review instruction example from Dr. Cohen's history course.

III. Critical Friend Model

Expanding on the peer review concept, the critical friend model can greatly enhance peer-to-peer support. Starting small and proceeding in a structured and methodical way helps students learn this process and give their peers better feedback. Costa and Kallick (1993) understands this is a process which needs time and we need to be realistic in this group process:

> Because the concept of critique often carries negative baggage, a critical friendship requires trust and a formal process. Many people equate critique

with judgment, and when someone offers criticism, they brace themselves for negative comments.... Critical friendships, therefore, must begin through building trust. (p. 50)

Building trust begins at the beginning of a course in small ways. For example, in a group discussion board in which group members use the critical friend model to review a low-stakes writing assignment and build up over the semester to a major, final paper. This will help build trust among the group and peers begin to learn their critical friend is not out to judge them but to offer constructive feedback and help their peers to be successful.

Asking nonthreatening peer review questions can also build trust; students also experience constructive comments instead of negative ones. Several UMSL instructors have embraced the critical friend model by utilizing the following guiding questions written by our Center for Teaching and Learning to help build trust and promote constructive feedback (K. Holmes, personal communication, February 9, 2021). Below are examples that offer constructive feedback:

1. What I like most about what you have written is this: _____ (Explain)
2. I would understand better if you clarify this: _____ (Explain)
3. I would know more if you add information about this: _____ (Explain)
4. I would like to offer these suggestions to improve grammar and writing style: _____ (Explain)

We found models such as this to be particularly successful in Spring 2020 when our face-to-face courses were quickly switched to online due to the pandemic. We found in follow-up surveys of our UMSL students, those who already had a connection with a peer or group of peers in their class were significantly more successful and had lower drop, fail, or withdraw rates than those that did not have that connection to the course.

BUILDING COMMUNITY WITHIN THE PROGRAM

Finally, we wrap up this chapter by stepping back and taking a broader look at the building of community, not just in a course, but at the program level. There are many connections to the program that can be generated. Consider creating a short welcome video from your dean or provost that can be incorporated into key gateway or feeder courses for the program. This helps set the culture of the program and stress the importance of the course. Courses could also end with a video from the instructor for the next course in the sequence welcoming them and introducing what will come next. Additionally, welcome opportunities for guest speakers from other courses or areas within the program such as advisors. The more connected students feel to the program, the more motivated they will be to be successful.

FUTURE DIRECTIONS AND RESEARCH

The COVID pandemic has really impacted higher education especially when many colleges and universities rapidly converted traditional classes to online or blended format. Through this rapid transformation of faculty, staff and student support and development, infrastructure, and educational paradigm shifts, many areas became evident for future research and recommendations. One area of future research is to examine inequities students experience in connecting and engaging online with their instructors, classmates, and content in their online or blended courses. A computer/laptop/mobile device and connectivity are vital in students participating in this way; this becomes vital in student retention and completion. Examining lessons learned in how we as a field approached these challenges during the COVID pandemic will inform the future. If case studies are developed on this topic, it can help inform institutions how to successfully support their online and blended students.

Another research recommendation is to conduct a qualitative study using the phenomenological method. Through this research, instructors can be surveyed and interviewed about their experiences rapidly transitioning from traditional instruction to online or blended with a special emphasis on how they incorporated teaching, cognitive, and social presences into their instruction. Through this research, processes and best practices can be developed to effectively enhance the teaching and learning process for large online and blended courses.

Finally, we recommend institutions examine and discuss in the appropriate professional organizations or accrediting agencies how colleges and universities effectively support their students remotely, especially how these institutions support students with physical or hidden disabilities. It is easy to make an online exam with extra time for students who need this accommodation, but how does an institution remotely support students with counseling who suffer from depression after losing their job or loved one? How does an institution support students who are mentally challenged or a student who has to decide how they are going to pay their bills, tuition, and support families during a crisis? These are essential questions to help build community in large online or blended courses.

REFERENCES

Anshu, M. S., Burdick, W. P., & Singh, T. (2010). Group dynamics and social interaction in a south asian online learning forum for faculty development of medical teachers. *Education for Health, 23*(1), 311–319.

Collison, G., Elbaum, B., Haavind, S., & Tinker, R. (2000). *Facilitating online learning: Effective strategies for moderators.* Atwood Publishing.

CoI Framework. (n.d.). https://coi.athabascau.ca/coi-model/

Costa, A. L., & Kallick, B. (1993). Through the lens of a critical friend. *Educational Leadership, 51*(2), 49–51.

Dewey, J. (1938). *Experience and education.* Macmillan. (Originally a Kappa Delta Pi publication)

Federman, D. D. (1999). Little-heralded advantages of problem-based learning. *Academic Medicine, 74*(2), 93–94.

Garrison, D. R. (2017). *E-learning in the 21st century: A community of inquiry framework for research and practice* (3rd ed.). Taylor & Francis.

Garrison, D. R., Anderson, T., & Archer, W. (2000). Critical Inquiry in a Text-Based Environment: Computer Conferencing in Higher Education. *The Internet and Higher Education, 2*(2/3), 87–105.

Gorsky, P., & Blau, I. (2009). Online teaching effectiveness: A tale of two instructors. *International Review of Research in Open and Distance Learning, 10*(3), 1–27.

Moore, M. G. (1989). Editorial: Three types of interaction. *American Journal of Distance Education, 3*(2), 1–7.

Novak, J. D., & Cañas, A. J. (2008). *The theory underlying concept maps and how to construct and use them* (Technical Report IHMC CmapTools 2006-01 Rev 2088-01). Institution for Human and Machine Cognition. https://cmap.ihmc.us/docs/theory-of-concept-maps.php

Palloff, R., & Pratt, K. (2007). *Building online learning communities* (2nd ed.). Jossey-Bass.

Palmer, P. (2005). The community of truth. In C. Anders & L. Runciman (Eds.), *Open questions: Readings for critical thinking and writing* (pp. 627–636). Bedford Books.

Palmer, P. J. (2017). *The courage to teach: Exploring the inner landscape of a teacher's life* (3rd ed.). Jossey-Bass.

Plotts, C. (2021, January 29). *Re-connecting to connectedness in online spaces: The importance of people, culture, and community* [Keynote address]. Keynote address presented at the 2021 University of Missouri-St. Louis Spring Forum, St. Louis, MO.

Porterfield, M., & Isaac-Savage, E. P. (2013). The formation of online wisdom communities amongst ministerial students. *Journal of Adult Theological Education, 10*(2), 116–131.

Richardson, J. C., Besser, E., Koehler, A., Lim, J., & Strait, M. (2016). Instructors' perceptions of instructor presence in online learning environments. *International Journal of Research in Open and Distributed Learning, 17*(4), 82–103.

Rogoff, B. (1994). Developing understanding of the idea of communities of learners. *Mind, Culture, and Activity, 1*(4), 209–229.

Rovai, A. (2002). Development of an instrument to measure classroom community. *Internet and Higher Education, 5*(3), 197–211.

Smith Budhai, S. (2021, February 10). Leveraging Bloom's Taxonomy to elevate discussion boards in online courses. *Faculty Focus.* https://www.facultyfocus.com/articles/online-education/online-student-engagement/leveraging-blooms-taxonomy-to-elevate-discussion-boards-in-online-courses/

Vygotsky, L. S. (1978). *Mind in society: The development of higher psychological processes* (M. Cole, V. John-Steiner, S. Scribner, & E. Souberman., Eds.; A. R. Luria, M. Lopez-Morillas, & M. Cole [with J. V. Wertsch], Trans.) Cambridge, MA: Harvard University Press. (Original manuscripts [ca. 1930–1934]).

Wenger, E. (1998). *Communities of practice: Learning, meaning, and identity.* Cambridge University Press.

Winkelmes, M., Boye, A., Tapp, S., Felten, P., & Finley, A. (2019). *Transparent design in higher education teaching and leadership: A guide to implementing the transparency framework institution-wide to improve learning and retention.* Stylus Publishing.

CHAPTER 6

STRATEGIES FOR COLLABORATIVE LEARNING IN LARGE ONLINE CLASSROOMS

Marcus Schultz-Bergin
Cleveland State University

Erin Avram
Cleveland State University

ABSTRACT

There is widespread agreement that collaborative learning, where students interact with each other toward a shared goal or project, enhances student learning when compared to traditional lecture techniques. Nonetheless, there is a great difficulty in incorporating these techniques into large courses and into online courses. Thus, there is even greater difficulty in incorporating these techniques into large online courses. Given the value of these techniques, however, it is imperative that we find methods to incorporate them whenever possible. In this chapter, we discuss the importance of collaborative learning in large online classrooms and then examine a variety of techniques and tools to identify general guidelines and best practices for effectively establishing collaborative learning environments. By drawing on, but abstracting from, specific collaborative techniques, we aim to show how faculty can incorporate collaborative learning into any online classroom. Additionally, we aim to show how this can be done in a way that simultaneously enhances student learning while reducing, or at least not increasing, the burden on faculty.

Most faculty prefer small, intimate class settings where they can engage personally with individual students and where students can engage with each other to develop a classroom community. However, it is a common fact of many universities that some courses will be delivered in a large format, consisting of over 100 students. During the COVID-19 pandemic in which this chapter was written, it was not uncommon for large format courses to be delivered remotely. For various reasons, going forward, it may become more common for large courses to be delivered online as well.

Despite some concerns about the effectiveness of teaching online, we believe that it is possible to establish an effective learning environment in a large online classroom. However, we admit that doing so can be more daunting than in smaller and/or in-person courses. In the next section, we examine three common problems that we might face in designing a large online course that may result in a less effective or engaging learning environment. Following, we go on to argue that a collaborative learning environment can be effective at remedying the three issues previously identified before moving, in the rest of the chapter, to outline how to organize a large online course around collaborative learning. Our aim is both to motivate and assist instructors in developing effective learning environments in large online courses through the use of collaborative learning techniques.

DRAWBACKS OF LARGE ONLINE CLASSROOMS

It can be exceedingly difficult to generate an effective learning community in a large online classroom. The online nature of the course already puts students at more of a distance to each other than a traditional classroom while the large class size further tends to increase feelings of isolation (Irwin & Berge, 2006). For many reasons, it is quite a difficult task to facilitate a 100-person discussion, especially via video chat or discussion boards. This is problematic given the significant research indicating the importance of community for student learning (Dewey, 1938; Vygotsky, 1978). The community of inquiry learning framework draws on research that identifies certain types of behaviors as valuable for both generating a sense of community (or "social presence" as it is called) and improving student outcomes (Swan & Richardson, 2017). Thus, there is both theoretical and empirical support for the importance of establishing community for the learning process. Creating a learning community in a large online classroom can be challenging, but with focused effort on incorporating structured group activities and fostering smaller learning activities, these challenges can be curtailed, increasing the quality of the learning experience for students.

An effective learning community can enhance the learning experience by providing opportunities for students to engage at a higher cognitive level with the course content (Gokhale, 1995). Through discussion, for instance, students can present and defend their interpretation of a concept or theory or its appropriate application and other students can interrogate that interpretation and offer alternatives. The process of debating proper interpretation or application requires students to draw more deeply on the course content as well as attempt to integrate it into their existing knowledge, forming connections which have been shown to help increase long-term retention of information (Ritchhart & Church, 2020). It can be difficult to ensure students are engaged in higher level thought in large online classrooms since, typically, the evaluation of, for instance, analytical work is more time-consuming for faculty than the evaluation of mere memorization.

A lack of higher-level engagement can further deteriorate the learning experience and make it difficult to achieve a course's learning outcomes, which often include higher-level thought, whether or not students are given the opportunity to practice such engagement. In particular, higher-level engagement via *active learning* is supported by constructivist learning theory as well as significant empirical research. According to constructivism, knowledge is constructed by the knower by building on past knowledge and experience, and engagement with new ideas. (Elliott et al., 2000). It is not typically built by mere recording of definitions; unless the student works with and applies the ideas, they are unlikely to come to know them in any meaningful sense (Phillips, 1995). Further, research comparing various active learning techniques to traditional lecture modes of transmission have found significant improvements in learning for students who were tasked with using the course content to solve problems or otherwise work through exercises rather than simply listen to a lecture (Deslauriers et al., 2019). Given all this, it is imperative that a classroom provide substantial space for active engagement, but for reasons stated above, that can be excessively difficult in large online classrooms.

One reason that it can be difficult to integrate higher-level learning experiences into a large online classroom is that such assignments can be much more time-consuming to evaluate. Multiple choice tests can be automatically graded by learning management systems (LMS), whereas written work or work that allows for multiple approaches or specifications of answers typically requires the instructor to manually evaluate. In a classroom of over 100 students, this can either lead to a complete lack of assignments focused on higher-level learning or the implementation of too few to truly facilitate student learning. This can be especially problematic if higher-level engagement is left to high-stakes assignments (like mid-term or final exams) without any real opportunity to practice and receive feedback throughout the course. More generally, we can recognize that large courses typically create a greater grading burden on faculty, at least if they are trying to do the same sort of activities and assignments that they would in a smaller classroom.

TOWARD A SOLUTION: COLLABORATIVE LEARNING

Given what we have said in the previous section, it should be clear that it is important to find methods for designing large online classrooms that engage and support a community of learners, ensure students ample opportunity for higher-level engagement with course content, and alleviate (or at least not exacerbate) the time required for grading. We believe that collaborative learning, understood most broadly as a learning process involving two or more individuals in interaction, is one such method for overcoming all three drawbacks common to large online classrooms. For our purposes, we will focus on small group learning rather than, for instance, pairing, since although pairing is a form of collaborative learning, it can still generate a lot of work for the instructor. Moreover, as we will aim to show in this section and beyond, small group collaborative learning produces some additional benefits beyond correcting for the typical drawbacks of large online classrooms.

While it is (nearly) impossible to generate a real learning community amongst 100+ people, it is certainly possible to do so with a group of 3–7 students. Thus, rather than attempting to host a full class discussion (either via video chat or discussion boards) one can ask students to engage in discussion only with their group mates. This can promote greater back-and-forth and, if the groups remain the same for an extended period of time, the development of understanding and empathy among the students (Michaelsen et al., 2002). The work on social presence in the classroom has suggested that *cohesive behaviors*, such as identifying oneself with the group through reference to things like what "we" have decided, enhance the sense of community. Small groups tasked with creating collaborative products will almost by necessity need to think about what "we" want or are doing. Moreover, *interactive behaviors* such as replying to or acknowledging a peer's work enhance social presence and help to generate a sense of community (Swan & Richardson, 2017). And while one can attempt to force interactive behaviors through, for example, demanding students "reply to at least 2 posts" on a massive discussion board, that neither guarantees that everyone is interacted with nor does it guarantee that the interaction is really meaningful (especially if the conversation just stops after a post and then reply). Students working in small groups, on the other hand, are more likely to naturally engage in interactive behaviors and, if the group activities are appropriately structured, a genuine back-and-forth can be all but guaranteed.

While small groups could be used for any type of work, they should be used (almost) exclusively for higher-level engagement. First, because small groups consist of multiple minds, they should have a greater ability to perform higher-level tasks than any given individual. Second, higher-level tasks like applying concepts/theories and analyzing situations can typically be done better by looking at the issue from multiple perspectives. Although a single individual can look at an issue from multiple perspectives, it is more difficult, and thus having multiple people each with their own perspective and experience is preferable. Third, the social constructivist approach suggests that students are much more likely to generate knowledge only through active, social interaction (Palincsar, 1998). They must integrate new ideas into existing knowledge and be able to do something with the new ideas. But, in order to ensure they understand the new ideas, they need to test their understanding in a social environment, in large part by testing the application of the ideas or elaborating on them in discussion with others. Finally, a substantial amount of empirical evidence has shown that students who engage in collaborative group work are typically more capable of engaging with course material at a higher level, largely because the collaborative group environment (when designed effectively) fosters such engagement (Michaelsen et al., 1982).

Finally, collaborative group work can allow for an instructor to create and assign activities and/or assignments that focus on higher-level skills without an increase in grading burden (or a minimal increase). This is because, in a classroom of 100 students, you can go from needing to evaluate 100 assignments to evaluating 20. Or, as we will discuss below, you can incentivize the group engagement in ways that do not require evaluating the group work at all but, nonetheless, motivates the students to engage in it. Additionally, group work can offload some of the feedback burden from the instructor to the groups themselves. If a group member misunderstands how to apply a theory, for instance, then that can come out during the collaboration and another group member may be able to correct it before it ever reaches the instructor. Given some of the evidence that students often learn more, or more deeply, from engagement with each other than engagement with the instructor, collaborative group learning is well placed to enhance student learning without thereby increasing the burden on faculty (Boud et al., 2001).

Thus far we have focused on the general value of collaborative group learning in a large online classroom. With that motivation in hand, we can now turn to the execution of collaborative group learning. Our goal is to identify both a variety of important principles for course design but also to indicate a variety of options and provide some considerations to keep in mind in selecting from among those options.

EFFECTIVE GROUP ACTIVITIES

Similar to the backward design approach to course design, we find it important to first have a clear picture of what you want students to get out of the group learning before working backward to identify how to organize groups, determining the size of the groups, and thinking about methods for accountability and effectiveness (Wiggins & McTighe, 2005). In this section we draw on a variety of existing models for collaborative learning in order to identify some key principles of designing effective group activities. Most centrally, our discussion draws on the models of team-based learning (TBL), project-based learning (PBL), and SCALE-UP. Crucially, however, we don't intend to provide a thorough explanation of any of these models but instead highlight some of their key insights for the design of effective group work. Below, we highlight three key insights before discussing a few of the activity design implications of those insights.

Many students (and faculty) balk at the idea of group work (whether in the class or online) because they have had terrible past experiences whereby they have been severely let down by their group mates not completing their share of the work. One reason this can happen is because the group work activity is designed around *cooperation* rather than *collaboration*.[1] Cooperation is merely a matter of multiple people contributing to a shared task—for instance, a group presentation where each person is responsible for a slide. Collaboration, on the other hand, demands *interaction*. Thus, to turn a group presentation into a collaborative endeavor, we could turn the focus to the group drawing a conclusion or making a recommendation and then defending it. Here, they must interact to decide on their conclusion/recommendation as well as to construct the best defense of it. They may still, in the end, divide up some portion of the presentation, but in doing their own part they must understand and take into consideration the whole.

Related to the focus on collaboration, it is also generally recommended that group work focus on *deliberation* rather than *discussion*. Discussion can be had without any common goal. Thus, a group activity that effectively amounts to "discuss amongst yourselves" provides little to no incentive for students to genuinely engage and interact with each other. Each can present their own view, but there is nothing encouraging them to hone in on disagreements and work through them. Deliberation, on the other hand, is always aimed at achieving a common goal. In this way, deliberation forces interactivity. Thus, rather than "discuss amongst yourselves" you may require a student group to "reach a consensus on a recommendation and justify it." This alternative approach demands students listen to each other, engage with each other, and work through disagreements. Assuming disagreements will arise partly due to differences in understanding of the course material, working through the disagreements is also a means of constructing knowledge and verifying understanding for each student. And so, whereas discussion can be done without ever moving to a higher level of engagement with the course material, deliberation simply cannot.

Finally, and following the emphasis on deliberation, group activities should be focused around a product rather than merely the process. This is not to say the process is unimportant, but rather that just as a focus on deliberation will generate discussion, but not vice versa, a focus on product can generate an effective and useful process whereas the opposite is not the case. So, once again, a requirement to "make one original post and reply to two other students" focuses purely on process and, as a result, does not incentivize interactivity or higher-level engagement, especially if it is done with a large group. Similarly, an activity to "discuss amongst yourselves" is process-oriented and so compatible with producing nothing of particular value. On the other hand, an activity that requires students to reach a consensus and be prepared to defend it emphasizes the result of a process, and in that way incentivizes an effective process, where effectiveness is (partly) defined by its ability to output a quality product.

As should be clear, each of these three insights—collaboration not cooperation, deliberation not discussion, and product not process—are deeply interrelated. An emphasis on a shared product almost by necessity generates the requirement to deliberate and not merely discuss while deliberation is itself necessarily an interactive process. By and large, then, each insight supports the same approach to course and activity design. This includes ensuring all activities have a clear and observable goal that all group members are responsible for. The observable goal can be the selection and defense of a recommendation on how to proceed in a case study, or the identification and explanation of relevant stakeholders for a project, or the collection of data from an experiment, and so on.

It also means that the observable goal must demand problem solving or other forms of high-level engagement with course material. Thus, whereas "define the concept" is technically an observable goal, it is not one that necessarily demands any analysis or problem solving amongst group members.[2] Again, since groups benefit from multiple brains, it is not only acceptable but strongly encouraged that group activities are designed to be too difficult or impossible for a single individual to complete on their own. To identify potential higher-level activities, it can be useful to draw on Bloom's taxonomy of cognitive complexity, with a focus on the *application* level and higher in the pyramid (Bloom, 1979). There are many versions of the taxonomy online that also include a set of action verbs describing the sorts of things students should be doing in order to be engaged in the relevant level of cognitive complexity, and those action verbs can form the basis of what students are asked to do in the group activity. In general, the higher the level of cognitive complexity, the more likely the activity is to demand deliberation and collaboration. One must be a bit careful, however, as "create" is generally considered the highest level of cognitive complexity but many activities aimed at that level, such as writing a paper, disincentivize collaboration. Thus, "apply," "analyze," and "synthesize" are typically the best levels to focus on, leaving the create step to individual work potentially based on the group work.

Group work should also typically be focused on "small" products, although the small products may be steps on the way to a larger project. This is because the common tendency for handling a significant project is to divide the labor, thus leading to cooperation but not collaboration. For instance, if students will be tasked, all at once, with researching the history of some activity, identifying various reforms, defending a particular reform, and putting this all together into a paper or presentation, it is likely different students will be tasked with each of those steps. Although some may still demand a degree of deliberation, such as the defense of a particular reform, the fact that the project, as a whole, does not demand deliberation will further disincentivize it even when it is called for. Thus, even if the ultimate aim of the group work is a large-scale project, as it often is in PBL, groups can be held accountable for completing specific steps at specific times, perhaps without any awareness of later steps, so that each group member is focused on the same task at the same time. For instance, if the final goal is a thorough report on some emerging technology and its social impact, groups could be tasked with answering specific questions related to the state of the technology one week, developing a list of stakeholders and their concerns another, and so on. Alternatively, both TBL and SCALE-UP tend to emphasize discrete activities that are introduced and completed in a single class period (or over a single week) and that have no strong relation to later activities, in the sense that earlier products don't get incorporated into later products. Of course, the learning that occurred with earlier activities is relevant for later activities.

Finally, and perhaps less obviously, the insights thus far discussed also suggest that all group members should receive the same grade on group work, assuming it is graded. If, instead, individuals either submitted distinct assignments (even though they were supposed to all draw on the same discussion) or individual grades for a group assignment were varied in some way, then there would be less incentive for collaboration and deliberation, as well as a reduced focus on generating a community. The product would no longer clearly be "our" product and the work no longer clearly "our" work. By solely focusing on the group product, and not individual member contribution and so on, we encourage true community development. Of course, this can generate its own problems related to free riders, but we will discuss how to handle that a bit later. The key, here, is that you need not handle such a problem by differentiating grades for group work and that there are significant costs to doing so.

EFFECTIVE GROUP FORMATION

Once it is reasonably clear what sorts of activities groups will be engaged in, it is now possible to think about the size of the groups and how to go about forming them. There are multiple considerations related to overall context. Much of the literature on groups suggests the ideal group size is 4–5 (Csernica et al., 2002). Some specific collaborative learning techniques, such as SCALE-UP and TBL deviate from this standard for specific pedagogical reasons (Beichner et al., 2007; Gaffney et al., 2008; Michaelsen et al., 1982). Additional considerations are technological limitations and realities of your course/university. For instance, it may be typical for students to drop out of the course and/or cease to participate, so it may be necessary to start with a larger group than what you consider to be ideal, so that the number of active participants settles in closer to the desired group size. The online setting can complicate matters further, where students may not be able to participate regularly or at specific times, in which case larger groups may help facilitate group progress.

The size of the group should match the types of activities students will be completing. TBL suggests groups of six to seven because the activities the groups are completing are designed to be quite difficult. These are typically tasks that no individual could do on their own, but rather those that require six to seven brains to complete. Relatedly, the SCALE-UP method typically suggests groups of 3 students, however in a physical classroom these groups are in close proximity to several other groups, encouraging intergroup collaboration. This is difficult to simulate in the online environment, so it is likely best to use larger sized groups.

Students can be assigned to groups randomly or can be pre-assigned based on set criteria. Most LMSs, such as Canvas or Blackboard, will provide a means of forming random groups. Randomization can be quick but can result in significant and potentially problematic inequalities between groups. For example, one group may end up with all upper-class majors in the relevant discipline whereas another may end up with all first-year students with little or no relevant experience. More deliberate group formation can be done reasonably well even for large courses. Groups could be assigned based on a topic of interest, availability, university status, and/or relevant skills and experience. Data can be collected through an information request to the university or by deploying a survey or pre-assessment to the students. A survey may contain questions such as "Have you taken 2+ university-level humanities courses?" or "Have you worked a full-time job for at least 6 months (or 1 year)." These questions will allow you to create groups with students with varied backgrounds, experiences, and expertise, which will encourage more rich discussions and learning experiences. A pre-assessment will allow students to be sorted based on ability level so that each group has at least one strong member. This is incredibly helpful with first-year courses where there is often a large disparity in preparedness and abilities. These mixed ability groups help provide more stimulating learning environments where more confident students can assist struggling students, providing benefits to all members of the group.

STRUCTURING GROUPS

Once groups are formed, it may be necessary to offer explicit group structuring rather than strictly relying on the structure of the activities to effectively funnel groups into particular structures. This structure may involve assigned meeting times, required methods of communication (such as discussion forum, group chat, shared workspace), group roles (such as recorder, facilitator, timekeeper), or a team contract.

The simplest form of group structuring is to establish clear modes of communication and meeting times. This is especially important for asynchronous courses where students are nevertheless expected to collaborate. You may require students to use a specific mode of communication or let them choose, only holding them accountable for the completed work, not the deliberations leading up to it. Having an established "meeting time" or, more broadly, a timeline for completing relevant work can be valuable. For instance, they may be required to use the discussion board, but then decide amongst themselves when each group member must first engage for the week. Alternatively, they may establish a policy of requiring text-based interaction earlier in the week in preparation for a video meeting later in the week.

When choosing group structures, it is important to keep in mind the aim and goals of the group assignments themselves. All group work should have the goal of producing some sort of artifact or deliverable, representing their learning. This may be a completed worksheet, escape room, approach to solving a problem, a presentation, or an infographic. If the aim of the group work is a product, then the instructor does not need to focus on the process, students will decide amongst themselves how best to achieve the goal. Asking for groups to describe their reasoning process or to show their work can be helpful to gauge how students are engaging with the material and help address misconceptions or potential discord within the group.

A team contract takes this establishment of communication and meeting times a bit further by asking students to establish broader expectations for participation, perhaps setting minimum participation thresholds for each group member, attendance expectations, and other strategies for ensuring work is completed on time and that each member contributes fairly. It is helpful to provide students with example contracts that have worked well in previous semesters because useful group norms will vary based on the types of activities and projects students are expected to complete.

Individual roles within the group can increase productivity by providing structure for how students engage with one another. These roles can be assigned arbitrarily such as based on whose birthday comes next or alphabetically by first name, alternatively, they could also be self-assigned. When choosing what roles to implement, it is important to consider the types of tasks groups will be asked to complete. Examples of possible roles can be found in Table 6.1, which are modified and compiled from Barkley et al., 2014; Johnson et al., 1991; Millis & Cottell, 1997; and Smith, 1996. These roles can, of course, be altered, combined, or eliminated based on the size of the groups and needs of the activity.

TABLE 6.1   Group Role Examples

Role	Description
Facilitator	Makes sure everyone is on task, moderates group discussion, distributes work
Speaker	Presents for the group
Recorder	Keeps a record of group work, posts work to the group space (such as a discussion board)
Questioner (Devil's Advocate)	Makes sure that the group has heard multiple points of view, introduces alternative explanations and solutions
Timekeeper	Encourages the group to stay on task, keeps track of how much time the group has left to work and due dates
Strategy-Analyst	Helps group members come to a common conclusion, does not get caught up in details
Encourager	Makes sure that each member of the group participates, recognizes each member's strengths and contributions
Quality Control	Checks to make sure all group members understand the concepts and the group's conclusions
Explorer	Uses problem-solving strategies to facilitate deeper thinking and explores new areas of inquiry
Wild Card	Assumes necessary role(s) if a group member is missing or needs assistance

ACCOUNTABILITY AND EFFECTIVENESS

Crafting appropriate group activities and providing assistance in structuring groups can go a long way to promoting both individual accountability to the group and effectiveness of the group. However, additional course design elements will likely be necessary to ensure everyone gets the most out of the group work. In particular, it is valuable to promote individual accountability through preparatory assignments and peer assessments. We discuss both techniques here, as well as a third, less common approach to ensuring individual contribution. We end this section with a discussion of one powerful tool for overall group effectiveness: the activity worksheet.

One method of ensuring individual accountability is to require individual group members to engage in some sort of relevant preparatory activity prior to engaging with their group. One option would be some sort of quiz, perhaps over the material students were to have already read in preparation for working with their group. Importantly, if using a quiz like this, it is worth keeping in mind, and making explicit to the students, that this is not a "reading quiz" merely aimed at compliance, but rather is a means of ensuring they have something to contribute to their group as well as helping them see where they may have misunderstandings that they can perhaps remedy with their group. This also means the sorts of questions asked on the quiz should be ones that are important for engaging in the group work. For instance, if the group work will involve evaluating a case by applying a set of related concepts, the quiz could ask students to select the correct definition of each concept, since it will be exceedingly difficult to contribute to the application of a concept without a basic grasp of its meaning. Similarly, if using a reading quiz in this way, it is important to keep in mind that the group work is the main location for students to engage in higher-level thought with the material, and so the quiz questions should remain at a "low" cognitive level, thus predominantly focusing on definitions and explanations. One additional value of a quiz of this sort, for a large class, is that you can usually use your course LMS or some alternative to create and automatically grade the quiz.

An alternative approach to individual preparation, which can be especially useful in courses focused on long-term group projects, is to have individual students attempt to produce some sort of work that will be directly relevant to helping their group complete that week's group work. For instance, if the group will be tasked with completing a stakeholder analysis related to their topic/issue, then individual students could be tasked with identifying two to three potential stakeholders. Presumably, the group will be expected to find a lot more, and perhaps explain their relevance in more detail, but if everyone comes in with a couple potential options, then each individual has something to at least start off the discussion with. So, the upside to this approach, in comparison to a quiz, is that it is a much more transparent form of ensuring individual accountability to the group since the work will directly tie in. The downside, of course, is that grading could be more difficult since these sorts of assignments would not clearly lend themselves to automatic grading. This can be partly handled by low-stakes and coarse-grained grading: For instance, so long as a student attempts to list two stakeholders, then they have "completed" the assignment, even if the two are inaccurate or not well detailed. But, even still, this approach does require more work on behalf of the instructor. It may also, depending on design, incentivize students to avoid any associated reading; so long as they can complete the preparation activity without completing the reading, they may very well do so.

Individual accountability can also be promoted "on the backend" with peer assessment. This is especially helpful if group work is being graded and every member is receiving the same grade. Since that can (appear to) be unfair to students doing more work, you can make the peer assessment available to them as a means of correcting for that unfairness. This is especially valuable since the group members are more likely to have a clearer picture of levels of contribution relative to group expectations. There are a variety of online peer assessment systems, some free and some which require a paid license, but with any of them you can upload the group rosters, set the relevant questions, and the window for completion, and the system will do the rest. There is a lot of scholarship on what peer assessments should look like, ranging from methods that necessitate ranking of group members to others that simply involve rating each member according to certain relevant behaviors. The best approach to use will largely depend on the sorts of activities students are engaged in. No matter the approach used, this is a pretty easy element to grade, as the system will produce some sort of numeric component that can be translated into a grade. For instance, if you have students rate each other across a variety of relevant behaviors ("this person contributes their fair share of the group's work") on a Likert scale and then have the system average across all the behaviors and all the group members, you can produce a number out of 5 or 10 that can be the basis of the peer assessment grade.

It is important, if using a peer assessment, to both give students an opportunity to provide constructive feedback before anyone's grade is impacted (such as through a "practice" peer assessment) as well as to review the peer assessment to ensure there aren't any clear problems. For instance, some students may misread the rating system, treating 1 as the highest rather than 5; or two group members may have a bit of a personality conflict and so tank each other's ratings while the rest of the group presents a different view. Most peer assessment systems provide a means for the instructor to moderate both comments and ratings before releasing reports to the students. Finally, the standard practice with peer assessments is to ensure all ratings and comments are anonymous as well as to limit the number of peer assessments done throughout a course. Too many peer assessments can generate antagonism among group members, but too few can under-incentivize involvement. In our experience, we have found that three peer assessments throughout a semester-long course is appropriate, with the first being a practice assessment that, while identical to the other two, is really used for students to get familiar with the peer assessment system and to provide some corrective feedback early (around Week 4 or 5) before continuing.

A further method of promoting individual accountability is providing groups with a means of excluding an unproductive group member. Depending on context, this may be referred to as "firing" or "divorcing" a group member. No matter the label, this approach should be used judiciously. Typically, for those who do use this, it is considered the "nuclear option": It is more aimed at simply being a threat that encourages involvement so that it never comes to pass. Hence those who refer to it as "divorce" emphasize that the group must go through "counseling" with the instructor prior to excommunicating a member. Further, depending on the overall structure of the course, a student without a group may be unable to pass the course—for instance, they may receive no credit for any group work—and/or may have to petition another group to accept them. Neither of the authors here have ever used this method, given its high stakes, but certain conditions may support its use.

Finally, more as a means of promoting group effectiveness than individual accountability, you'll want to consider the degree of structure you provide groups to complete an activity. This could range from no structure—you simply pose a question that they must answer and leave it up to the group to figure out how to work through the issue—to very precise structure where students are led on their deliberations, by specific questions, culminating in something like the main answer or recommendation. If students are more advanced and/or part of the learning outcomes for the course involve figuring out how to work through complex problems, then less structure may be appropriate. On the other hand, with less advanced students or just as a means of putting the focus on different learning outcomes (such as applying theories) more structure would be appropriate. One of the best ways to provide structure, as supported by recent empirical work, is through a group worksheet (Weir et al., 2019). In designing such worksheets, it can be helpful to simply break down the process you, or any expert in the relevant field, would go through to answer the "big question" that you are trying to get students to answer. For instance, if the final goal is for groups to make a recommendation in a case but you want to ensure they examine the case in all the appropriate ways, you can break down each step into its own question/prompt.

Although worksheets can be a powerful tool no matter the size or delivery method of the course, they are especially helpful in large online classrooms for two reasons. First, evaluating or providing feedback is more straightforward on a worksheet than on an unstructured activity. You are able to examine each question along the way, perhaps noting where the group went astray, and, if the build-up questions are such that they have truly correct answers, then you can also easily mark which they got correct or not. Since many of the most effective group activities, especially in the humanities or social sciences, do not lend themselves to singular "correct" answers (but rather focus more on the reasoning/application to get to or support an answer), having build-up questions that do so lend themselves helps students more immediately develop from feedback. Second, since it can be difficult to be constantly available for all groups in a large course, the worksheet doubles as a secondary "instructor" by appropriately prompting the groups and providing focus. A more unstructured activity may result in students feeling lost and/or constantly reaching out to the instructor for assistance.

EVALUATING GROUP WORK

Group activities may serve as formative or summative assessments (or both). Formative assessments are typically aimed at facilitating learning through practice, and therefore carry little to no grade impact. Many instructors who use TBL, for instance, do not grade the group's work, but rather regard it as a means for individuals to practice relevant skills and receive immediate feedback (both from peers and the instructor) in order to improve prior to individual summative assessments. Problem-based learning (PBL), on the other hand, treats the groupwork, or at least the final product of the groupwork, as a summative assessment. Students in a PBL course will not typically have individual summative assessments alongside the group product, although they may have individual formatives assessments or graded peer assessments. Put another way, when groupwork is used for formative assessment, it is typically understood as a means to an end, the end being the individual performance. When it is used as a summative assessment, it simply is the end. Which approach you choose may partly depend on the outcomes for the course—do they include a heavy focus on collaborative production? If so, at least some group work should function as a summative assessment. If, on the other hand, none of your course learning outcomes emphasize collaborative engagement, then group work could be seen as purely formative. There are, of course, middle positions as well. Additionally, although there is value in ensuring individual preparation and accountability no matter the role of the group work, it may be less important if the group work is simply practice, rather than the major element of a student's grade.

Feedback to students is important but providing individual feedback in large classes is a challenge. The use of groups eases this burden because feedback can also be provided by other members of the group in addition to the faculty member. It is also possible to incorporate self-grading "quizzes" either through in-class polls or online forms that can provide students with immediate feedback regarding their accuracy. An answer key for a group worksheet can also be provided after class for students to verify their approach and their answers. Another option is to feature the work of a few of the groups and encourage feedback from peers. These no-stakes or low-stakes activities keep the emphasis of the group space on the process of learning, allowing students to take risks and work through problems without the pressure of getting the answer correct on the first try.

For summative assessments, the use of rubrics may be helpful. This not only streamlines the grading process, but also communicates expectations and objectives to students allowing them to weigh their final product against the rubric as well. Well-written rubrics can be challenging to design, but many universities have example rubrics for various types of projects that are useful as a starting place. It may be helpful for a component of the grade to reflect the individual performance of a student perhaps based on a self and peer evaluation of fellow group members, but this should be communicated effectively at the start of the summative assessment.

CREATING THE GROUP SPACE

The most direct way to set up a group working space, for most faculty, will be to use their university provided LMS. These systems typically provide a method of organizing students into groups and then providing each group with its own designated discussion board area as well as allowing for group submission of assignments. The group discussion board can be used as the main method of facilitating group deliberation and provides an instructor-facing record of what the group has discussed. Group submission of assignments can be helpful, especially for speeding up grading, since it usually allows the instructor to grade the single submitted assignment and that grade will apply to all members of the group automatically. Some LMS also have methods for synchronous text or video chat, which tend to be better for promoting true deliberation, but which may not produce a record of the group's work. Finally, using the university-wide LMS can be beneficial for students because they will typically already have some understanding of how the system works, or at the very least, their learning of the system will be relevant to other courses they take as well. This can help to reduce the overall cognitive load on students, especially early in the semester, and thus allow them to focus more on the course learning and less on the technology learning.

The use of an LMS may have drawbacks. Depending on the specific system, they are often not the most intuitive or inviting for students. The use of LMS discussion boards, in particular, can feel quite isolating to students and result in very sterile discussions as a result. Thus, in this way, they can work against the fullest development of social presence for students, especially by encouraging, by design, more formal engagement. While some level of formality is certainly preferable, as we discuss later in this section, groups that have opportunities for informal engagement tend to be more effective in the long run. An additional potential issue is that the LMS may not allow for the sorts of collaboration you are looking for. For instance, they tend not to have a built-in way for students to collaborate on the same document or maintain a shared set of persistent notes. This can be remedied by incorporating some outside systems, such as Google Docs or Office Online, but then students are being asked to make use of more than one technological ecosystem, which can increase cognitive load and thus have a negative effect on learning.

There are many benefits to creating a synchronous group space where students meet at an assigned time. This helps to build instructor presence and a learning community, where students can make connections with other students in the course as well as the instructor. These meetings can involve a mixture of active learning activities with the entire class, such as with polls and debriefing sessions, interspersed with group space activities. Depending on the platform used to coordinate the meetings, breakout rooms can be pre-assigned or students can choose their group's specific breakout room. An additional option is for breakout rooms to be randomly assigned, but due to the time it takes for group norms and productivity to establish, this is not recommended. For the large classroom, pre-assigning groups can be challenging due to constraints of the meeting platform, it is also necessary for students to log in with a predictable email address, but this can be done. Manually assigning more than 30 students during a live class is not recommended, necessitating either pre-assigned groups or students being able to select their assigned room. Once the breakout rooms are assigned, the instructor can open and close the breakout rooms many times during a class session, allowing for small group discussions as well as whole class debriefings.

While students are in breakout rooms, the instructor can float from room to room to check progress and offer suggestions. From personal experience, students seem much more apt to ask questions in these more intimate settings rather than in front of the entire class. As the number of groups increases, it is more difficult for the instructor to make it to each breakout room during class, but students can "ask for help," which prompts the instructor to visit that specific breakout room. It is also helpful for the instructor to set up an informal rotation to make sure that over the course of a few class meetings the instructor visits each group. When designing activities for students to complete in the breakout room, it is best if they have a deliverable, such as a discussion board post, a post to the meeting chat, a verbal share out, preparation for a class discussion, or an online form submission.

A final option for creating and organizing the group space is to leverage the ever-increasing domain of project management software. These are software platforms, like Microsoft Teams, Slack, and Trello, that are sometimes used in large organizations to help members of those organizations manage projects and swiftly communicate, especially in a remote environment. One immediate benefit of such systems, then, is that it is becoming increasingly likely students will need to be reasonably familiar with such software in order to effectively contribute in the workplace. Additionally, these systems typically provide multiple modes of communication that are more natural for students than LMS discussion boards, including persistent chat (a mixture of text messaging and discussion boards) and audio/video chat. They can also often be combined with shared documents or workspaces; for instance, Microsoft Teams integrates Microsoft OneNote to allow for a shared "notebook" where designated people can contribute and view each other's contributions. Thus, these systems are especially helpful if you will be leaving the modes of communication largely up to the students, as they can then engage in multiple ways as needed. Typically, these systems are also platform-agnostic, allowing students to access them from any type of computer or smartphone operating system.

A further, but perhaps unusual, benefit of a project management system is that it can better encourage informal or "off-topic" discussions among group members than (for instance) an LMS discussion board. It is, predominantly, the persistent chat feature that can permit this, as it feels more like texting with friends than writing a formal post. Now, it may seem unusual to want to encourage such off-topic discussions, but the work on social presence in the classroom has suggested that informal engagement is valuable in developing social presence and helping groups to form a shared identity that has a positive effect on their overall performance and learning.

FUTURE RESEARCH AND RECOMMENDATIONS

We have endeavored to both make the case for collaborative learning and to identify some best practices for effective collaborative learning. Along the way, we have drawn on learning theories, existing empirical studies of pedagogical methods, and our own experience. Based on the existing evidence, we believe there is a strong case for focusing on collaborative learning, no matter the learning environment. However, there are at least two areas of relative weakness in the existing literature that merit further exploration and the findings in those areas may justifiably alter our conclusions.

First, it would be helpful to research the comparative benefits of online collaboration between synchronous and asynchronous course designs. Collaboration is possible in both cases but must be done differently in each. For instance, collaboration in a synchronous online course is necessarily constrained by the set meeting time while collaboration in an asynchronous online course can permit more intermittent and free-flowing collaboration across a longer period of time. It should be reasonably clear that each of these approaches has its benefits and drawbacks, and so an overall comparison of the two approaches and their impact on student learning would be helpful in progressing the discussion of how best to integrate collaborative learning into online courses and how to structure online courses more generally.

Second, there has been relatively little focus on how different techniques for collaborative learning, or collaborative learning as a whole, affect students at different educational levels. Do first-year students benefit more from direct instruction than seniors, who are perhaps in a better position to benefit from collaborative learning? Is there any major difference in learning outcomes between majors and nonmajors when using collaborative techniques in higher-level courses? While the extant research has been carried out on students from a variety of different educational levels, it has not typically been the aim of that research to provide comparisons. Rather, the foci are typically on the techniques and the relevant course. However, comparative research may show us that certain conditions must be met for collaborative work to be (highly) successful. This would, then, help us develop a more comprehensive approach to educational experiences that may combine collaboration with other techniques when appropriate given the relevant student population. Currently, since most research draws conclusions based on the studied population, which may be diverse in terms of the factors here described, it largely covers any of these potential differences.

Even granting the need for further research, our aim in this chapter has been to synthesize widespread literature encompassing a variety of collaborative learning techniques to identify general best practices for collaborative learning. These best practices can be summarized thusly:

1. *Fixed Teams:* To get the most out of collaborative learning, students need to interact with the same people regularly over an extended period of time.
2. *Deliberation:* To ensure true interactivity, ensure activities engage teams in deliberation that require agreement on certain decisions.
3. *Higher-Level Thought:* To further promote team interaction, ensure teams are engaged in activities that no member is likely to be able to do on her own. This typically means higher levels of thought—

analysis, synthesis, evaluation—rather than simple memorization or verification of understanding.
4. *Transparent & Deliberate Group Formation:* If possible, deliberately organize groups around transparent criteria aimed at promoting diverse thought and disagreement.
5. *Ensure Individual Accountability:* Provide a means, prior and/or posterior to the relevant teamwork, for ensuring individual preparation and involvement.
6. *Promote Team Building:* Use activities, such as team contracts and team performance reports, to promote team building and team effectiveness.

CONCLUSION

It is not uncommon for faculty to express dread at having to teach large courses, and especially large online courses. This is understandable, since such environments pose challenges for establishing the sort of learning community and experiences faculty typically aim for. Even in cases where faculty embrace the challenge, the result can often be an excessive grading or other administrative burden. Nonetheless, in this chapter we have suggested that the use of collaborative learning can help to overcome these challenges so that instructors can simultaneously create high impact learning experiences and ease their own burden. Readers now motivated to adopt some of these practices are encouraged to think clearly about what students should get out of their courses and how best to organize collaborative learning so that students achieve those outcomes. With a keen focus on an observable group product, with the right accountability structures in place, it is possible to provide students a learning experience that feels like a small seminar, even if the course as a whole is populated by hundreds of their peers.

NOTES

1. The literature on the difference between collaborative learning and cooperative learning is quite poor on maintaining a standard distinction. While some (e.g., (Laal & Laal, 2012; Michaelsen et al., 2002) of the literature tracks the difference in the way we describe here, other work flips the labeling, thus treating cooperative learning as the interactive approach (e.g., (Paulson, 1999)). And still others identify cooperative or collaborative learning with there being a shared goal, rather than with any particular process or engagement (e.g., Johnson & Johnson, 1999). Other distinctions, for instance about whether students have assigned roles or not, are also discussed. Nothing

much hangs on the terms we use, so long as we keep in mind the same meaning. Thus, for our purposes, the key issue is the degree of interactivity.
2. Importantly, some "provide a definition" activities could demand higher-level thinking, just so long as students are being required to craft a definition (or choose from among a set of reasonable possibilities) and defend it by appeal to other (course) ideas.

REFERENCES

Barkley, E. F., Cross, K. P., & Major, C. H. (2014). *Collaborative learning techniques: A handbook for college faculty.* John Wiley & Sons.

Beichner, R. J., Saul, J. M., Abbott, D. S., Morse, J. J., Deardorff, D., Allain, R. J., Bonham, S., Dancy, M. H, & Risley, J. S. (2007). The student-centered activities for large enrollment undergraduate programs (SCALE-UP) project. *Research-Based Reform of University Physics, 1*(1), 2–39.

Bloom, B. S. (1979). *Taxonomy of educational objectives: The classification of educational goals handbook I.* Longman.

Csernica, J., Hanyak, M., Hyde, D., Shooter, S., Toole, M., & Vigeant, M. (2002). *Practical guide to teamwork.* College of Engineering, Bucknell University.

Deslauriers, L., McCarty, L. S., Miller, K., Callaghan, K., & Kestin, G. (2019). Measuring actual learning versus feeling of learning in response to being actively engaged in the classroom. *Proceedings of the National Academy of Sciences, 116*(39), 19251–19257.

Dewey, J. (1938). *Experience and education.* Collier Books.

Elliott, S. N., Kratochwill, T. R., Littlefield Cook, J., & Travers, J. (2000). *Educational psychology: Effective teaching effective learning.* McGraw-Hill College.

Gaffney, J. D., Richards, E., Kustusch, M. B., Ding, L., & Beichner, R. J. (2008). Scaling up education reform. *Journal of college science teaching, 37*(5), 48–53.

Gokhale, A. (1995). Collaborative learning enhances critical thinking. *Journal of Technology Education, 7*(1), 22–30.

Irwin, C., & Berge, Z. (2006). Socialization in the Online Classroom. *E-Journal of Instructional Science and Technology, 9*(1), 1–7.

Johnson, D. W., & Johnson, R. T. (1999). *Learning together and alone: cooperative, competitive, and individualistic learning.* Allyn & Bacon.

Johnson, D. W., Johnson, R. T., & Smith, K. A. (1991). Cooperative learning: Increasing college faculty instructional productivity. *ASHE-ERIC Higher Education Report, 4.* https://files.eric.ed.gov/fulltext/ED343465.pdf

Laal, M., & Laal, M. (2012). Collaborative learning: What is it? *Procedia–Social and Behavioral Sciences, 31,* 491–495. https://doi.org/10.1016/J.SBSPRO.2011.12.092

Michaelsen, L. K., Knight, A. B., & Fink, L. D. (Eds.). (2002). *Team-based learning: A transformative use of small groups in college teaching.* Praeger.

Michaelsen, L. K., Watson, W., Cragin, J. P., & Dee Fink, L. (1982). Team learning: A potential solution to the problems of large classes. *Exchange: The organizational behavior teaching journal, 7*(1), 13–22.

Millis, B. J., & Cottell, P. G. J. (1997). *Cooperative learning for higher education faculty*. Oryx Press.

Palincsar, A. S. (1998). Social constructivist perspectives on teaching and learning. *Annual review of psychology, 49*(1), 345–375.

Paulson, D. R. (1999). Active learning and cooperative learning in the organic chemistry lecture class. *Journal of Chemical Education, 76*(8), 1136–1140.

Phillips, D. C. (1995). The good, the bad, and the ugly: The many faces of constructivism. *Educational researcher, 24*(7), 5–12.

Ritchhart, R., & Church, M. (2020). *The power of making thinking visible: Practices to engage and empower all learners*. Jossey-Bass.

Smith, K. (1996). Cooperative learning: Making "groupwork" work. In T. Sutherland & C. Bonwell (Eds.), *Using active learning in college classes: A range of options for faculty* (pp. 71–82). Jossey-Bass.

Swan, K., & Richardson, J. (2017). Social presence and the community of inquiry framework. In A. L. Whiteside, A. G. Dikkers, & K. Swan (Eds.), *Social presence in online learning: Multiple perspectives on practice and research* (pp. 64–76). Stylus Publishing.

Vygotsky, L. S. (1978). *Mind in society: Development of higher psychological processes*. Harvard University Press.

Weir, L. K., Barker, M. K., McDonnell, L. M., Schimpf, N. G., Rodela, T. M., & Schulte, P. M. (2019). Small changes, big gains: A curriculum-wide study of teaching practices and student learning in undergraduate biology. *PLOS ONE, 14*(8), e0220900. https://doi.org/10.1371/journal.pone.0220900

Wiggins, G., & McTighe, J. (2005). *Understanding by design* (2nd ed.). Association for Supervision and Curriculum Development.

CHAPTER 7

ENGAGEMENT AND CRITICAL AND ETHICAL THINKING—EFFECTIVE ONLINE TEACHING WITH LARGE ONLINE STUDENT COHORTS

Anti-Racist Pedagogy and First Nations Studies

Mary Frances O'Dowd
Educational Research and Consultancy

ABSTRACT

Large online cohorts can have minimally engaged students who feel unengaged and isolated. This chapter indicates how the large online environment can be a very effective and rewarding teaching context. It provides proven strategies and techniques to foster student engagement and to promote deep critical and ethical thinking. The chapter identifies four critical periods; these are (a) Preparation (the most important); (b) Engagement and Week 3; (c)

Assessment & Feedback; and (d) Final 2 Weeks & Improving Evaluations. The context is a discipline noted for student resistance—a mandatory 12-week unit in First Nations' Studies where 85% or more of students are non-Indigenous. The strategies and insights described have been acquired and refined over 10 years of tertiary teaching, brought into large scale online teaching contexts and received university awards. The chapter enables those new to large scale online teaching as well as skilled practitioners to extend their pedagogical efficacy.

This chapter extends discussions on fostering engagement and deep critical and ethical thinking in large online teaching classes (120 students upward). There is a need to focus on student engagement (Cooper & Robinson, 2000), to develop a sense of academic community (Chapman et al., 2005), and have quality materials to enable critical thinking (Tsui, 2002). Online teaching is not primarily about technological wizardry, it is about applying and embedding good educational practice such as reflection and other active learning strategies (Brown et al., 2014; Lang, 2016). The chapter begins with an explicit background reflection on how pedagogical knowledge from other formats informs planning. It sequentially discusses four critical periods. Critical Period 1 covers preparation for managing a large cohort, structuring of the large cohort into teachable groups, staff ratios, and tutorial sizes. It details the important work of tutor preparation. It indicates how assessments design, online forums, unit design, lectures, and deliberate relationship building work together to maximize engagement and critical thinking. In Critical Period 2, it provides key strategies for the critical threshold in engagement of Week 3, which Salmon (2013) identifies as the last significant point to actively engage students who up to that point have remained marginally involved. Assessment marking is privileged in Critical Period 3; and Critical Period 4 discusses continuing momentum to the last weeks to ensure students have a clear understanding of their learning journey and are enabled to provide a more thoughtful evaluation. The recommendations for further research and conclusions draw attention to the key role of lecturer advocacy to ensure large scale online teaching strategies and praxis are adequately resourced and, that units focused on social justice and anti-racist pedagogy are not marginalized by institutional practice focused on profit before quality.

BACKGROUND REFLECTION ON PEDAGOGY IN THE SUBJECT

Experienced teachers bring important pedagogical knowledge into the online environment. It is useful to reflect on the learning difficulties students frequently experience in this subject, and how to embed responses to student needs in the design of the large online pedagogy. Planning and preparation are key as it is harder to win back student engagement in a large impersonal online environment than in a face-to-face context or in a smaller online space.

The discipline I teach is First Nations Studies (Indigenous Studies); I am based in Australia. Most of the students (about 85%) who enroll in this subject are non-Indigenous and enroll, not out of interest, but because it is a *mandatory* component in several professional degree courses, including the Bachelor of Social Work, Bachelor of Health Sciences, and Bachelor of Education. The non-Indigenous students often tend to regard the unit as a "tick the box" requirement, an unnecessary exercise in political correctness, and perceive it as a place of threatening knowledges that infer racism (Aveling, 2006). This subject is noted for non-Indigenous student resistance and poor student evaluations—even in face-to-face learning (Aveling, 2006; Tate & Bagguley, 2017). The history of the invasion and colonization of Australia (the unit content) is a contested narrative (Bekerman & Zembylas, 2011) and "troubling knowledges" (Zembylas, 2013) because it creates affective, as well as cognitive, challenges. Student resistance often masks ignorance, insecurity, and vulnerability, which form barriers to engagement and to interrogating racism. Students need to be engaged, supported, and challenged to think critically so the online teaching pedagogy must be planned and approached with a deliberate focus on engagement and support, to enable critical thinking and ethical reflection (O'Dowd, 2010).

Non-Indigenous students begin to critically engage with racism. They consider how racism is embedded in foundational White history of the nation and in "taken for granted beliefs" that typically exclude ideas of invaders dispossessing sovereign Indigenous peoples.

Student engagement is critical and forums and discussion boards are established to enable reflection on the historiography of formative national history, and master narratives that have created rather that described what is (Bell, 2014; Berger, 2009; Thijs, 2008).

The students' belief and imagining of a benign heroic national identity and pioneer mythology have to be critically engaged with and history unlearned (O'Dowd, 2012) as part of unlearning racism (Cochran-Smith, 2000). Yet the pioneer imagining has saturated generations of settlers–colonizers' sense of self and history in art, film, story, poetry, and formal education (O'Dowd, 2011). Learning is assisted by scaffolding students' awareness of the mythology of settler colonialism as not exclusively national (Australian). The mythology runs through the foundational national histories and White national identities in each AANZCUS nation (Australia, Aotearoa/New Zealand, Canada and the United States); they share the commonality of an imagined legitimate possession and the construction of "a problem" and "a savage primitive" Indigenous people.

Understanding the United States's "wagon train imagining" of good honest folk opening up the frontier, facing "savages," and the resulting construction of a problematization of Native Americans (Rifkin, 2012), enables the Aussie students to then engage with Australian history that has similiar constructions of First Nations people as "the problem" (Russell, 2001) and begin to see the problem of a settler invasion. Students begin to understand master narratives as more than national and so are less likely to react affectively and assume their personal/national identity is being attacked. Students are thus supported into engaging with the newer revised academic history which details of the brutality of dispossession and the attempted genocide of First Nations peoples (Reynolds, 2006; Wolfe, 2006). The online pedagogy discussed here enables students to critically engage with former historical understanding and to understand and interrogate the racist assumptions that enabled dispossession and violence. Bringing pedagogical understandings of the discipline's strengths and challenges into planning a large online environment is a transferable strength, but there are techniques that assist.

Next, the chapter contributes to understanding effective techniques and strategies. The pedagogy discussed embraces: peer education, supporting and challenging students to develop critical and ethical thinking; fostering respectful relationships (teacher with student [Freire, 1996] and student with student [Major, 2015]) and a developing a sense of engagement and community (Conrad, 2005). Further, it is designed to enable students to be reflective and informed students and future professionals, able to work respectfully with First Nations people and willing to address racism. The chapter now moves sequentially through the four critical periods

CRITICAL PERIOD ONE: PREPARATION

The weekly format in my units is an online lecture, a two-hour tutorial which develops on the lecture through discussion topics and activities (drawing on pre-existing online media). Students are expected to prepare for the tutorial by completing two mandatory (provided) academic readings. The preparation, lecture, and tutorial (and its discussion forums) focus on integrating engagement (and relationship building as part of this) to foster and practice critical and ethical thinking. Important components are staffing ratios and unit organization, lecturer and tutor roles, effective assessment, stimulating forums, and dialogical lectures designed to foster key learning relationships to build a learning community. Additionally, in a large online unit, the elements above maintain student and lecturer/tutor time on task and reduce unnecessary email traffic. Ideally the lecturer also works as a tutor to a cohort, as this deepens awareness of how the students are engaging.

Core to effective teaching in large online cohorts is staffing and *organizing students into reasonable sized learning communities*. Students are divided into tutorial groups, and they stay in these groups all semester. They go to the larger unit for the lecture and learning resources and return to their tutorial group. Staffing and the ratio of staff to students are important considerations. The lecturer needs to ensure that the tutorial size is appropriate. In large online cohorts, numbers of students often exceed 120 so tutors are required to ensure students receive timely support and feedback in the discussion forums and assessments. The math determines the number of tutors required. Essays and reports (1,500–2,000 words) are a major assessment tool in my units (usually two per semester) and a marking time of 30 minutes is required with a university stipulated 2-week turn around period. Given the other responsibilities of lecturer and tutors, marking for 30 hours a week is a maximum; it takes 2 full weeks for one person to mark 120 assessments.

The tutorial group size may vary. In my discipline, a tutorial size for the weekly discussion group of about 35–40 students per tutorial is a reasonable number for quality teaching and learning and recognizes that some online students prefer not to post more than required. The size of the tutorial group can vary depending on the year level and the discipline; for example, units with first-year, first-semester students may require more support (Tinto, 2009); and units with "troubling knowledges" such as racism (Cochran-Smith, 2000; Wagner, 2005; Zembylas, 2013) require more contact time. When discussion forums are working well, they are sites of significant engagement and critical and ethical thinking and require careful monitoring. In this context then, the engagement and tutoring is at least equivalent to face-to-face time and generally more intensive, particularly in the first half of semester when gaining engagement is key (Salmon, 2013).

The lecturer has to be explicit on the *roles and responsibilities of the lecturer and the tutor* from the outset. Institutions need to support tutors in their role with the provision and payment for preparation time. The lecturer's role embraces orientation and preparation time for the tutors so they acquire a good knowledge of the unit content and pedagogy—if they do not already have this. It includes raising the tutors' awareness of issues including that students often feel apprehensive coming into this unit as it addresses racism, so it is important they feel welcomed and that the tutor's role explicitly involves relationship building. The tutors are guided into how the unit content scaffolds the students, how the forums are designed to function, and how their role is to support, monitor, and respond to students. The importance of the pedagogy underpinning the unit, in this case ethical reflection (O'Dowd, 2010) is made clearer; as is the importance of the unit requirement for students to support their online posting with an academic reference and a basic ethical justification. An ethical justification moves a response from assertions, such as "I disagree," to a reasoned response that considers the social good "this advantages society because..." and an academic reference (e.g., from the unit's academic readings). This enables less acrimonious and more open discussions which is important in the context of racism.

The tutor's role has to be explicitly provided by the lecturer and with strategies. The role includes consciously fostering relationships with students, each other and the subject matter; to monitor and respond carefully in forums because this is the cornerstone of learning; they must understand the assessments as this is frequently raised by students in week 1; and provide quality feedback in assessments. They must have a clear picture of how to navigate and locate the online materials.

The tutor reinforces what is expected from students, including the time commitment required by students each week and understands that this often needs to be gently reinforced. The tutor is familiarized with electronic tracking of student online contact and how this facilitates awareness of who needs encouragement and support (outlined later in Critical Period 2).

The lecturer informs tutors that they are supported throughout semester, including with formal sessions in week 2 and prior to assessments. Tutors also need to be informed of university services that support students so they can direct students to services (e.g., to a free online university counseling service for personal or academic skills). The preparation ensures the tutor is clear on their role and responsibilities and the support available. Tutors will have a manageable and clear workload and adequate teaching time for their role. The time allocation, as discussed, should be comparable to face-to-face tutorials.

It is important to privilege the requirement for good tutors *and* resourcing tutors is a foundation stone for success when teaching large online cohorts. The lecturer has to ensure, or try to ensure, good tutors. But this is where institutional factors may form significant barriers if tutor recruitment is poorly done, and tutors without discipline expertise are appointed; in this situation, an excellent unit becomes less than adequate. It is where large online teaching units run into problems and gain a poor reputation. Tutors must have discipline expertise in the subject. It sounds obvious, but is not always the practice. The issue is compounded when a university fails to provide sufficient (or any) preparation time for the tutor to engage with the unit material. Some faculties have been known to appoint markers at the last moment (Week 3 of semester) as a stop gap. Hence the lecturer in large online cohorts has a critical advocacy role because any unit is only as good as its tutors and resourcing.

The assessment design needs careful consideration as a pedagogical tool to foster engagement in the unit and assess knowledge and understanding. The assessment does not operate in isolation but should be consciously linked with the discussion forums and building peer relationships. It is useful to consider assessments in this relationship because in large online units significant numbers of students often need motivation to post and engage. Assessments are more effective and relevant when they require engagement with the weekly lectures, tutorials, readings, and discussion forums. By engaging in the unit discussions and content students' knowledge deepens. Therefore, it is useful to make explicit links between the assessment and the weekly content and the discussion forums. It is not difficult to craft the first assessment task so it has a component that requires posting in the weekly discussion forum. Thus students need to engage in weekly content and active thinking.

My first assessment asks for five posts in four different weeks in the first half of the semester, and two of these posts must be replies to other student's posts. This part of the assessment also requires the student to support their post on the discussion forum with an academic reference. When responding to a peer's post, the student has to affirm what was good in the post and provide a respectful suggestion on how the post might be improved, such as providing a reference or quote. This fosters academic skills, critical and ethical thinking, and reinforces academic writing. Importantly it establishes student engagement early in the unit. It is purposeful as when the students are ready to write their assessment they already have part of it complete and some references. The other major component of the first assessment is an essay or report that requires content knowledge, a conclusion that includes their critical and ethical reflection on their ethical position, and how the latter has been influenced by their reading or thinking in the unit. This further reinforces the value and practice of the discussion forum. The assessment marking rubric further fosters intellectual engagement by one of the assessment criterion including, "engagement with unit readings and lectures as relevant to the question."

Forums facilitate engagement and critical and ethical thinking. Tutors must be made aware of the function of each forum and their key role in posting (as indicated below). The *weekly discussion forum* is the core forum where students draw on their ideas arising from the lecture (and its "pause and consider" points—discussed later). Here students post their response to the key ethical questions and ideas arising from the lecture and tutorial reading material. The specified requirement, stated above, of an academic reference, as well as furthering scholarship, enables a cognitive response to the affective issues that the content generates. The reference and the ethical thinking assists in reducing racist posts as it reinforces the discourse required by academia. Monitoring and responding to the discussion forum is the tutor's task, but not policing it, as students often respond with sensitivity to each other and peer learning is facilitated. Students typically listen more readily to the lived experience of each other; for example, the lecture might indicate there was a silence in Australian history (Stanner, 1969) that often continues in the current education system. One student might post, annoyed or outraged, that this was not her experience but others respond that this was their experience. This sharing broadens experience and knowledge.

Importantly, the student can post as much as she/he wishes but selects which four of their posts they wish to present for assessment so they have control. The discussion forum typically moves from a requirement into a site of interested commentary, serving peer learning and participatory community building. Student evaluations of the unit regularly emphasize the important role of the discussions. The critical and ethical thinking skills acquired and developed in the discussion forum transfer to the assessment.

Another useful forum is the *introductory forum*. It is not compulsory, but in Week 1 students are asked to post their transformative vision for society—the changes they would like to see and achieve and to consider how this subject might assist. This promotes interest in the subject and with each other. These "Why am I here?" questions and "How I want to transform the world," enable the students to link to big issues, express their ideals, and so link the subject to their life. Many students post and many more read the posts.

A *key learnings to date/ethical reflections' forum* enables students to post ideas, affective reactions, and resulting cognitive positions that have impacted on them as they engage in learning and ethical reflection. It slowly develops over the semester and functions as an important site for reinforcement, motivation, and revision. It operates best when optional.

A *question and answer forum (Q&A)* is best as a tutor only answer site to questions so no mistakes are reinforced. At the start of semester the tutors are required to inform the lecturer and students which days they will be online as a timely response to student queries is important.

Tutors need to be sensitive to culture and history and the risks of trauma. In the units I teach about 10–15% of students identify as First Nations Australians. Typically, they do not demonstrate resistance to content; they understand the nation's history as including invasion and dispossession; the national narrative of "noble White pioneers" is already problematic. They do not need to be convinced that racism exists. However, First Nations students may experience affective responses, including trauma, that arise from the content history which embraces the brutality of colonialism, including, "Stolen Generations" (Boarding schools being a similar North American equivalent assimilationist abuse). While First Nations students should have the option of own unit run by an Indigenous lecturer, meeting the United Nations Declaration on the Rights of Indigenous People (UNDRIP) is still not routinized in all universities. In lieu of this, I provide a forum that is exclusive to First Nations Australians, if they chose to use it, in an attempt to provide some cultural safety. Here students can discuss their concerns without non-Indigenous peoples' gaze or input.

The forums, particularly the Q&A forum, have another important implicit function which is *reducing email traffic*. One of the big dangers in a large scale unit is that too much teaching time becomes email time responding to individual students. Tutors have to be strategic and from Week 1 the lecturer and tutor encourages and socializes students into their responsibility to look for the material in the online unit/resources, using the Q&A forum for routine questions, and posting their reflections in other forums as their contribution to peer learning. It is useful pedagogy to guide students firmly to the practices required. It must be done supportively with a reply to any individual student email but while replying directly pointing out that the email should go to, for example, Q&A forum as it is valuable and their response assists other students. The reply must be done in a kindly and respectful manner, without rebuke, and indicating only clarification. Clarity, in the use of email and forums, avoids drowning in emails and losing quality teaching time. It is useful to imagine that the minority of students who fail to follow the email protocol have a full-time job, an unsupportive partner, a major tragedy, and care for their elderly bedridden parents. This facilitates patience and reminds one that when you have many students, such hardship and tragedy are part of some students' lives.

Zoom tutorials can augment tutorials. These are live and then recorded for those who cannot attend. This chapter does not focus on this due to space restrictions. It is normal for engagement on the discussion forum to ease after the compulsory posting ends, and Zoom tutorials can be more valuable at this time.

A primary relationship is the lecturer with tutor (and vice versa) and is formed with preparation time and support through semester (as previously discussed).The tutor's role is to foster three student relationships: tutor and student, student with student, and student with the subject content. Relationships foster students' sense of membership, community belonging, and engagement with learning (Tinto, 2010; Wehlage & Rutter, 1985). Relationships between students facilitate engagement and peer learning (Boud et al., 2014). These relationships are structurally embedded by the lecturer through the above strategies. The three key relationships require respect and highlight the importance of a tutor with discipline expertise (this a cornerstone) in order to respond to both the cognitive and the affective needs of the students. Tutor guidance and affirmation deepens this culture of support: some individual-posted responses from the tutor, but also a systemized and reasonably detailed summative weekly response based on the previous week's discussion forum postings. A tutor can group email responses in key themes, indicating the commonalities, but always using the student's first name which indicates the post has been read and appreciated. The tutor adds and reinforces learning by asking questions that prompt deeper critical and ethical thinking, encouraging students to move their thinking, perhaps from a locally based ethical position of self and family to community; to region, state and nation—and also globally. Students both strong and weaker can be affirmed and guided with questions that would assist them to think more deeply. This scaffolds and extends all students. Through the part of the assessment requiring forum posting to a peer, peer dialogue is fostered and the students begin forming relationships with peers and the subject. The relationship to the subject is encouraged by the ethical reflection. The unit is not about political orthodoxy but about fostering the capacity to think justly and support views with academic literature. The student explains why they have reached a view and the online peer and tutor culture enables and fosters support in extending or modifying that view. As the semester progresses the tentative membership with the subject deepens with new academic ideas and reflection.

The lecturer's distinct role is preparing and designing the 12-weeks unit; setting up content purposefully (as indicated above). Therefore, in designing the unit online navigation should be as intuitive as possible for students and all required information and resources easily accessible. The layout of a unit is assisted by simplicity and consistency in how content is presented each week and from week to week. Students should learn quickly in Week 1 how to access the lectures, readings, tutorials, and discussion forums and the function they hold. The lecturer sets the culture as one of support. In the tutorial discussion forum questions that the lecturer sets, there should be an example response of what is required in the first few weeks; the assessment needs discussion; the philosophy needs explanation; and of course, information needs to be reinforced as few students absorb advice in one iteration. Click links with key information provided as PDFs or videos reduces unnecessary repetition. This facilitates student time on task and minimizes time wasted in navigation and clarification.

When Week 1 begins, the unit should have capable and resourced tutors who understand the what, when, where, and how of the unit (as discussed earlier in preparation time). The online explanations may be in several formats, such as a recorded introduction and optional links to textual PDF detail. Students will learn what will occur and what is required. They will know their tutorial group and have a tutor who has introduced herself/himself.

The lecturer writes and delivers the lectures to reinforce the culture of engagement and critical and ethical thinking through academic justification and support. An introduction to the lecture in Week 1 might advise students,

> You are beginning a learning journey where your thinking and ideas will be extended- as you expect. Here is an outline of what to expect. Each week you have a recorded lecture that is in four 15-minute segments, two readings, tutorial (academic) readings, and a topic and a discussion forum. The lecture has accompanying PDF PowerPoint slides that have core summary points. The recorded lecture contains key critical ethical questions for you to consider. You

will hear "pause and consider" before these ethical issues are posed—sharing your thoughts on a discussion forum is important.

After the lecture and prior to the tutorial, read the two provided academic readings for preparation as they will assist your thinking. There are notes to guide your reading of the article to make this more engaging. Once you have finished the lecture and readings, you go to the tutorial which includes a weekly discussion forum. Don't worry, you are guided with examples for how to post on the tutorial discussion board. Posting responses in the tutorial discussion forum is important and part of the assessment (see assessment link). Remember, in the discussion forum you support each other—no one has all the answers. Your ideas change and develop. Your post to a peer should acknowledge the strength in your peer's comments, and you share one idea of what might improve the ideas (it may just be a reference or a quote). As future professionals, it is important to be respectful. Respect might include providing an alternative perspective if it is supported by literature. We are here to extend our learning on how to be respectful across cultures as well as understanding the formative non-Indigenous culture and its impact and legacies.

The lecture pedagogy will also reinforce engagement and foster critical and ethical thinking explicitly, through use of the strategies including a practice for the lecturer to begin each week of semester with short questions to remind and reinforce learning from the previous weeks. The traditional lecture, speaking for 50 minutes, is not an effective pedagogy and it adapted by breaking up the lecture into four 10–15 minute parts. Each with quality content and challenging and engaging deep questions that assist cognitive engagement. The weekly lecture topic can have a key question; for example, this week consider, "What is a master narrative?" To this sub-questions are asked as the lecture progresses building in "pause and consider" statements, such as, "If you did not know about the brutality during First Nations' dispossession, why was this?"; "If you have not heard this history before write a few words on how you feel hearing it now"; or "Was it ethical to keep this history silent?" This works well in the online environment, but must be linked to purpose so the student uses their reflection in the forum's discussion board, which in turn, may be used in the assessment. The focus on an ethical reflection means students have to justify their views, and they learn how to do this from each other and, as stated, the student is required to reference an academic article to support her view. This referencing links again to the assessment and builds the student's capacity in essay writing.

With a large online cohort, I prefer to record the weekly lectures only one week ahead for the first five weeks. I try to draw on comments that tutors provide on interesting posts and reflections and use tutor's names and student's names. In this way, a link is made to the tutorials. Redoing the lecture each year enables asides to be made to current events which fosters engagement. Each year has its own moments. As I write in July 2020, current issues embrace Black Lives Matter, COVID-19, lockdown, and mask-wearing. Current "asides" provide learning relevance to the now. They facilitate student thinking and transference: how this knowledge connects with other subjects. When "asides" reflect that the lecture was recorded the previous year, it informs the students this was last year's lecture, and they might as well be last year's student; this is not scaffolding and not love (Freire, 1996).

CRITICAL PERIOD 2: ENGAGEMENT AND WEEK 3

Salmon (2003, 2013) notes that after Week 3, it is much harder to engage students who have not already participated. Week 3 in a 12-week unit is a critical week to look at the students' engagement range. This is when the online technological tracking tool that records each student's individual online engagement is important when used in conjunction with a supportive email. Online platforms vary in their capacity and accuracy of recording student contact into the online unit, but tutors are required to use this tool for Week 3, ideally in conjunction with a technological platform that allows you to send a personalized email. (A personalized email is one that may be sent to perhaps 700 plus students that begins with the student's name, for example, "Hi Mohammed,..." So, it is personalized and not, "Dear Student"). At Week 3 the tutor looks at the engagement of the whole cohort and groups the cohort by level of online engagement; for example, no/very little engagement (5% or less), well-below average (6–25%), below average (26–49%), average (50–65%), above average (65–75%), excellent (76–85%), in top 15%. The tutor will draft an email for each of the categories or focus on the two weakest categories (depending on time). For students whose engagement is low to well-below average, the idea is to motivate them to engage and catch up and indicate concern (relationship). The email to the low to minimal cohort would read something like:

> Hi Maria, just to let you know I am worried as I have noticed you have engaged very little in the unit. Perhaps something is wrong or there is something you do not understand? You may be apprehensive to ask. I am here to help you. It might help to know the university provides a free counseling service (email link). Perhaps it got too hard to start—that happens. There is time to catch up. Let me know how you are traveling, no pressure, but I am concerned. Despite being a large unit, I care about your success. I am here to help. Remember you have time to catch up now but after this week it will be tough. Here's hoping all is well.

The tutor's email to the next grouping (in low attendance) is adapted. It is useful to add, "what did you like about the unit so far?" Further, by asking what the students like about the unit, they have to think about this, write it, and this also can assist motivation to engage. In this, the tutor (and lecturer) gets feedback on what works well. For those engaging well, affirmation is appreciated. Congratulating them and reinforcing their involvement indicates they have a good work ethic, commitment, and suggests great promise as a future professional. The medium contact students are sometimes surprised to learn that almost 50% of the cohort are more involved than they are, and it motivates them. The lowest contact groups often are prompted into action. Because the 3-week period is the critical window to engage or lose students, it does not need to be replicated but obviously can be. Most students will reply and yes, the process often becomes a short dialogue, but this is a positive communication exchange. In summary, writing a compassionate and/or affirming email in week 3 prompts students' engagement and/or ongoing engagement. The process conveys the tutor's professionalism, and it fosters engagement and relationship. This technique is extremely valuable. I have had only positive to extremely positive and grateful responses to the range of emails. The emails also provide important information and motivation to tutors and lecturers.

CRITICAL PERIOD 3: ASSESSMENTS AND FEEDBACK

The assessment purpose was outlined earlier, but feedback in online assessments is a very important part of pedagogy. It provides critical feedback. The feedback should contain three positives about the assessment, and it should contain at least two ways to improve. The focus should be on improvement. Feedback must be personalized to be meaningful. It should be timely, that is, the assessment should be returned within 2 weeks. This is a key place for the tutor to provide clear individual advice that is critical (for the second assessment and/or learning). Assessment moderation has to be undertaken (but this is not detailed here due to space considerations).

CRITICAL PERIOD 4: FINAL WEEKS AND IMPROVING EVALUATIONS

Continuing efficacy and improving student evaluations is undertaken when continuing the above practices. The final two weeks merit some special consideration. Continuing efficacy, reinforcing learning and improving student evaluations of a good unit is enhanced by drawing the students' attention to how and where the unit's learning outcomes were met and how much they have learned. The students' posts in the *key learnings to date/ethical reflections forum* should be drawn on as it again reinforces, acknowledges, and reminds the students what they have learned. I have often found that many students become deeply engaged, including some who may lack the academic skills to get a high grade. Consequently, the offer of a reference affirms appreciation of this. I invited these students to write his/her own reference in a "fill in the gaps" format where the student states what they have learned as part of the reference. As well as prompting students to recall what they have learned, the written reference preserves the record of their learning and their commitment into the workplace where such references are useful. It is rare that one has to moderate the assertions students' make. It is time consuming but worthwhile.

FUTURE DIRECTIONS AND RESEARCH

Gray (2001) makes an important point that online teaching does not have a 1,000-year history. In fact, the history of large scale online teaching is often less than 20 years. To that end, given large scale online teaching is a new and developing area of pedagogy, educators have the capacity and duty to not only contribute to innovation (as this chapter and book do) but to advocate for adequate staffing and time allowances on a par with face-to-face teaching. Large online units get a poor reputation when they are not provided with time for organization, adequate tutor preparation time, and/or lack teaching time to enable a pedagogy responsive to the discipline needs.

This chapter provides a comprehensive overview of strategies in a large online unit that produce quality teaching and learning. It includes descriptions and analysis of the complexity and support required, for a unit to run well. It also provides evidence that staffing ratios and tutorial size are critical. The discipline this chapter discusses requires engagement and critical and ethical thinking for deep engagement: each part of the unit is crafted (including tutors, forums, assessments) to this goal. It is time-intensive work. When that time is not provided by a faculty, it creates unrealistic demands on the lecturer and tutors, including an implicit and unethical pressure to provide free labor, and this reduces the academic's research time and so the situation is perpetuated. Disciplines concerned with social justice, like First Nations Studies, are of critical importance to professions and citizenry. Currently, many citizens and academics are saying, "Black lives matter." But where an institution approaches large scale online units focused on social justice and anti-racist pedagogy as a place to make profit by reducing staffing, it indicates "Black lives do not matter"—and institutional racism. In Australia, First Nations Studies were not given by the academy but won by political advocacy, mostly by Indigenous peoples, and their allies, to bring justice. In my teaching career, they have moved from adequately resourced face-to-face units into large online cohorts that can be poorly resourced. Lecturers in large online learning cohorts arguably have an ethical responsibility to speak up and back to inadequate institutional resourcing. But we need research into staffing and time demands in this area to be powerful. Classroom size is a hot topic in school classrooms but largely flies under the radar in the university. It needs consideration. The pedagogy is only as powerful as the resourcing and the research that establishes the time that is required.

REFERENCES

Aveling, N. (2006). 'Hacking at our very roots': Rearticulating White racial identity within the context of teacher education. *Race Ethnicity and Education, 9*(3), 261–274.

Bekerman, Z., & Zembylas, M. (2011). *Teaching contested narratives: Identity, memory and reconciliation in peace education and beyond.* Cambridge University Press.

Berger, S. (2009). On the role of myths and history in the construction of national identity in modern Europe. *European History Quarterly, 39*(3), 490–502.

Boud, D., Cohen, R., & Sampson, J. (Eds.). (2014). *Peer learning in higher education: Learning from and with each other.* Routledge.

Brown, P. C., Roediger, H. L., III, & McDaniel, M. A. (2014). *Make it stick: The science of successful learning.* The Belknap Press of Harvard University Press.

Chapman, C., Ramondt, L., & Smiley, G. (2005). Strong community, deep learning: Exploring the link. *Innovations in education and teaching international, 42*(3), 217–230.

Cochran-Smith, M. (2000). Blind vision: Unlearning racism in teacher education. *Harvard Educational Review, 70*(2), 157–190.

Conrad, D. (2005). Building and maintaining community in cohort-based online learning. *International Journal of E-Learning & Distance Education/Revue internationale du e-learning et la formation à distance, 20*(1), 1–20.

Cooper, J. L., & Robinson, P. (2000). The argument for making large classes seem small. *New directions for teaching and learning, 2000*(81), 5–16.

Freire, P. (1996). *Pedagogy of the oppressed* (Revised ed.). Continuum.

Gray, H. H. (2001, January 17). The university in history: 1088 and all that. Presented at the *Idea of the University Colloquium*, University of Chicago.

Lang, J. M. (2016). *Small teaching: Everyday lessons from the science of learning.* Jossey-Bass.

Major, C. (2015). *Teaching online.* Johns Hopkins University Press.

O'Dowd, M. (2010). 'Ethical positioning' a strategy in overcoming student resistance and fostering engagement in teaching aboriginal history as a compulsory subject to pre-service primary education students. *Education in Rural Australia, 20*(1), 29–42.

O'Dowd, M. (2011). Australian identity, history and belonging: The influence of White Australian identity on racism and the non-acceptance of the history of colonization of Indigenous Australians. *International Journal of Diversity in Organizations, Communities & Nations, 10*(6), 29–44.

O'Dowd, M. (2012). Engaging non-Indigenous students in Indigenous history and "un-history." *History of Education Review, 41*(2), 104–118.

Rifkin, M. (2012). The Transatlantic Indian Problem. *American Literary History, 24*(2), 337–355.

Reynolds, H. (2006). *The other side of the frontier: Aboriginal resistance to the European invasion of Australia.* UNSW Press.

Russell, L. (2001). *Savage imaginings: Historical and contemporary constructions of Australian Aboriginalities.* Australian Scholarly Publishing.

Salmon, G. (2003). *E-moderating: The key to teaching and learning online.* Psychology Press.

Salmon, G. (2013). *E-tivities: The key to active online learning* (2nd ed.). Routledge.

Stanner, W. E. H. (1969). *After the dreaming: 1968 Boyer lectures.* ABC.

Tate, S. A., & Bagguley, P. (2017). Building the anti-racist university: Next steps. *Race Ethnicity and Education, 20*(3), 289–299.

Tinto, V. (2010). From theory to action: Exploring the institutional conditions for student retention. In J. C. Smart & M. B. Paulsen (Eds.), *Higher education: Handbook of theory and research* (pp. 51–89). Springer, Dordrecht.

Thijs, K. (2008). *The metaphor of the master: 'Narrative hierarchy' in national historical cultures of Europe.* Palgrave Macmillan.

Tsui, L. (2002). Fostering critical thinking through effective pedagogy: Evidence from four institutional case studies. *The Journal of Higher Education, 73*(6), 740–763.

Wagner, A. E. (2005). Unsettling the academy: Working through the challenges of anti-racist pedagogy. *Race Ethnicity and Education, 8*(3), 261–275.

Wehlage, G. G., & Rutter, R. A. (1985). *Dropping out: How much do schools contribute to the problem?* https://files.eric.ed.gov/fulltext/ED275799.pdf

Wolfe, P. (2006). Settler Colonialism and the elimination of the Native. *Journal of genocide research, 8*(4), 387–409.

Zembylas, M. (2013). Affective, political and ethical sensibilities in pedagogies of critical hope: Exploring the notion of 'critical emotional praxis'. In V. Bozalek, B. Leibowitz, R. Carrolissen, & M. Boler (Eds.), *Discerning critical hope in educational practices* (pp. 33–47). Routledge.

CHAPTER 8

INSTRUCTIONAL DESIGN AND FACULTY PARTNERSHIP FOR A STANDARDS-ALIGNED ONLINE COURSE DESIGN FOR LARGE CLASSES

Manuella B. Crawley
Cleveland State University

Vivian LeAnn Krosnick
Cleveland State University

ABSTRACT

According to the U.S. Department of Education, National Center for Education Statistics (2018), in 2015, of the nearly 20 million students enrolled in a degree-granting postsecondary institution, 29.8% were enrolled in at least one distance education course. As online learning becomes more prevalent in higher education, it is important to discuss effective ways to design and develop courses for higher student success. Intentional design with emphasis on learning outcomes, pedagogy, course alignment, and the potential value of the online learning environment itself supports a student-centered approach to virtual learning. This chapter will discuss the benefits of a partnership between the instructional designer and faculty member throughout the course design, implementation, and evaluation process for online course design for large classes.

According to the U.S. Department of Education, National Center for Education Statistics (2018), in 2015, of the nearly 20 million students enrolled in a degree-granting postsecondary institution, 29.8% were enrolled in at least one distance education course. In 2020, online learning grew exponentially due to the coronavirus pandemic (COVID-19). Primary, secondary and postsecondary classes shifted online to decrease social contact and virus spread (Burke, 2020, Goldstein, 2020). This rapid shift to online learning placed many faculty and students in an unfamiliar learning environment. In addition, the shift also generated the need to clarify terminology related to online teaching and learning. According to Hodges, Moore, Lockee, Trust, and Bond (2020), *online learning* has been studied for decades. The research has proven repeatedly that effective online learning is a product of a carefully planned systematic instructional design process, and that design decisions have an impact on instructional quality. Craig (2020) explains that what students experienced in response to the COVID-19 pandemic is *remote learning*, not online learning. Hodge et. al. (2020) propose a specific term for this type of instruction, suggesting it should be called *emergency remote teaching*. This remote teaching is not representative of the systematic instructional design process that can take months of careful planning and design and can lead to standards-aligned courses. Reacting to an emergency and being forced into remote teaching was not a welcome situation; however, this period may eventually be recognized as transformative for education. According to McKenzie (2020) remote teaching has given us the opportunity to rethink teaching practices, the increased ability to use instructional technology, and the foundational knowledge that may lead to more faculty who are motivated to develop rigorous online or blended academic experiences with an instructional design partner. For the remainder of this chapter, we will use the term *online* to refer to any form of distance education, including remote teaching.

The popularity of online courses can be attributed to many factors, among them (a) the potential to reach more learners (increased enrollment), (b) flexibility with scheduling (no physical classroom needed), and (c) flexibility for the learner (learning from your living room and when it is the most convenient; USDOE, 2010). Further, online classrooms do not have the limitations of a traditional classroom, in the number of seats available. The number of students enrolled is only limited by the instructor's capacity to manage the course, making it a cost-effective use of an instructor's workload. This, in addition to demand and interest in online learning, are the driving forces behind large online course offerings.

A large online class is generally defined as those consisting of 60–149 students, while those with 150+ are considered "very large" (Arbaugh &Benbunan-Finch, 2005; Bocchi et al., 2004; Leufer, 2007; Ryan et al., 2001). The large number of students participating in online learning means that instructors must shift how they think about their courses, re-evaluate their teaching effectiveness, and discover new and innovative teaching strategies to adapt to the online environment. Instructors are learning to "translate" their in-person courses into an online learning environment, often with little to no training or knowledge about this new environment. To an instructor who has been teaching for many years, this shift to the online learning environment cannot only be intimidating, but also may feel like they are starting over as a teacher (Johnson, 2013). Teaching online involves much more than the posting of PowerPoints and initiating discussions; much like in-person teaching is more than telling students to read the book. It involves carefully designed lessons, supporting materials, and evidence-based activities appropriately designed for the online learning environment. The teaching part is the key. In online classes, the teaching is what makes the difference between a great class and a not so good one. But how to "effectively teach" in that environment? The answer is creating an active learning environment, where students (while not in the same geographical place) can create connections with the instructor, learn from peers, and participate in activities that will enhance their learning.

Active learning is defined as a learning experience in which the learner increases knowledge by actively engaging in activities, interacting with other learners and teachers, and participating in simulations or projects. This type of learning, in which the students are actively engaged in the experience, has the potential to activate deeper learning (Twigg, 2003a, 2003b). In an online learning environment, active learning and teaching can pose a challenge. Intentional course design can be the starting point in the creation of an active learning environment in online instruction. Intentional course design consists of building online courses from the ground up, using existing quality standards and best practices, and not simply moving the existing traditional in-person course to an online platform.

Online courses may not have clearly established enrollment caps or instructor-to-student ratios that are typical of traditional courses. Intentional design, with emphases on learning outcomes, pedagogy, course alignment (ensuring materials, activities, and assessments support learning objectives), along with the potential of a socially connected and active online learning environment, support a learner-centered approach. As the demand increases for online learning in higher education, there is a need for a systematic course design process led by instructional design professionals who join forces with faculty to develop online courses (Hsu, 2020). This partnership is quickly being recognized as key to helping faculty transition courses to an online learning environment (Beirne & Romanoski, 2018). One can trace the roots of systematic instructional design in the United States to the 1940s, when thousands of World War II soldiers were trained by the military. Having proven its value to the military, instructional design, defined as "a systematic process that is employed to develop education and training programs in a consistent and reliable fashion" (Reiser & Dempsey, 2007, p. 11), gained a foothold. With the rapid growth of online learning in recent years, instructional designers are increasingly in demand for higher education and are commonly expected to provide leadership and support in the following areas (Schwier & Wilson, 2010, pp. 137–144; Rowland, 1992, pp. 80–82):

1. Build and maintain professional relationships with faculty and team members within diverse contexts.
2. Consult with faculty on instructional design and development projects.
3. Manage instructional design and development projects—serve as a liaison for communication, time management, and task coordination with all project team members.
4. Advocate for instructional design—be vocal about the instructional designer's role and value to the institution.
5. Teaching and learning can benefit all team members—instructional designers may find themselves guiding subject matter experts to use effective active learning strategies; conversely, instructional designers may find themselves at the receiving end of studying a content area that is foreign to them.

It is critical that instructional designers possess the skills needed to foster faculty collaboration and the knowledge base to guide the design, development, and leadership of high-quality, engaging online instruction (Munzenmaier, 2014). As a rule, instructional designers should have foundational knowledge based on the online teaching and learning research (Lack, 2015; Means et al., 2009; Wu, 2015). Two nationally recognized organizations, the Online Learning Consortium and Quality Matters provide research-based standards to help ensure the quality of online course design and online teaching and learning (Shelton, 2019). The rigorous guidelines provided by these organizations help to ensure an active, learner-centered approach to course design. A partnership between faculty and instructional designer, grounded in these evidence-based standards, is a solid starting point for a well-planned approach to designing high-quality online courses.

The delivery or teaching of an online learning course, especially one with high enrollment, can present many challenges. Opportunities for social, cognitive, and instructor presence, which naturally take place daily in a traditional classroom, may look very different in an online learning environment. Instructional design with a standards-aligned focus, or in other words, intentional planning for what the research has proven, works for social and active learning, instructor presence, and communication in a large online class can help build the framework toward ensuring your instructional goals are achieved. The book *Small Teaching Online* (Darby, 2019) discusses several strategies that have been shown to have a positive impact on student learning in high-enrollment online courses. These simple strategies, though beneficial for all online courses, are particularly well-suited to large online classes. These strategies include:

1. *Design for persistence*—Build activities into your course that lead to student success. Do not assume that students already have all of the skills needed. Plan activities and assignments that will scaffold students as they develop the characteristics and skills of a successful learner.
2. *Assign a goals contract*—Helps students commit to the requirements of the course and accept responsibility for their own learning. A contract may include agreements about reading and understanding the syllabus, course schedule and deadlines, expected hours per week, expectations for logging in, and where students can ask questions about the course.
3. *Nudge selected students*—Reach out to students who may be struggling. A personal email sent to students early in the semester has the potential for a positive impact on students. Something as simple as contacting students who are not logging in or have low test scores can be the support that can motivate students to turn things around.
4. *Help students make cognitive connections*—Use strategies that help students create an organizational structure, activate prior knowledge for students to make this connection.
5. *Provide a framework*—This can be something as simple as giving students a worksheet to accompany readings, videos, or other activities. A note-taking worksheet for use during synchronous sessions may be useful for students.
6. *Be flexible and compassionate*—to your students and to yourself. Showing your human side can go a long way toward connecting with online students (Darby, 2019, pp. 131–151).

Intentional planning for the design and teaching of large online classes is essential and is frequently a team-based approach where an instructor and an instructional designer work collaboratively. This systematic process and the benefits of this collaborative partnership are discussed in the next section.

SYSTEMATIC INSTRUCTIONAL DESIGN

Program Planning

Instructional design begins with a systematic planning process that analyzes a project request and asks pertinent questions related to overall program purpose and overarching goals. An instructional designer, a professional with training and experience in designing and developing educational programs and managing educational projects, can be a key member of an instructional team. Early engagement with an instructional designer can begin to uncover critical details that impact an entire program. An instructional design team in higher education typically includes the following persons in some capacity (college dean, department chair/director, faculty/subject matter expert [SME], instructional designer, media developer). According to Booth (2018, p. 1–3), an instructional design team should begin an online program by analyzing four critical areas:

1. *Who are your learners?* Despite some obvious learner diversity (age, gender, background, experience) determine if your learners share some common characteristics (educational goals, experience, desire for success)? Knowing your learners' characteristics can be a good starting point for making important instructional program planning decisions.
2. *What are the program goals?* Designing with the *end in mind*, an instructional development framework from Wiggins and McTighe (1998) is central to making program planning decisions. Early on, this type of backward design planning will lead to many sound instructional decisions related to content and delivery.
3. *What is the learning methodology?* Working as a key member of the instructional team, the instructional designer's role is to carefully analyze the information gleaned from the program analysis. Based on this preliminary information, the designer will be able to recommend the learning methodology to achieve program goals. For online learning, this methodology combines effective pedagogy seamlessly integrated with instructional technology.
4. *What is the best way to evaluate a program?* How will we know when learners have gained the desired outcomes—for a program, a course,

or a unit of instruction? Considering this question early in the planning process connects us back to the idea of backward design. What is it that learners will know or be able to do at the completion of a learning experience? How do we know that learners have achieved those outcomes? Analyzing this question from the very inception of a program can help establish a framework for good online course design. Although the outcomes may be different for a program (pass a licensing exam), for a course (diagnose a viral infection), or for a unit of instruction (recommend a treatment plan), the importance of evaluation cannot be overstated in relation to continuous improvement of learning experiences and outcomes.

In a 2014 webinar, *Online Engagement Strategies for Large Classes*, an instructional designer and faculty member from the University of Central Florida discussed their instructional design collaboration in some detail. Given the job of developing an online undergraduate business program with high enrollment courses, they were charged with a focal institutional goal—increase engagement for large (average of 600 students) online courses (Massiah & Howard, 2014). As a result of their early program planning, the team proposed three critical questions that they used to help guide their program and course design. These questions informed many of the decisions for both the faculty member and the instructional designer as they moved forward with the design and development of this online program. These questions as discussed by Messiah and Howard (2014) were:

1. How do I reach individual students when there are so many?
2. How can I engage students in large online and blended classes on a limited budget?
3. How can I serve my students while still having time for everything else I need to do?

This approach helped to inform not only the instructional strategies that the team would design, but many other decisions related to the teaching and learning experience in these high-enrollment online classes. This is an example of a systematic instructional design process that began with three key questions—the answers to which would inform the design and development of every aspect of this online program.

Although Massiah and Howard's (2014) experience is an example of a successful faculty/instructional designer partnership with positive outcomes, we recognize this is not always the case. Tensions can arise between the two and according to Wilson (2019), instructional designers report that working with faculty is one of their biggest challenges. Several reasons were noted, ranging from a lack of knowledge about an instructional designer's role to a lack of faculty incentive to collaborate with an instructional designer. In her article, "Easing Instructional Designer-Faculty Conflicts," Tate (2017) discusses several ways to "anticipate, address and avoid tension or conflict between designers and faculty members" (p. 1). At one university, the instructional design manager intentionally pairs a designer with a faculty member based on personalities; the manager makes his best guess at matching for compatibility and success. However, he is not hesitant to move designers around if needed. A few more strategies for relationship building include calling on other faculty to demonstrate a successful project, asking faculty to talk about their collaboration with an instructional designer, and finally, asking instructional designers to facilitate a quick "win" early in the collaboration. This may be something as simple as demonstrating a course template that contains pre-populated information for learners (such as disability services, library links, writing center, etc.). Thus, eliminating the time that might be required for faculty to collect all these student resources. Another important relationship builder is to clarify the roles of project team members. Early in a project, this clarification step helps to avoid misunderstandings about who does what. Lastly, it is important to be clear with faculty about time commitments. Experienced designers and team leaders can be fairly accurate in estimating time commitments for faculty, and it is important to share this information at the onset of a project.

Instructional Design: Course Planning

From its early roots dating back to World War II, the field of instructional design has continued to expand and evolve. Colleges have been increasingly employing instructional designers to support online teaching and learning opportunities on their campuses (Beirne & Romanoski, 2018; Kilgore et al., 2019). Following a systematic instructional design process provides a design and development model that helps to ensure program and course consistency, ensures that high quality instructional design standards are met, and guides the work of course design teams. Wagner (2011, p. 34) quite aptly defines systematic instructional design as a process with the following three elements:

- systematic design and development of instruction using learning and instructional theory to ensure the quality of instruction;
- analysis of learning needs and goals and the development of a delivery system to meet those needs;
- development of instructional materials and activities; and
- opportunities for evaluation of all instruction and learner activities, before, during, and after the instruction.

Instructional design in higher education is a relatively new partnership. As with any new working relationship, there may be a period of adjustment as faculty adapt to a team-based approach to course design and instructional designers navigate the academic landscape. Team members may experience new roles, there will most likely be new processes and workflows, and a need for more open communication and sharing. Instructional designer and instructor alike may occasionally find themselves taking a step back in order to focus on the big picture and not get lost in the "process" itself. The cost of losing this focus may be greater in an online course where attrition rates are typically higher and student relationships and communication can be more challenging (Lorenzetti, 2018). Maintaining a focus on student engagement and outcomes (i.e., learner centeredness) is critical to student achievement and success. A search of the current instructional design literature allowed us to further narrow the scope to the design of high-enrollment online courses. Systematic instructional design helps an academic team make sound decisions about the pedagogy, management, and support for effective learning for large online courses.

For a closer look at an instructional design process, we return to our team from the University of Central Florida (Massiah & Howard, 2014). Benefitting from their early program planning, the design team was able to make several strategic instructional design decisions at the course level for online courses that could potentially have up to 1,500 students. These instructional decisions included the following:

1. *Message students who...* (early warning system with pre-set criteria)
2. *Targeted office hours* (invite groups of students to meet based on determinants—low exam scores)
3. *Efficient scheduling* (student sign-ups for meetings)
4. *Video conferencing opportunities with students* (connecting with many students)

You may notice similarities to some of the strategies that Darby (2019) suggested earlier in this chapter for engaging learners in large online classes. It is important to recognize that the Central Florida University instructional team did not have immediate answers for how they would achieve the institution's focal goal—which was to have more engagement in large online courses. Instead, we can trace these decisions to a careful planning process that began with higher-level program goals and progressed into individual course decisions. This type of systematic instructional design process is common to online learning (Al Mamun et al., 2020).

A systematic course design project is a cyclical process—with the initial phase of the cycle focused on *analysis*, followed by *design* and *development* of the course. During mid-cycle, the course goes through the *implementation phase* (teaching). During implementation, instructors should be collecting formative feedback and adjusting as needed. Finally, the instructional design process moves into the *evaluation* phase, wherein the faculty and instructional designer analyze all course findings, both formative and summative (what worked, what needs changed, student feedback, student performance). This systematic instructional design process, also known as ADDIE, was developed in the mid-1970s by the educational technology team at Florida State University (Branson et al., 1975). The ADDIE model (analysis, design, development, implementation, evaluation) incorporates a succession of iterative steps, an approach instructional designers, developers, educators, and others use to continually improve a design or a product (Eby, 2019). The use of the ADDIE model for instructional design has withstood the test of time and allowed for the adaptations necessary to meet a growing understanding of how people learn, the need for more rapid and responsive design, and the ability to customize the model to meet specific instructional projects. This and other instructional design models will be discussed later in the chapter. For now, we will look at a systematic design process in relation to the work of this collaborative faculty-instructional designer partnership (see Figure 8.1). The following iterative instructional design model is designed based on an instructional designer's experience working with faculty in designing and developing online coursework at a higher education institution center for e-learning:

1. *Analysis*—During the first iteration of the analysis phase, the design team (faculty/SME, instructional designer, media developer) examines the relevant data and information related to an online course request. Beginning with the all-important course outcomes as the foundation, the team then examines other areas of the course such as enrollment levels and caps, course delivery method, semester rotations, instructional content, materials available, any publisher resources used, unit and course evaluations, technology tools, target audience, and other components important to course design. After teaching the course, during subsequent iterations of the analysis phase, the faculty and instructional designer will examine the data collected during course implementation and recommend revisions and updates for continuous improvement of the course. This process should continue throughout the life of a course.
2. *Design/Redesign*—During the first iteration of the design phase, the instructional team will work on the design of appropriate learning experiences and assessments that are aligned to learning objectives. During the design phase, the instructional designer must have a persistent focus on instructional design standards. The instructional designer should be well-versed in these standards and be able to

make standards-based design recommendations during this period. In subsequent iterations, the team will be recommending design improvements during the redesign phase. Improvements should be based on the evaluation and analysis of learning outcomes, student feedback, surveys, evaluation of what worked well, current events, and updated resources. This information should be an outcome of teaching the course, noting your experiences throughout, tracking revisions, and evaluating the feedback and outcomes after you teach.

3. *Develop/Revise*—During the first iteration of the development phase the course itself is built. This may involve adding materials to a learning management system, developing multimedia content, recording lectures, and procurement of other course resources that will populate the learning environment. During subsequent iterations of a course, expect that there will be some revisions to the course as the team evaluates the data from previous implementations. Continuous course improvement is an ongoing goal in teaching and learning.

4. *Implementation*—During implementation you will teach the course, collect formative feedback, revise as you teach based on the feedback and exam scores. As discussed, this is cyclical and you will continue to teach, evaluate, and revise during the life of a course.

5. *Evaluation*—The evaluation phase is a critical step both during and after you teach a course. Throughout this process, you will be testing

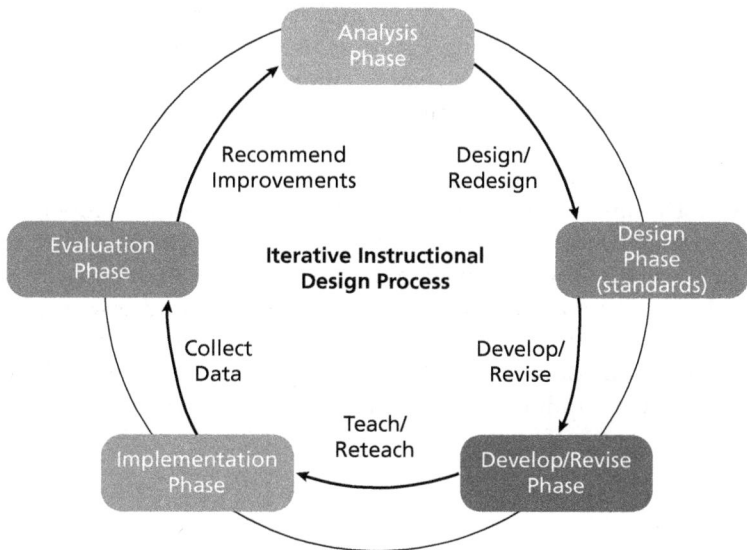

Figure 8.1 An iterative instructional design model.

out your teaching methods and materials, you will be gathering data: collecting feedback from student surveys (formative and summative), evaluating student performance, observing the overall experience, and determining successes and where you may need revisions. Analysis of the outcomes takes the course full circle, it enables you to continue on in this iterative process, armed with knowledge, experience and valuable data as you begin a new semester with the information needed for continuous course improvement.

The process above clearly shows the important collaborative relationship between the instructional designer and the faculty member. While the faculty member will guide the content portion of the development and design, the instructional designer facilitates the delivery of the content in a way that is appropriate for the online learning environment by helping the instructor to design and implement the content. The instructional designer's technical knowledge complements the faculty member's content knowledge. Together they can create and deliver content driven, pedagogically sound and technologically effective lessons for the online environment.

Instructional designers may choose from a variety of systematic instructional design models (Culatta, 2020). Earlier in this chapter, we discussed a systematic course design process known as ADDIE. Most instructional designers will incorporate best practices from several models and learning theorists, including: ADDIE model (Kurt, 2017), backward design (Wiggins & McTighe, 1998), Dick and Carey model (Dick & Carey, 1985), theory of andragogy (Knowles et al., 2011), and Bloom's revised taxonomy (Anderson et al., 2001). The design process used for online course planning should be replicable and yet dynamic enough to allow for customized design as determined by the institution and the project context and goals. It should also be iterative so that continuous improvement becomes a part of the process. Now that we know a little more about the instructional design process, let's jump in and walk in the shoes of a faculty member who has limited experience with online teaching—someone who may have utilized the institution's learning management system in a limited capacity but has not yet designed an online learning course. Keep in mind as we explore this process that each situation is unique, and that you are encouraged to explore, experiment, and modify this process in a way that works for you, for your academic discipline, and for your college, department, or institution.

Where Do We Start?

When your department chair or director asks you to work with an instructional designer to develop an online learning course, you probably have a lot of questions. "Why do I need to work with an instructional designer?"; "What does an instructional designer do?"; "What will this mean to my workload?"; "To my teaching?"; and "I have taught this class for years in a traditional classroom, why do I need to work with a designer now?" These questions and others will be addressed during a project initiation or kickoff meeting, typically the starting point to begin an online course development project. It is here, in this initial meeting, that the instructional designer will work to establish a rapport with you and to ease any concerns you may have. The designer will also answer your questions and discuss the various ways that he or she may be able to help you with online course design and development goals. Hopefully, during this early phase, the faculty–designer partnership will begin to form, with initial introductions and an exploration of various aspects related to online course design. This conversation will most likely touch on the following as part of the initial analysis:

- *instructional design (ID) roles*—how an instructional designer can help;
- *overarching goals* for this course;
- introduction to the *course template*;
- *enrollment*—knowing early that you will have high enrollment in this course is beneficial for planning;
- *course delivery*—traditional 16-week course, accelerated 8-week, summer, or other delivery formats;
- your *background* as it relates to designing and teaching an online learning course;
- *professional development*—training opportunities for designing and teaching an online learning course;
- *timelines*—"When do you plan to offer this course, timeline, milestones, and so on?";
- *availability*—"How much time will you have to collaborate with a designer?";
- *memo of understanding*—agreement on who does what–when, delivery dates, and so on;
- *materials*—text, videos, articles, other; and
- *course development*—an agreement about who will build the course in your learning management system (LMS).

These are just a few of the important areas that may be discussed during an analysis meeting. Think of these questions as a framework that will evolve and expand as a faculty/instructional designer team works together. As part of good design planning, many higher education instructional designers rely on design standards from organizations that study and aggregate the research behind high quality instructional design. One such organization mentioned previously is *quality matters (QM)*. QM was formed from the work of a federal grant (FIPSE, 2003–2006) awarded to analyze the peer-reviewed research behind high quality online course design. From this grant, QM developed a set of instructional design standards that help guide faculty and designers as they design an online learning experience. QM continually analyzes the peer-reviewed literature related to online learning design and updates the standards on a 3-year cyclical basis. This ensures that their academic subscribers are using the most current research to inform their online course design ("Quality Matters Rubric," 2018). QM addresses eight general standards:

1. course overview and introduction
2. learning objectives
3. assessment and measurement
4. instructional materials
5. learning activities and learner interaction
6. course technology
7. learner support
8. accessibility

Within each of the QM general standards, there are specific review standards that provide further detail and examples of "how this may look in your course." These thorough descriptions and examples give you multiple exemplars of various ways to meet QM standards and help ensure that the online course provides a high-quality, student-centered learning experience (Martin & Bolliger, 2018). Meeting these standards will not only help the faculty in their own organization and design of the course, but it will also allow students to focus on the content rather than spending much of their time learning to navigate the course and struggling to find the content. Working with the instructional designer ensures that the standards are followed and result in a user-friendly, learner-centered course for students.

As a starting point to meeting standards, a course alignment map provides a visual representation for course design. Creating a course alignment map allows you to break down a course into its component parts and helps to align course and unit learning objectives to course materials, activities, and assignments. Intentionally charting a course to verify alignment is an efficient and effective way to ensure that you are addressing and measuring the desired learning outcomes (Caruana, 2017). As shown in Figure 8.2, a course map can be as simple as a table you create with a word processor.

Once the design team maps the course and completes the design planning, you are ready to move forward. You have done the prework, you can see the big picture in your course map, and you are ready to begin gathering your course materials and developing the course in your institution's LMS. If you have not used your institution's LMS, now might be a good time to get formal training or work with a colleague on the basics of the

Course ID and Title				
Course Learning Objectives 1. 2. 3.				
Module Name	Module Learning Objectives	Assessments	Materials	Activities
Module 1: Intro	1.			
	2.			

Figure 8.2 Course alignment map example.

system. This can alleviate some of the frustration from not knowing a system well and struggling through the layout and mechanics as you build a course. The instructional designer or an online learning team member could quickly get you up-to-speed on the basics of the LMS, and most institutions offer formal training on their educational technology tools.

Engaging and Connecting With Students in an Online Learning Environment Through Instructional Design

More important than class size is the quality of the interaction between student–student, and student–instructor (Arbaugh & Benbunan-Finch, 2005; Drago & Peltier, 2004; Nagel & Kotze, 2010). Engaging and connecting with students can be beneficial to both students and instructor in a large online class environment. This is where the benefits of a clearly defined, standards driven design are most clear.

In an online learning course, small design mistakes can be amplified. In a large online course, that is then multiplied and will take considerable instructor time to correct. Minor issues that could be easily addressed in an in-person class can become a time-consuming logistical nightmare in an online learning environment. Something that would take perhaps a few minutes to address and rectify in a traditional classroom, can quickly entail answering several emails and phone calls (Elison-Bowers et al., 2011). In a large online class, the management of such issues can mean a much larger workload for the instructor. Further, once mistakes—large or small—are made in an online learning classroom it can be difficult for the instructor to regain control and the trust of the students and recover within the course timeline (Berry, 2009; Dykeman & Davis, 2008). Working with an instructional designer will likely result in avoiding many of these unfortunate events. The instructional designer is trained to identify, and problem-solve these small mistakes. For example, the designer may suggest the use of a detailed rubric to clarify any confusion that may come from grading. The designer can then incorporate the rubric into the LMS and make it available to students. This simple action can result in a clearer description of the assignment expectation and eliminate any confusion related to the student submission. It will also streamline the course grading, leaving less room for error.

According to Berry (2009), to be successful in developing, teaching, and managing a large online class, a shift in focus from teaching to learning is required. This shift encompasses many parts of the course design and delivery. Berry (2009) uses the example of the PowerPoint slide presentation to illustrate this idea. In a traditional face-to-face course, PowerPoint is designed with teaching in mind. The instructor uses it as an outline to guide his/her lecture. In an online learning environment, the PowerPoint must be developed from the learner perspective, including what students need, rather than what the instructor needs to deliver the material (Berry, 2009). Voiced-over PowerPoints or video lectures can be effectively used in the online environment to deliver lectures and to create a connection between the student and the faculty member. Instructional designers facilitate the process of creating the videos and embedding them into the course LMS for seamless viewing for students.

Another key factor for online course success is establishing time frames and deadlines. Part of the appeal for online classes is the flexibility it provides for students, especially those juggling a full-time job, family responsibilities, or simply a large workload to complete their studies within an expected timeframe. This flexibility, however, means that students must manage their time and work on their own to complete the course without the constant reminder and guidance of the traditional classroom. It is therefore important that students have a clear understanding of the expectations and deadlines of the course (Bocchi et al., 2004). Providing students with complete and clear calendars for the course, sending weekly announcements introducing the week's content—including assignments due dates for the week are just some ways to help students stay on track. Among the standards instructional designers follow, the incorporation of these calendars and timeline tools are key to creating a compliant course.

In a large online class, these simple practices will not only help the student to manage their course load but will also save the instructor considerable time and frustration. Large class sizes in an online learning environment, instructor-student engagement and individualized interaction may become a challenge. While most course management systems support individual emails or discussion interaction, the sheer volume of routine emails with which instructors will be faced (e.g., simple and clarification type of emails) may diminish the instructor's ability to allow time for individualized conversations with students. As a result, interactions may happen in a general discussion forum, in the form of a class announcement or weekly wrap up/or introductory emails rather than a personalized interaction. Further, instructor workload is generally decided based on course credit hours. The number of students enrolled in each course can be a factor in workload decisions. This can create a challenge for those instructors teaching a high enrollment course. The number of students in a course will undoubtedly have an impact on workload for grading and course management. Large class size is likely to affect many aspects of the class and its content. Specifically, class size may interfere with aspects related to instructor–student engagement and instructor workload.

Instructor Presence and a Sense of Community

Level of instructor presence during an online learning course varies, and it may be an issue that instructors struggle with when developing and managing their courses (Sheridan & Kelly, 2010). Instructor presence can vary wildly based on instructor preference and teaching style. For example, while some instructors may not actually participate in course discussions and only provide the original question and observe while students interact, others may actively participate in discussions and provide individualized feedback or comments on each student's post (Sheridan & Kelly, 2010). Research has indicated that instructor presence can represent several factors, including but not limited to, the instructor's communication with students in discussion boards and outside of the discussions, instructor sharing information related to instructor professional interests and efforts taken by the instructor to create a sense of community among students (Garrison et al., 2000; Palloff & Pratt, 2003). Further, students tend to put high value on instructor responsiveness, clarity of information presented in the course, timeliness of information, and feedback (Sheridan & Kelly, 2010).

Creating a sense of community has been repeatedly found in the literature as a key factor in enhancing learning in online classes (Garrison et al., 2000; Palloff & Pratt, 2007; Rovai, 2002). A sense of community could mean different things to different students and instructors, but generally, it seems that a feeling of shared interests and purpose, collaborative learning, reflective presence, and social presence has been identified as important in the online environment in enhancing student learning (Palloff & Pratt, 2005). Instructional designers are key in facilitating the use of different tools to create this sense of community and engagement between students and faculty. Depending on the LMS and other available apps and software to each university, the instructional designer will integrate these tools into the LMS and the course.

Key Takeaways

Research has shown that students learn more and retain what they have learned longer if the knowledge acquired is done so actively (Fink, 2003, 2013). Instructional designers guide faculty members in the development of active learning courses, following national standards resulting in a more effective and complete online course. Key takeaways for instructors for course design to promote student success include:

- Shift the focus from instructor-centered material development to student centered. Remember that much of asynchronous online course is self-guided by students. Materials and organization of the course must be easily accessible and organized for students.
- Provide clear and explicit course goals, objectives, policies, assignment descriptions, and overall course expectations. The less room for error and misunderstanding, the less time and effort will be needed by the instructor to clarify and manage once the course is started. Small mistakes can often be costly as far as time and student perceptions and trust for the instructor.
- Work to create a sense of community within the online course. This can often be missing in an online learning class, but it is important and has an influence on student learning.
- Identify ways to assess if students are perceiving the online course to be engaging and connecting to the material and instructor.

Bocchi et al. (2004) suggest that in order to prevent students from feeling isolation often felt in online coursework, students must interact with other students, with faculty, and with the course content. But how can you know if students are connecting with the material, the instructor and classmates? Course management systems allow several opportunities for instructors to know that students are engaging in a large online course. Instructional designers facilitate the use of these tools and ensure those tools used are evidence-based and contribute to the overall course goals and objectives. Instructional designers can be a valued partner to faculty from the start of an instructional design and development project. Developing this partnership and learning to trust the professional expertise of each team member draws on the strengths of each and forms a design team that ensures standards-aligned course design and consistency across courses. Partnering an instructor, who has extensive subject matter expertise, an understanding of learners' needs and his or her own unique teaching experiences, with an instructional designer who has a background in pedagogical design, experience with the effective integration of instructional technology, and in-depth knowledge of online learning standards, forms a mutually beneficial partnership—one that focuses on high quality learning experiences and learner-centered instruction connected to measurable outcomes.

FUTURE DIRECTIONS AND RESEARCH

A major research initiative related to online learning was undertaken in March 2020 as a response to the pandemic. The U.S. Department of Education, Institute of Education Sciences, announced a call for nominations of existing research studies in the field. From this initiative, 932 studies were nominated by researchers, technical experts, and other online learning professionals. These studies were then classified according to rigor, design, sampling, learner audience (post-secondary, high school, middle school, K–4), and other important characteristics. This quick response by the federal government clearly points to the importance placed on online learning during an international crisis. This database is in the public domain and one would anticipate that these studies will continue to expand in number and scope as the importance of online instruction has become clear at both a national and international level (USDOE, 2020).

QM, as mentioned previously, is an organization dedicated to the research and standards development for high quality online course design. They maintain a repository of current online learning research and fund research studies undertaken by their own membership. In addition, QM continually reviews updated peer-review research studies and subsequently updates their design standards on a 3-year cycle. Subscribers have the benefit of knowing that meeting the QM design standards outlined by the QM rubric certifies that their courses meet high quality, standards-aligned online courses. The Online Learning Consortium, also mentioned previously, is another organization that maintains a research repository comprised of current research studies, white papers, journal articles, and many other materials related to online teaching and learning. In addition, OLC has developed a Scorecard Suite that enables faculty and instructional teams to evaluate online learning in an expanded way. Their OLC Scorecard includes rubric tools for the instructional design of online and blended courses (like the QM Rubric). OLC has also developed tools to evaluate the practice of teaching online, as well as the administration of online programs. Just as with QM, OLC is an organization dedicated to the research supporting high quality online learning. Becoming familiar with both organizations and their research initiatives is an important step that your instructional designer can help facilitate. Knowing and understanding the value of this peer-reviewed research contributes greatly to the design and development of outcomes-based, learner-centered online courses.

Previously in this chapter, we noted that the partnership between faculty and the instructional designer is not always a unified one. However, the 2020 global pandemic appears as if it may be a game-changer for this partnership. Leveraging on this, (Milosch, 2018) offers us some helpful tips to strengthen the faculty–instructional designer collaboration:

- Provide opportunities for instructional designers and faculty to experience one another's worlds—reverse roles and have designers *teach* an online course and instructors *design* online activities.
- Build on a meaningful collaboration—a respected partnership between faculty and an instructional designer not only builds understanding and cooperation, but also helps facilitate a shared effort toward the goal of high-quality online learning for students.

In a qualitative study titled, "Faculty and Instructional Designers on Building Successful Collaborative Relationships" (Richardson et al., 2019), investigated relationship perceptions between instructional designers and faculty at higher education institutions. They found some noteworthy views from both faculty and the instructional designer perspective. It seems that faculty want an instructional designer who is knowledgeable and can challenge them and support that challenge with the literature, while instructional designers typically desire an egalitarian relationship with faculty. Like any working relationship, this takes effort, time, and a common goal. The following key elements from this study point us to ways that instructional designers may avoid barriers and encourage this equal partnership with faculty (Richardson et. al., pp. 865–869):

- *Build trust and rapport*—Instructional designers should spend time getting to know their faculty partner, be clear that you would like to help, that you care about student learning, and be respectful of their experience and expertise.
- *Be an active listener*—Begin your collaboration as a fact-finding mission. Do not assume you know what faculty want. Tease out the information, ask good questions, take copious notes, and always listen with respect to the faculty member. You do not have to have all the answers, this is a time to gather data and then later analyze your findings. Recognize that faculty are smart, talented people and that your goals are most likely the same.
- *Be a coach and facilitator*—Give faculty time to accept and internalize suggestions. Provide several options for them to consider and always recognize that this is their course, they have the final say.
- *Be open-minded and flexible*—Instructional designers should be adaptable and always ready to change direction and look for acceptable

solutions. Be patient in faculty relationships, understand that faculty have many demands and pressure, and that not all of these can neatly fit in a project timeline. Be prepared for some delays and interruptions and adjust accordingly.
- *Know your strengths*—Being flexible and open-minded does not mean that you do not rely on your own education and experience to support your work. Faculty respect instructional designers who challenge them and can support these challenges with the research and their own range of experiences with online learning.
- *Be sensitive to cultural diversity*—As an instructional designer, you may work with faculty from various disciplines, from other countries, even from various teaching backgrounds and philosophies. Get to know your faculty, "What are the styles of different faculty in different places, and what are the effective ways of interacting with faculty who may be at a different place along the continuum of understanding what good instruction is?" (p. 868)
- *Advice for new instructional designers*—Do not fall into the trap of feeling as if you must have all the answers, that you need to prove your knowledge. The best course of action is to listen and to have a dialogue with faculty that will lead to a much more meaningful exchange. Know that sometimes it is not going to be a perfect match and that sometimes a project may not be successful. Be confident of your knowledge and abilities, know that you did everything you could to make it successful, and that sometimes external factors are out of your control.

As we consider the future of online learning, growth seems predictable, as does higher enrollments in online and blended courses. On the horizon, expect there to be rapid changes in the technology supporting online learning. As it relates to high-enrollment courses, watch for improvements in collaborative and group tools, streaming bandwidth, and more apps that support active and social learning. We should also see many of these tools become closely integrated with mainstream LMS systems, which makes them easier to access and use. Expect there to be more research about online teaching and learning, and because of their unique challenges and solutions, more research about effective instruction for large online and blended classes. Coinciding with this projected growth, we anticipate that we would also see a growth in effective high enrollment teaching practices, as well as modeling the active learning techniques we are asking our faculty to embrace. A culture of change and growth in online learning is upon us—expanded research, growth of engagement and active learning strategies, social connections, and instructional technology—all seem to be moving faster than we can keep up sometimes; but know that you are leading a revolution that would have been beyond our imagination just a few years ago. Keep up the good work!

REFERENCES

Al Mamun, M., Lawrie, G., & Tony, W. (2020). Instructional design of scaffolded online learning modules for self-directed and inquiry-based learning environments. *Computers & Education, 144*. https://doi.org/10.1016/j.compedu.2019.103695

Anderson, L. W., Krathwohl, D. R., & Bloom, B. S. (2001). *A taxonomy for learning, teaching, and assessing: A revision of Bloom's Taxonomy of educational objectives* (Complete ed.). Longman.

Arbaugh, J. B., & Benbunan-Fich, R. (2005). Contextual factors that influence ALN effectiveness. *Learning together online: Research on asynchronous learning networks, 1*, 123–144.

Beirne, E., & Romanoski, M. P. (2018, July 26). Instructional design in higher education: Defining an evolving field. OLC outlook: An environmental scan of the digital learning landscape. *Online Learning Consortium.* https://onlinelearningconsortium.org/instructional-design-in-higher-education-defining-an-evolving-field

Berry, R. W. (2009), Meeting the Challenges of teaching large online classes: Shifting to a learner-focus. *Journal of Online Learning and teaching, 5*(1), 176–181.

Bocchi, J., Eastman, J. K., & Swift, C. B. (2004). Retaining the online learner: Profile of students in an online MBA program and implications for teaching them. *Journal of Informational Systems Education, 79*(4), 245–253.

Booth, J. (2018, March 18). Why instructional design matters in elearning. *Learning Solutions.* https://learningsolutionsmag.com/articles/why-instructional-design-matters-in-elearning

Branson, R. K., Rayner, G. T., Cox, J. L., Furman, J. P., King, F. J., & Hannum, W. H. (1975). *Interservice procedures for instructional systems development* (Vols. 1–5). U.S. Army Training and Doctrine Command.

Burke, L. (2020, June 9). Colleges move online amid virus fears. *Inside Higher Ed.* https://www.insidehighered.com/news/2020/03/09/colleges-move-online-coronavirus-infectsmore

Caruana, V. (2017, September 08). How a course map puts you on track for better learning outcomes. *Faculty Focus.* https://www.facultyfocus.com/articles/course-design-ideas/how-a-course-map-puts-you-on-track-for-better-learning-outcomes/

Craig, R. (2020, April 02). What students are doing is remote learning, not online learning. There's a difference. *EdSurge.* https://www.edsurge.com/news/2020-04-02-what-students-are-doing-is-remote-learning-not-online-learning-there-s-a-difference

Culatta, R. (2020, January 14). Instructional design models. *Instruction Design.* https://www.instructionaldesign.org/models/

Darby, F. (2019). *Small teaching online: Applying learning science in online classes.* John Wiley & Sons.

Dick, W., & Carey, L. (1985). *The systematic design of instruction.* Scott, Foresman.

Drago,W., & Peltier, J. (2004). The effects of class size on effectiveness of online courses. *Management Research News, 27*(10), 27–41.

Dykeman,C., & Davis.,C. (2008). Part one: The shift toward online education. *Journal of Information Systems Education, 19*(1), 11–16.

Eby, K. (2019, January 2). The power of the iterative design process. *SmartSheet.* https://www.smartsheet.com/iterative-process-guide

Elison-Bowers, P., Sand, J., Barlow, M. R., & Wing, T. J. (2011). Strategies for managing large online classes. *The international Journal of Learning, 18*(2), 57–66.

Fink, L. D. (2003). *A self-directed guide to designing courses for significant learning.* Jossey-Bass.

Fink, L. D. (2013). *Creating significant learning experiences: Revised and updated.* Jossey Bass

Garrison, D. R., Anderson, T., & Archer, W. (2000). Critical inquiry in a text-based environment: Computer conferencing in higher education. *The Internet and Higher Education, 11*(2), 1–14.

Goldstein, D. (2020, March 13). Coronavirus is shutting schools: Is America ready for virtual learning? *New York Times.* https://www.nytimes.com/2020/03/13/us/virtual-learning-challengs.html

Hodges,C.,Moore,S.,Lockee,B.,Trust,T.,&Bond,A. (2020,March27).The difference between emergency remote teaching and online learning. *Educause.* https://er.educause.edu/articles/2020/3/the-difference-between-emergency-remote-teaching-and-online-learning

Hsu, H. K. (2020). Developing online engineering courses: A resource kit for collaboration between faculty and instructional designers. *Journal of Educational Technology Systems, 49*(1), 49–58. https://doi.org/10.1177/0047239520905773

Johnson, A. (2013). *Excellent online teaching: Effective strategies for a successful semester online.*

Kilgore, W., Prusko, P., & Gogia, L. (2019, August 8). A snapshot of instructional design: Talking points for a field in transition. *Educause Review.* https://er.educause.edu/blogs/2019/8/a-snapshot-of-instructional-design-talking-points-for-a-field-in-transition

Knowles, M. S., Holton, E. F., & Swanson, R. A. (2011). *The adult learner: The definitive classic in adult education and human resource development* (7th ed.). Elsevier, Butterworth-Heinemann.

Kurt, S. (2017, August 19). ADDIE model: Instructional design, in educational technology. *Educational Technology.* https://educationaltechnology.net/the-addie-model-instructional-design/

Lack, K. (2015). *Current status of research on online learning in postsecondary education.* https://doi.org/10.18665/sr.22463

Leufer, T. (2007). Students' perceptions of the learning experience in a large class environment. *Nursing Education Perspectives, 28*(6), 322–326.

Lorenzetti, J. (2018). *Seven ways to combat attrition in online courses.* https://www.academicbriefing.com/administration/seven-ways-combat-attrition-online-courses/

Martin, F., & Bolliger, D. U. (2018). Engagement matters: Student Perceptions on the importance of engagement strategies in the online learning environment. *Online Learning, 22*(1), 205–222. https://doi.org/10.24059/olj.v22i1.1092

Massiah, C. A., & Howard, C. (2014, April 6). *Online engagement strategies for large classes* [Webinar]. University of Central Florida. https://cdl.ucf.edu/faculty-seminar07/

Mckenzie, L. (2020, May 27). Ramping up for remote instruction. *Inside Higher Ed.* https://www.insidehighered.com/news/2020/05/27/new-resources-help-support-faculty-quality-online-instruction

Means, B., Toyama, Y., Murphy, R., Bakia, M., & Jones, K. (2009). *Evaluation of evidence-based practices in online learning: A meta analysis and review of online learning studies*. U.S. Department of Education.

Milosch, T. (2018, January 17). Building a collaborative instructor-instructional designer relationship. *Inside Higher Ed.* https://www.insidehighered.com/digital-learning/views/2018/01/17/building-collaborative-instructor-instructional-designer

Munzenmaier, C. (n.d.). *Today's instructional designer: Competencies and careers: Research library.* https://www.elearningguild.com/insights/178/todays-instructional-designer-competencies-and-careers/

Nagel, L., & Kotze, T. G. (2010). Supersizing e-learning: What a CoI Survey reveals about teaching presence in a large online class. *Internet and Higher Education, 13,* 45–51.

Palloff, R. M., & Pratt, K. (2003). *The virtual student: A profile and guide to working with online learners.* Jossey-Bass.

Quality Matters Rubric. (2018). *Standards from the Quality Matters Higher Education Rubric.* (6th edition). Quality Matters. https://www.qualitymatters.org/sites/default/files/PDFs/StandardsfromtheQMHigherEducationRubric.pdf

Reiser, R. A., & Dempsey, J. V. (2007). *Trends and issues in instructional design and technology* (2nd ed.). Pearson Education, Inc.

Richardson, J. C., Ashby, I., Alshammari, A.N., Cheng, Z., Johnson, B. S., Krause, T. S., Lee, D., Randolph, A. E., & Wang, H. (2019). Faculty and instructional designers on building successful collaborative relationships. *Education Tech Research Dev, 67,* 855–880. https://doi.org/10.1007/s11423-018-9636-4

Rovai, A. P. (2002). Development of an instrument to measure classroom community. *Internet and Higher Education, 5*(3), 197–211.

Rowland, G. (1992). What do instructional designers actually do? An initial investigation of expert practice. *Performance Improvement Quarterly, 5*(2), 65–86. https://doi.org/10.1111/j.1937-8327.1992.tb00546.x

Ryan, M., Hodson-Carlton, K., & Ali, N. (1999). Evaluation of traditional classroom teaching methods versus course delivery via the World Wide Web. *Journal of Nursing Education, 38*(6), 272–277.

Schwier, R. A., & Wilson, J. R. (2010). Unconventional roles and activities identified by instructional designers. *Contemporary Educational Technology, 1*(2), 134–147. https://doi.org/10.30935/cedtech/5970

Shelton, K. (Ed.). (2019). *A practical handbook to implement the quality scorecard for the administration of online programs.* Online Learning Consortium.

Sheridan, K., & Kelly, M. A. (2011). The indicators of instructor presence that are important to students in online learning courses. *Distance Education Report, 15*(3), 6–8.

Tate, E. (2017, June 3). Easing instructional designer-faculty conflicts. *Inside Higher Ed.* https://www.insidehighered.com/digital-learning/article/2017/05/03/easing-conflicts-between-instructional-designers-and-faculty

Twigg, C. (2003a). Improving learning and reducing costs: New models for online learning. *EDUCAUSE Review, 38*(5), 28–38.

Twigg, C. (2003b). Improving quality and reducing cost: Designs for effective learning. *Change, 35*(4), 22–29.

U.S. Department of Education, Institute of Education Services. (2020). *Studies of distance learning.* https://ies.ed.gov/ncee/wwc/DistanceLearningStudy

U.S. Department of Education, National Center for Education Statistics. (2018). *Digest of education statistics 2016* (NCES 2017-094), Table 311.15. https://nces.ed.gov/pubs2017/2017094.pdf

U.S. Department of Education, Office of Planning, Evaluation and Policy Development. (2010). *Evaluation of evidence-based practices in online learning: A meta-analysis and review of online learning studies.* www.ed.gov/about/offices/list/opepd/ppss/reports.html

Wagner, E. (2011). In search of the secret handshakes of ID. *The Journal of Applied Instructional Design, 1*(1), 33–37.

Wiggins, G. P., McTighe, J., Kiernan, L. J., Frost, F., & Association for Supervision and Curriculum Development. (1998). *Understanding by design.* Association for Supervision and Curriculum Development.

Wilson, A. (2019, September 11). Conquering the challenges of instructional design in education. *GoReact.* https://blog.goreact.com/2019/09/11/instructional-design-in-education/

Wu, D. D. (2015). *Online learning in postsecondary education.* https://doi.org/10.18665/sr.221027

CHAPTER 9

FACULTY LEARNING ABOUT TEACHING LARGE ONLINE CLASSES REMOTELY

Reflections of Faculty Developers

Joanne E. Goodell
Cleveland State University

Shamone Gore-Panter
Cleveland State University

Judith Ausherman
Cleveland State University

Selma Koç
Cleveland State University

Marius Boboc
Cleveland State University

Sarah Rutherford
Cleveland State University

Marcus Schultz-Bergin
Cleveland State University

ABSTRACT

The purpose of this chapter is to describe and reflect on how three professional development courses at a Midwestern higher education institution were implemented, particularly as one of them relates to teaching large online classes. These professional development courses included over 60 full-time and part-time faculty participating in each course during the summer of 2020. The courses focused on: Flipping your remote classroom, small teaching online, and engaging students in online learning. In addition, we discuss the future impact of such faculty development and future lines of inquiry.

In March 2020, educational environments around the world were significantly impacted by the COVID-19 pandemic-related closures, and the rapid switch from face-to-face to emergency remote, fully online settings (Hodges et al., 2020). In our university, a medium-sized comprehensive urban public institution with around 16,000 students, over 500 full-time and 900 part-time faculty in the Midwest of the United States, the faculty had just over one week's notice to make this transition. To remedy the needs of the faculty, particularly for faculty who haven't taught online or used the university's course management system, the university's Center for e-Learning and the Center for Faculty Excellence quickly responded to provide support for the faculty to teach online. These two centers collaborated frequently to ensure faculty development is provided in areas of need and a comprehensive practice of programs and support available and accessible to faculty.

The university administration was supportive in terms of funds for the initiatives suggested to help provide services and support to faculty and students. To provide continuous support to faculty for effective teaching, a large number of professional development activities and programs were developed by the university's Center for e-Learning and the Center for Faculty Excellence. The purpose of this chapter is to describe and reflect on how these professional development courses were implemented, particularly as one of them relates to teaching large online classes. We provide a contextual description of our setting leading up to the pandemic, and describe and reflect on how we responded with these particular professional development courses. In addition, we discuss the future impact of such faculty development and future lines of inquiry.

CONTEXT

While size differentials have been documented in terms of traditional, face-to-face classes, no similar findings have been reported in relation to online courses, pointing to the fact that the current state on online education has shifted its focus to quality rather than course size (Ellison-Bowers et al., 2011). However, given the significant differences between the two modalities of instruction delivery, further analyses indicate that student engagement in online learning environments could be impacted by class size based on social interactions and information overload as parameters (Chen et al.,

2017). Using massive open online courses (MOOCs) as examples of the greatest magnitude when it comes to the number of enrolled students, the design, implementation, and evaluation of high-quality instruction should address some of the limitations related to learner support, inclusive pedagogy, and enhanced lived experiences (Amemado & Manca, 2017). Moreover, a closer look at commonalities among the negative impacts of class size on student engagement, irrespective of modality of instruction delivery, highlights course design and pedagogical strategy considerations that should be the emphasized, such as overuse of lecturing, unequal and inconsistent student participation, lack of student involvement in higher thinking skill opportunities, overall student performance and satisfaction with learning experience (Zhong, 2018). In the same vein, balancing social presence with cognitive load mediated by teaching presence and immediacy could lead to an effective learning experience in virtual settings (Nagel & Kotzé, 2010).

Like many universities in the United States, we had a number of support for faculty already in place (O'Keefe et al., 2020). We had offered a range of fully online classes across all seven academic colleges for more than 15 years using the BlackBoard learning management system. We had a Center for Faculty Excellence that provided faculty teaching development opportunities for both online and traditional instruction and a well-funded center for e-learning. Despite this apparent level of preparedness, there were still many faculty members who were in need of significant assistance in moving to remote teaching. The center for e-learning responded by increasing support for their existing asynchronous professional development known as the Faculty Online Teaching Development course. They also offered a range of predominantly technically focused live webinar sessions in March and April 2020 that were well attended and were made available through their website for asynchronous viewing after the live event. The Center for Faculty Excellence (CFE) collected previously recorded content related to teaching and learning in online contexts and publicized those to faculty in March and April. While these efforts were appreciated, it was by no means enough to meet the need for in-depth professional development around critical issues faculty were encountering in synchronous and asynchronous emergency remote teaching. As Bidwell, Boyle, and Boyle (2020) report, faculty appreciate the professional development opportunities provided by centers; however, they want better incentives to participate. This is particularly true for part-time (contingent) faculty, many of whom work in multiple universities to cobble together the equivalent of a full-time position with far lower compensation and few, if any benefits. With funding for stipends made available from federal Pandemic assistance funds through the CARES act, the CFE planned and implemented three blended (online synchronous and asynchronous) professional development opportunities open to both full-time and part-time faculty. All three began on July 10 and ended on August 14th of 2020, each took the form of a book discussion. The response was much greater than expected with 185 registrations from 105 people.

A communities of inquiry (Garrison et al., 2010) approach was adopted for the implementation of the three courses over 3 weeks in July and August 2020. The participants were recruited via email and web-based notices in early June, and included faculty holding part-time (adjunct), visiting, lecturer (nontenure track full time) and tenure-track appointments, with between 1 and 30 years of experience. What follows in this chapter is a short description of each of the three book discussion groups including details of the requirements to earn the stipend, the strengths and weaknesses of the resources used, the participant feedback, the facilitator reflections on the format, lessons learned about teaching large online classes, and suggestions for future such offerings.

Professional Development Courses

To support faculty online learning needs, three professional development programs implemented were:

- Flipping Your Remote Classroom
- Small Teaching Online
- Engaging Students in Online Learning

The director of the Center for Faculty Excellence (CFE) designed the three courses with the assistance of two faculty with expertise in the content of each professional development activity. The planning process was collaborative and occurred over Zoom. The CFE director selected the book for each course and obtained electronic versions for the respective facilitators for planning purposes. The CFE director worked with each team to plan the synchronous and asynchronous activities in all three courses. Each course chose slightly different activities, lengths of meetings, numbers of required artifacts and final products.

All the courses had two or three synchronous meetings over a 3-week period, with asynchronous activities in between. Synchronous meetings were held in Zoom while asynchronous activities were housed in Blackboard. Faculty had to successfully complete a minimum of the 80% of the assignments to be eligible for the stipend. Participants each received an electronic version of the book upon signing up and were eligible for a $300 stipend if they completed all of the requirements. Participants completed readings, posted written reflections and reacted to other participants offline in the Blackboard environment. There was a summative assessment for each course.

Participants and Large Class Management Strategies

The large number of participants in each of the three courses necessitated grouping them into smaller discussion groups managed by one facilitator. Each course was divided into three discussion groups. The facilitators graded the work of the participants in their subgroup. Synchronous meetings began in one large group and then broke into subgroups. Blackboard discussions were also separated into subgroups to enable participants to build rapport with each other. As noted above, there was considerable diversity in the experience and type of appointment of the participants, and this added to the richness of the ensuing discussions. The synchronous components of the course were beneficial in that they allowed faculty from each small group to intermingle and build camaraderie. In the midst of teaching challenges caused by the pandemic, this interpersonal connection created a space not just for faculty to learn, but to commiserate with and support each other.

Group 1: Flipping Your Remote Classroom

Flipped learning has been defined as "a pedagogical approach in which direct instruction moves from the group learning space to the individual learning space, and the resulting group space is transformed into a dynamic, interactive learning environment where the educator guides students as they apply concepts and engage creatively in the subject matter" (Flipped Learning Network [FLN], 2014). This course was organized using a flipped course structure. This was intentional in order to model how a course might be set up this way and to allow faculty participants to experience the model from the student perspective. Evaluations after the course reflected an appreciation for not only the way the course was structured, but for the experience of learning in a flipped learning environment.

The three facilitators of this group had worked together on previous faculty book discussion groups, one on flipped learning and the other on desirable difficulties. All had implemented some elements of flipped learning in online and face-to-face settings. The goals of this faculty learning community were for participants to be able to:

1. Describe flipped learning and its benefits.
2. Write a module plan that involved flipping some elements of instruction.
3. Discuss the benefits of using flipped learning models in remote teaching environments.

The course was based on the book *Flipped Learning: A Guide for Higher Education Faculty* by Robert Talbert (2017). It is a particularly well-suited resource to guide the process of defining learning outcomes and planning the group space and individual activities. The three modules in this course corresponded to the three sections of the book. There were five discussion forums for which participants had to post a response to the questions and reply to at least two other posts. The summative assessment was a unit or module plan (or part of one) that illustrated their understanding of the flipped learning design principles.

Of the 61 participants who signed up, all but one logged into the course at least once. Eighteen did not complete all of the requirements to earn the stipend, although 10 of the non-completers did some of the activities. Participants reported liking the structure and content of the book, which gave much practical advice based on Talbert's own experiences in using a flipped approach with many of his classes over a number of years. They also liked the clearly defined steps for determining objectives and planning the in-class and out-of-class activities.

Grading rubrics facilitated efficient grading and consistency among instructors. In course evaluations some participants connected facilitator grading comments to the efficacy of their performance in the course. A short evaluation survey was administered at the end of the course, and we received 23 responses, and 15 of those included comments. There were no negative comments, and a number of helpful suggestions for future courses. Two responses mentioned that it was very helpful to experience this in the hybrid online format because it made them realize what their students were experiencing. Some expressed an appreciation for how the course structure enabled self-directed learning. One commented that the asynchronous discussions were extremely helpful.

This course group was offered again in the Spring 2021 semester. We also invited the author of the book Robert Talbert to give a virtual seminar open to all faculty in February 2021, which was very well received. In addition, some of the weekly CFE seminars led by CSU faculty have focused on flipped learning, which is helping to keep discussions of flipped learning going across campus.

Group 2: Small Teaching Online

The concept of small teaching has its beginning in the work of Brown, Roediger, and McDaniel's (2014) *Make it Stick*, which synthesized a range of research findings from the cognitive and psychological learning sciences and provided suggestions for both faculty and students as to how they could improve learning by making relatively minor changes in teaching or study methods. James Lang (2016) built on this in his book *Small Teaching*, in which he related the Brown et al.'s (2014) work and other findings to brief classroom or online learning activities, one-time interventions in a course, or small modifications in course design or communication with students.

We had offered three previous well-received book discussion groups on the Lang (2016) *Small Teaching* book, and James Lang visited CSU in 2018 and did a half-day workshop on elements of the book. The book *Small Teaching Online* by Darby and Lang (2019) applied the techniques distilled by Lang to online learning.

Faculty facilitators for this group had taught numerous fully online asynchronous courses, one for over 10 years, the other 4 years. Both had been recommended by the director of e-learning, and both had participated in previous CFE professional development opportunities, although none of them had worked together on any project prior to this experience. The goals of this module were to:

- Reflect on and discuss the models, principles, and tips for incorporating small changes in teaching that will increase student success in remote, blended, or online classes.
- Plan and implement (if possible) at least two suggestions from the reading or discussion board posts aimed at improving student success in remote, blended, or online classes.

The modules for the *Small Teaching Online* (Darby & Lang, 2019) focused on three guiding principles that were explored in the text. The first was to engage participants in a discussion about the design for learning in an online environment. Second was to explore how individuals participate in online courses. In the last module, the purpose was to explore what motivated online participants.

Facilitating large online groups requires organization and management. In order to have productive academic discussions, it was important to utilize breakout rooms and have a planned role for all the participants. Prior to assigning participants to specified breakout rooms, a summary of expectations was distributed (Johnson, 2020). Designated roles ensured participants have more structure for more in-depth conversations, as well as shared responsibility for learning. Before moving into breakout rooms, participants were reminded to designate a facilitator, recorder, and timekeeper and to limit their comments to allow everyone an opportunity to participate. The facilitator directed the group discussion, the recorder captured the main ideas of the discussion and presented the main ideas to the large group upon return. In some cases, notes were posted to the discussion board as a record of the session for people who were not able to be in the synchronous session.

The summative assessment asked participants to differentiate their reflection among three levels of reflective thinking, technical, contextual, and dialectical (Taggart & Wilson, 1998). More specifically the participants were asked to reflect on (a) "What have you learned?"; (b) "Discuss how what you learned will impact your future remote, online, or blended teaching"; and (c) "Discuss plans to follow-up on learning, either on your own, with a colleague, or in other professional opportunities."

The evaluation survey was completed by 19 participants, 11 of whom provided written feedback. There were no negative comments, while two comments provided suggestions about improvements for future courses and three participants commented on the value of the book. Participants reported appreciation for the opportunity to experience something similar to what their students may have felt in the transition to online learning.

This group provided real-world tips and tricks to assist educators forced to modify the structure of their class due to the pandemic. Not only did the participants gain new tools but the facilitators as well. This forum allowed faculty to work with others from different departments and colleges which does not happen as often as maybe it should. Facilitators reported enjoying the small groups breakout sessions. Participants asked thoughtful questions and many times a facilitator and other participants were able to help their fellow colleagues work through a challenge. This forum also allows all of us to share our frustrations in a safe space and receive support from others sharing similar experiences/frustrations. There is something comforting about shared challenges that lets you know that you are not alone and that this too shall pass.

Group 3: Engaging Students in Online Learning

This faculty learning community was built around learning about social, cognitive, and teaching presence, and utilized the communities of inquiry framework (Garrison et al., 2010). The premise of the Engaging Students in Online Learning program was balancing social presence with cognitive load mediated by teaching presence and immediacy could lead to an effective learning experience in virtual settings (Nagel & Kotzé, 2010). Additionally, formative assessment was taken into account as a set of procedures intended to augment establishing social presence. *Social Presence in Online Learning: Multiple Perspectives on Practice and Research*, edited by Swan, Whiteside, and Dikkers (2017) was used as the main source for discussions in addition to the Web resources and PowerPoint presentations by the workshop facilitators.

The three facilitators were the director of the Center for Faculty Excellence and two colleagues of hers who had researched online instruction and the range of design considerations applicable to student-centered pedagogy and assessment practices. In preparing for this professional development opportunity, the facilitators took into account how to structure content that would engage faculty in sharing their own expertise as well as questions they may have based on their experience pivoting completely to virtual teaching caused by the pandemic. As expressed previously, both formally and informally, faculty felt that their pedagogical content knowledge had been put to the test by students who had to embrace online teaching and learning in spite of their wide range of abilities to perform well in Web-based settings.

The goals of this faculty learning community were for participants to delve into the components of the community of inquiry (CoI; Garrison et al., 2010) framework as a way to allow faculty to propose their own definitions, coupled with examples of their own strategies that support those definitions, followed by facilitated small group activities, and a wrap-up session at the very end of the 90-minute period. The modules were designed to engage faculty in constructive conversations bridging theory and practice focused on the three types of presence—social, teaching, and cognitive—promoted by the CoI (Garrison et al., 2010) framework. Moreover, formative assessment strategies that positively impact social presence were a main focus. Through the assigned and recommended readings, coupled with participation in the two synchronous sessions, faculty were prompted to reflect on and explain changes they would make to their teaching to increase social, teaching or cognitive presence in a future class. Furthermore, participants were asked to elaborate on how they would implement the proposed change and the context in which that would occur. As expected, class size came up as a major consideration, as faculty had a range of courses in mind for their enhanced pedagogical strategies, including large online classes. It was clear from the discussions that large classes were in particular need of the establishment of a student-centered CoI.

The course consisted of two modules. The first was focused on understanding the CoI framework. There were a number of readings from the Swan et al. (2017) book, and links to videos and other resources for participants to access asynchronously. The synchronous sessions conducted in Zoom provided an opportunity for participants to meet each other and discuss the applications of the content of the module. A module reflection took place in the Blackboard discussion board, and a written assignment based on a short case description facilitated participants' application of the CoI framework to the case. Module two was focused on assessment techniques that have been shown to increase student engagement. After reading a variety of materials, participants responded to four questions focused on how they would connect the concepts to their own practice. A final summative assessment asked participants to describe how they were intending to incorporate one aspect of the CoI framework and one new type of formative or summative assessment into their teaching. A pre-assessment was used to determine faculty's familiarity with the three components of the CoI (Garrison et al., 2010) framework, followed by a couple of assigned readings on social presence. Further topical points addressed teaching presence, assessment, and the high-impact practices for assessment supported by the American Association for Colleges and Universities (Kuh, 2008).

During the first synchronous session, participants were prompted to reflect on affective behaviors and how they would define and model them in the classroom. Based on examples generated by faculty themselves, the conversation shifted to considerations needed to ensure an effective transfer of such strategies from face-to-face to virtual learning environments. Participant engagement then centered on teaching presence and how online class design principles, coupled with relevant technological and assessment tools/strategies could inform student-centered teaching, as highlighted by OLC's Faculty Playbook (O'Keefe et al., 2020). Similarly, a pre-assessment on social presence encouraged faculty to comment on how they structure their classes to provide students with opportunities to interact by being visible, accessible, and responsible in the learning environment. Participant feedback identified the need for instructors to build and sustain a course climate that supports discourse, based on which faculty were then asked to elaborate on and share examples of social, teaching, and cognitive strategies from their own practice. Finally, formative feedback was focused on as a way to apply faculty-generated examples of formative assessment to student-centered instructional environments. All along, assessment was defined along a spectrum ranging from didactic, teacher-centered to constructive design that focuses on co-construction of knowledge and relevant applications to the world outside the classroom. Under these circumstances, class size and the transfer of pedagogical skills between face-to-face and virtual courses were included in participant exchanges during synchronous sessions as well as in Blackboard postings.

There were 67 participants who signed up, and all but three accessed the course at least once. A total of 47 completed the requirements to earn the $300 stipend by the end of the summer, with 6 more completing some but not all of the requirements. The evaluation survey was administered at the end of the program to all enrolled participants. There were 26 responses and 19 comments, including 15 with some negative feedback, one with neutral feedback, and nine with positive feedback. There were six participants who commented that the Swan et. al (2017) book was too dry, had too much educational jargon and lacked practical suggestions. Two comments noted that participants wanted better and more timely feedback, while one said there was too much work. Positive feedback included wanting more time, appreciating the experience with Zoom breakout rooms, and provided good additional resources.

The facilitators realized that the book for this course was not suitable as a discussion group book for the same reasons as the faculty. This book was written by educational technology researchers for educational technology researchers. The facilitators also felt that the course could have been more interactive. This could take the form of having more synchronous sessions that focused on critical reflection of participants' teaching practice, much of which had occurred in the discussion board posts. There could also have been more content delivery in the asynchronous mode to make more time for group discussion in the synchronous sessions, essentially applying a flipped classroom model to this faculty learning community.

Social, teaching, and cognitive presence is often discussed among faculty with respect to strategies and technology tools to engage students in activities that facilitate and support these aspects that are desired in an online course, particularly in large online courses. Given the importance of establishing and maintaining social, teaching, and cognitive presence in online teaching, it would be desirable to find a book that focused more on practical matters related to how to develop a community of inquiry with their classes.

DISCUSSION

Responding to the need for professional development opportunities prompted by the COVID-19 pandemic created the impetus for these three courses. It was the first time the Center for Faculty Excellence had offered professional development in the summer, and the first time it had used a blended learning format. Given the short time frame in which the planning and implementation had to occur, the feedback from the participants was remarkably positive. It is unclear what impact the availability of the stipend had on the enrollment, but there were more part-time faculty who completed the courses than in professional development opportunities offered during the academic year.

Some common themes were found in both the faculty feedback and facilitator reflections across the three different groups. First, faculty reported appreciating the opportunity to experience remote learning just like their students had done in March and April. In particular, those who had signed up for more than one course commented that they now more fully appreciated how difficult it was to keep the requirements for multiple courses straight in their mind, and that they would make more effort to be clear and transparent in their expectations and communications with their students in coming semesters.

Second, participants requested more timely feedback on the discussion board posts. Facilitators reflected on the amount of time it took to provide useful and meaningful feedback to so many students and on the challenges of co-teaching, which few of them had experienced before. Facilitators discussed using more of a flipped learning approach in which the participants would acquire course content on their own in an individual learning space, and then have the discussions in the group space during the synchronous meetings. That would alleviate the need to provide extensive feedback in discussion board posts but necessitate the use of some other forms of assessment in order to provide formative feedback throughout the course.

As the only facilitator of all three groups, the CFE director was able to compare the features of the three books used in these courses. The clearly defined outcome that was the focus of the *Flipping Learning* (Talbert, 2017) book made ideal for this kind of professional development. Talbert's extensive classroom experience with flipped learning came through clearly in the narrative and examples he used to illustrate the concepts of flipped learning. *Small Teaching Online* (Darby & Lang, 2019) was quite accessible in its style and language use, and definitely appealed to the participants, but it lacked a specific focused outcome, instead presenting nine different approaches for planning courses and lesson, teaching, and motivating students, a comprehensive overview of many aspects of being a teacher. Perhaps it was this broad focus that made it difficult for some participants to connect as well to this book as to the Talbert book on flipped learning. Finally, the Swan et al. (2017) book was clearly out of reach to many of the participants, as evidenced by the six comments received about the "dry" nature of the book with too much jargon. It is somewhat surprising that given how much has been written about it and how well used the CoI framework has become since it was developed in 2000 (Swan & Ice, 2010) that there are not more articles or books directed at faculty who have little or no experience with educational literature or teaching, which was definitely the case for quite a number of participants in this course. On reflection, it may have been better to not use a book for this course and instead rely on other resources. The facilitators are considering working together to produce an edited volume that is more focused on the practical issues of developing social, teaching and cognitive presence for faculty developers to use in courses such as this.

The use of Zoom was particularly impactful on both participants and facilitators. Like most educators, we all had virtually no experience with Zoom until mid-March 2020, so being part of a large Zoom group was an excellent opportunity to not only see things from the other side, but to discuss its use in real time with colleagues. Facilitators used Zoom and demonstrated at the same time by forming breakout groups randomly, pre-assigning breakout groups, using reactions, using the chat feature and using Zoom polls.

The format and timing of the sessions worked well for this type of activity. Given the short timeframe available to complete the courses, those participants who signed up for and completed all three courses (13 people) were quite busy keeping up with the work. A further 23 people completed two of the three courses, with the remaining 50 completing one course. There were only two negative comments about the amount of work required, and one comment that indicated the author thought there should be more work!

Facilitators were in agreement that attendance at the synchronous sessions should not be compulsory, so no attendance records were kept, and there was no credit given for attendance. All of the sessions were recorded and posted on the Blackboard site for those who were not able to attend. Most of the synchronous sessions had between 30 and 40 participants, although the first one was usually more than 40. Facilitators graded the work of the discussion group they had facilitated, which ended up being around 14 people in each group. Credit was given for initial postings and replies to other posts in Blackboard, although the co-facilitators did not use specific criteria related to the length or quality of writing. Overall, the faculty responses were thoughtful and reflective.

FUTURE DIRECTIONS AND RESEARCH

The professional development courses brought teams of faculty to design, implement, and assess each professional development program based on their expertise on the topic. Thus, the team-teaching model with large groups of participants showed value for use in online learning. The team-teaching model can be implemented with guest or expert visitors in addition to bringing together different cultural groups that have similar learning goals. As an example, teaching councils could be created to tap into faculty expertise that could serve as mentors to fellow online instructors.

As seen in the above examples, the CFE continuously assesses and evaluates the programs it implements based on faculty needs, with a consideration toward new or emerging educational technologies. The CFE courses are supported with expert speakers and faculty who have implemented effective ways of teaching online. As evidenced in these program assessments, faculty sought practical applications rather than theoretical discussions based on assigned readings. Consequently, the literature chosen for faculty readings should emphasize practice. Understandably, faculty perceive learning about practical applications to be more essential and immediate in terms of transferring skills to their own teaching practice.

Future research needs to focus on strategies and technology tools that work in a variety of parameters based on which to form groups, such as size and experience. Further, faculty support and training programs should become part of the system by which they are supported institutionally. Consequently, centers for teaching and learning can collaborate with other administrative support centers on campus to share best practices for faculty training. Online teaching and learning during the pandemic render technology-focused pedagogical training and development essential. Strategies for large online classes are very likely to stay long after the pandemic is over. Successful incorporation of advanced virtual technology in future curricular models relies on institutions and faculty working together to face future realities and plan accordingly.

REFERENCES

Amemado, D., & Manca, S. (2017). Learning from decades of online distance education: Moocs and the community of inquiry framework. *Journal of e-Learning and Knowledge Society, 13*(2), 21–32. https://doi.org/10.20368/1971-8829/1339

Bidwell, L. M., Boyle, K., & Boyle, D. (2020). Pedagogy in a pandemic: Emergency remote teaching during COVID-19. *Virginia Social Science Journal, 54,* 65–73.

Brown, P. C., Roediger, H. L., & McDaniel, M. A. (2014). *Make it stick.* Harvard University Press.

Chen, B., DeNoyelles, A., Zydney, J., & Patton, K. (2017). Creating a community of inquiry in large-enrollment online courses: An exploratory study on the effect of protocols within online discussions. *Online Learning, 21*(1). https://doi.org/10.24059/olj.v21i1.816

Darby, F., & Lang, J. M. (2019). *Small teaching online: Applying learning science in online classes.* John Wiley & Sons.

Ellison-Bowers, P., Sand, J., Barlow, M. R., & Wing, T. J. (2011). Strategies for managing large online classes. *International Journal of Learning, 18*(2), 57–66. https://scholarworks.boisestate.edu/psych_facpubs/150/

Flipped Learning Network. (2014). *What is flipped learning.* https://flippedlearning.org/wp-content/uploads/2016/07/FLIP_handout_FNL_Web.pdf

Garrison, D. R., Anderson, T., & Archer, W. (2010). The first decade of the community of inquiry framework: A retrospective. *The Internet and Higher Education, 13*(1/2), 5–9. https://doi.org/10.1016/j.iheduc.2009.10.003

Hodges, C., Moore, S., Lockee, B., Trust, T., & Bond, A. (2020, March 27). The difference between emergency remote teaching and online learning. *Educause Review.* https://er.educause.edu/articles/2020/3/the-difference-between-emergency-remote-teaching-and-online-learning

Johnson, A. (2020). *Online teaching with Zoom: A guide for teaching and learning with videoconference platforms.* http://excellentonlineteaching.com

Kuh, G. D. (2008). *High-impact educational practices: What they are, who has access to them, and why they matter.* AAC&U.

Lang, J. M. (2016). *Small teaching: Everyday lessons from the science of learning.* John Wiley & Sons.

Nagel, L., & Kotzé, T. G. (2010). Supersizing e-learning: What a CoI survey reveals about teaching presence in a large online class. *The Internet and Higher Education, 13*(1/2), 45–51. https://doi.org/10.1016/j.iheduc.2009.12.001

O'Keefe, L., Rafferty, J., Gunder, A., & Vignare, K. (2020). *Delivering high-quality instruction online in response to COVID–19: Faculty playbook.* http://www.everylearnereverywhere.org/resources

Swan, K., & Ice, P. (2010). The community of inquiry framework ten years later: Introduction to the special issue. *The Internet and Higher Education, 13*(1/2), 1–4. https://doi.org/10.1016/j.iheduc.2009.11.003

Swan, K., Whiteside, A. L., & Dikkers, A. G. (Eds.). (2017). *Social presence in online learning: Multiple perspectives on practice and research.* Stylus Publishing LLC.

Taggart, G. L., & Wilson, A. P. (1998). *Promoting reflective thinking in teachers: 44 action strategies.* Corwin Press.

Talbert, R. (2017). *Flipped learning: A guide for higher education faculty.* Stylus Publishing, LLC.

Zhong, L. (2018). Strategies and practices related to teaching large online classes. *Journal of higher Education Theory and Practice, 18*(1), 152–166. https://doi.org/10.33423/jhetp.v18i1.541

CHAPTER 10

BUILDING AN ADAPTIVE ONLINE LEARNING ENVIRONMENT

Learners' Perspectives and Satisfaction

Emre Emrah Özkeskin
Anadolu University

Cengiz Hakan Aydın
Anadolu University

ABSTRACT

Massive open online courses (MOOCs) have been around for more than a decade, and the COVID-19 pandemic boosted their integration into formal education. Those institutions which get involved in the MOOCs movement have different motives for doing so. Anadolu University in Turkey is one of those institutions that has been using MOOCs as a test bed environment for experimenting applicability and effectiveness of innovative technologies and strategies in its large-size formal distance courses and programs. The main purpose of the study is related to testing the effectiveness of an adaptive learning environment and a course, which included an automated notification system and content presentation based on holist-serialist cognitive styles of the learners, as well as the MOOC participants' persistence to complete the course as well as exploring their reactions to and perspectives on these notifications. This chapter summarizes some of the major results of a large-scale study. For instance, the study has shown that learner modeling is a complex and complicated process, while learners' characteristics may change during learning. It seems better to adapt the system based on learners' characteristics that were performed during the learning process. Another major finding is about automated personalized notifications. The study presented evidence of effectiveness of those auto-generated and shared personalized notifications on MOOC participants' retention.

Open and distance learning (ODL), as a field of study, focuses on formal, informal, and nonformal flexible learning opportunities in which learners are, in general, separated from learning resources, including instructors, other learners, and resources by time and/or place, and interact with these resources via telecommunication systems (Aydin, 2011). Since the beginning, ODL providers have been struggling to find innovative ways to offer open, flexible, and personalized learning experiences that address each learner's personal needs, preferences and characteristics. According to Ozgul (2015), the major chronological milestones were (a) the establishment of open universities, starting Open University in the UK in 1969 and others during 1970s and 1980s; (b) the increasing interest among traditional institutions in online learning during late 1990s and early 2000s; (c) the open courseware (OCW) project, popularized with the Massachusetts Institute of Technology's project (MIT OCW) in 2002; (d) the launch of massive open online courses (MOOCs) in 2008; and (e) almost at the same time, the transformation of open textbook, open courseware projects into open educational resources and their rise in 2010s.

Anadolu University in Turkey is one of those providers which has been in an ongoing search for exploring new implementations for more open, flexible, and personalized education opportunities for all who wish to learn. It was established as a traditional higher education institution in 1958, and it transformed into a dual mode university in 1982. Since then, it has been offering distance higher education opportunities to millions. A self-paced learning strategy has been employed in almost all of its distance certificate and undergraduate (2 or 4 years long) programs since the beginning. Textbooks delivered in print or online format are the main material, but the learners can use around 14 different online support materials presented in the learning management system, which is also customized, produced in-house. Centralized exams organized throughout the country, Europe, Azerbaijan, United States, UK, Saudi Arabia, and Egypt two times (midterm and final) in a semester are the main assessment tools the university uses. However, based on the requirement of the program or course, various assessment methods, such as portfolio, practicum, internship, lab performance, oral exams, and so on, are also employed. Approximately 1 million learners enroll in Anadolu University's 60 distance programs (41 associate degree, 19 BA degree programs) and roughly 100,000 in certificate programs (Anadolu University, 2020). This large body of learners makes Anadolu University one of the mega universities of the world.

However, the size of a learner group brings several limitations to the system. Providing enough personalized learning opportunities and support for learners is one the major limitations that Anadolu University has been struggling to solve due to the large student enrollment in their distance learning programs. Strategies such as evening and weekend face-to-face sessions, email, discussion boards, and an on-demand online support system (AOS), have been implemented and are still in place. In addition to these supplementary programs, the university continued to seek alternative ways to meet the needs of the learners and their preferences. One of the latest solutions considered by Anadolu University was the MOOC project, called AKADEMA.

The AKADEMA platform was established during late 2014, and it requested university professors to offer short learning courses to anyone, of any age, who wants to learn. It started with 2,500 learners in four courses and reached more than 100,000 learners in 120 courses. In the majority of these courses, a guided-study approach is employed, which means that learners have a chance to interact with real university professors. This has been considered as one of the main strengths of the AKADEMA courses (Bozkaya & Aydin, 2019). Meanwhile, this project and the courses included in it served areas of interest: (a) to train and motivate professors about teaching online; (b) to showcase that online teaching is possible in science, music, physical education, and many other fields; and (c) to create a test bed environment for innovative pedagogies that might be integrated into regular large size formal ODL courses.

Based on the agenda focused on creating a test bed environment, one of the AKADEMA courses, entitled as Introduction to Data Mining, was used to test a course that provided adaptive content presentation and notifications. The main goal of the study was to explore learners' reactions to these personalized content presentations and notifications sent based on their participation in learning activities. This chapter summarizes the design and implementation processes as well as the participants' perspectives and conclusions drawn from this test bed evaluation. The chapter is organized into three major sections: an introduction to MOOCs and the adaptive learning environments; an insight about the test bed evaluation; and lessons learned in the evaluation study.

MASSIVE OPEN ONLINE COURSES (MOOCS)

The OpenupEd initiative of the European Association for Distance Teaching Universities (OpenupEd, 2015) defined MOOCs as "courses designed for large numbers of participants, that can be accessed by anyone anywhere as long as they have an internet connection, are open to everyone without entry qualifications, and offer a full/complete course experience online for free" (p. 1). Although there are different variations and classifications, there are mainly two major MOOCs types: cMOOCs and xMOOCs. The former ones are actually the original version that follows a connectivist approach and learning is shaped by student preferences and the networks they are in. On the other hand, xMOOCs employ traditional online course elements and mainly include video-based lectures, peer interaction activities, quizzes, and reflections (Margaryan et al., 2015).

The success of cMOOCs led to an increase in the number of MOOCs (xMOOC) produced by many profit/nonprofit organizations in different countries. Some examples for MOOCs are Udacity, Udemy, EdX, FutureLearn, J-MOOCs, and OpenUpEd. The number of MOOCs in Europe is increasing, but most of the MOOCs are offered by initiatives from the United States of America. FutureLearn of UK, France Université Numérique (FUN), Miriadax, ECO and EMMA can also be exemplified as European MOOC initiatives (Aydin, 2017). Commonly, it is possible to have a completion certificate based on a MOOC. Some programs offer participants certificates accepted as credits in formal programs (Zhang, 2016).

Although the courses are usually independent of each other, there are some specializations comprising several courses and a capstone project. Coursera and FutureLearn, for example, offer many certified specializations or short learning programs. On the other hand, many MOOCs providers look for ways to integrate MOOCs into formal curricula. For instance, Edx, founded by Harvard University and MIT, offers micro-master's degree alternatives along with professional and xSeries certificates.

MOOCs are also considered a platform for trying out innovative online pedagogies (Diver & Martinez, 2014; Freitas & Paredes, 2018). For instance, video-based learning (Giannakos et al., 2014), mobile learning (Sharples et al., 2015), gamification (Rincon-Flores et al., 2020), self-directed learning (Zhu et al., 2020), virtual and augmented realities (Kabtane et al., 2020), and similar innovations were tested in MOOC environments. Adaptive learning is also among these innovative learning technologies tested in MOOCs (Ewais & Samara, 2020; Lallé & Conati, 2020; Wan & Yu, 2020). However, in order to understand the value of adaptive learning and adaptive learning environments in MOOCs and online learning, it would be beneficial to establish a knowledge base on these terms, as addressed in the following section.

ADAPTIVE LEARNING ENVIRONMENTS

Adaptive learning refers to applications in which the learning process differs and becomes flexible in line with the learner's individual needs, characteristics, and learning behaviors. There are various teaching approaches that underpin adaptive learning. Mödritscher, Garcia-Barrios, and Gütl (2004) gather these approaches under four headings: macro, ability-method, micro, and constructive-collaborative approaches. Adaptive learning environments can be defined as learning spaces where learning resources, activities, interactions, and strategies can be presented according to the learners' individual or group needs. The most popular adaptation implementations are about the content presentation and navigation in the learning environment; but there is a growing interest in adapting assessments tools and strategies, media preferences, and gamification elements based on the learners' characteristics, needs, and preferences (Salahli et al., 2013; Stoyanov & Kirchner, 2004; Truong, 2016). Different adaptation systems provide different benefits for learners. For example, while presentation adaptations increase learners' comprehension level of learning content, adaptive navigation support makes it easier for learners to search and navigate content (Brusilovsky, 1997).

Adaptive learning environments in which computers are used to support learning processes can be examined in two groups as intelligent tutoring systems and Web-based adaptive learning systems. Intelligent tutoring systems are generally used for curriculum organization, problem-solving analysis and problem-solving support. Web-based adaptive learning environments, on the other hand, basically provide content presentation and navigation support to learners (Brusilovsky & Peylo, 2003,). Adaptive learning environments may be open to learner intervention at different levels. In this context, Oppermann, Rashev, and Kinshuk (1997) have positioned adaptive learning environments on a bipolar scale as adaptable and adaptive systems. According to this view, while adaptations in adaptive systems are carried out completely by the system (computer) without any intervention of the learner; in adaptable systems, changes are managed directly by the users.

There are three main components in an adaptive learning environment: learner model, course content model, and adaptation engine (Nguyen, 2012). The learner model is the core component of an adaptive learning environment. Studies on adaptive learning environments in the literature show that learner models can be based on different variables like learning styles, cognitive styles, and knowledge level or computer experience. According to Brusilovsky and Millán (2007), the most common and useful adaptation variables are the learner's level of knowledge, interests, goals, experience, and personal characteristics. Adaptive learning environments can be open to the learner intervention at different levels. Oppermann,

Rashev, and Kinshuk (1997) have positioned adaptive learning environments according to openness to user intervention on a bipolar scale: from fully open to interfering to learner never interferes.

THE STUDY

As indicated above, one of the major issues of Anadolu University's distance education is related to providing personalized flexible learning experiences that directly address the learners' needs, characteristics, and preferences. Transforming the university's courses into adaptive learning environments seemed like a solution for this problem. However, past experiences have shown that due to a large body of students in each distance course, any small change may create important problems in the system. Consequently, a MOOC offered via the university's MOOC platform, AKADEMA, was used as a test bed environment to test effectiveness, efficiency, appeal, and sustainability of an adaptive learning solution.

The main purpose of this study, in general, was to design, develop, and evaluate an adaptive open and distance learning system. Specifically, it intended to examine how a MOOC in the Anadolu University open and distance learning system can be presented in a way that supports adaptive learning, and to explore learners' perspectives and satisfaction with the course. The following questions were sought during the study:

1. How can we model the learners?
2. What kinds of technological infrastructure components should the environment include?
3. What are the learners' perspectives about the system and the course?
4. How did the system satisfy the learners?

In order to identify the learner modeling strategy, we conducted a focus group interview with the participation of three international and four Turkish experts who have implemented some sort of adaptive learning environments and published articles on this topic. Based on the results of the focus group, we decided to create a learner-modeling based on two variables: (a) the cognitive styles of the learners based on Pask's holistic and serialistic classification (Pask, 1976); and (b) time-spend on tasks. At first, we intended to use Witkin's field-dependent, field-independent classification and gather data with the online version of the embedded ground figure test (Witkin et al., 1971). We created an online version of the instrument but could not get approval from the copyright holders of the test and had to give up. Later, Pask's classification and the scale was adapted because it was found to be the closest to Witkon's classification, and also there was a Turkish adaptation, whose reliability and validity had already been proven (see Figure 10.1). Therefore, the holist-serialist scale was adapted and integrated easily into the learning environment. According to this classification, holistic learners tend to have an overall learning approach and serialists are inclined to have a one point at a time approach (Ford, 2000).

As it has been mentioned above, the study was conducted in a course offered via AKADEMA platform at Anadolu University. To be able to reach a large group of learners, we chose to offer a course on a popular topic. Previous analyses of the AKADEMA learners' preferences of topics had already uncovered data mining as one of the most frequently mentioned topics. So, the course was designed to help learners acquire introductory level knowledge base and skills on data mining, and, accordingly, entitled as *Introduction to Data Mining*. It consisted of six modules, including orientation (the first module) and a warm-up (the last module). In the orientation module, the participants were asked to fill out a survey which included holist-serialist cognitive style scale as well as a few more questions regarding the participants' demographics and other characteristics. Based on the results of the survey, the learners were classified into three groups and received different navigation and content options. An explanatory self-regulated learning

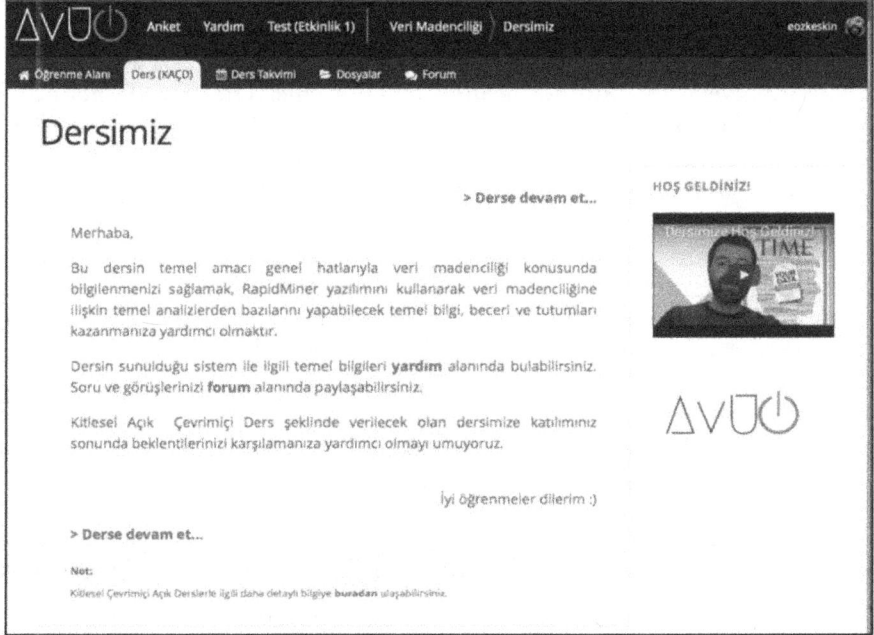

Figure 10.1 Welcome page introducing the course.

approach was employed as the instructional strategy for all groups. In other words, in each module, the learners received lectures about the topic of the module after an introduction and followed by a series of interactive activities, such as drag and drop, multiple choice, or fill-in-the-blanks questions, drawings, and so on. The modules also included a summary and a short quiz at the end.

The learners were heterogeneous in terms of different prior experiences in data mining, varying educational levels from high school and middle school graduates to master's degrees in varying fields (from computer science to fine arts), different age groups from 16 to 50 years old. They, as mentioned before, divided into two groups based on their serialist-holist characteristics. Each group was assigned randomly under three subgroups: (a) fixed, (b) all, and (c) flexible. The learners in the "fixed" group had to follow the content structure organized according to their holist-serialist characteristics. The learners in the "all" group were able to access all the navigation and content possibilities free from their cognitive style, and the learners in the "flexible" group were first faced with the content and the navigation according to their cognitive style but had the chance to switch between holist or serialist content and navigation structures. Table 10.1 shows the number of learners in each group.

The course environment was based on a widely used content management system (CMS) Drupal which provided rich modules that offered various possibilities to the developers. However, a professional programmer was used to add more components and features for securing the adaptive content, navigation, and notification components. The environment also included structured preset pop-up notifications and automated emails attached to each content page. It automatically provided warnings and different learning content suggestions to each learner, depending on the time she or he spent on the page. If the learner exceeded the threshold time on a page, a pop-up message was displayed and for certain pages an email sent to the learners. We have identified these threshold times by using Çetinkaya-Uzun's readability formula (Çetinkaya, 2010). The aim was to let learners self-assess and decide on their own learning needs.

While designing these pop-up notifications and emails, we used the flow theory, which suggested that an individual is at her/his full capacity when she or he is in a flow. Nakamura and Csikszentmihalyi (2009) expressed that an individual stays in the flow only when her/his abilities and the difficulty

TABLE 10.1 Number of Learners in Each Group

Holist				Serialist				
Fixed	Changing	All	*Total*	Fixed	Changing	All	*Total*	TOTAL
141	146	142	429	105	115	115	335	764

of the activities are balanced. To help the learner stay in flow, we used pop-ups with motivational text and supportive learning content. We have also tracked if the learners opened the e-mails and clicked the links.

The pop-ups consisted of a personal salutation (e.g., Hello John); a warning message like, "For some time, you have lost your interest! Are you OK? What happened? Are you bored?"; study tips; and alternative learning materials (easier and more advanced). This field was often included personalized motivational/informational messages. The other parts of the notifications included various content alternatives, such as (a) adaptive learning components, (b) book page which had the structure of sub-pages, (c) content which was a static content page, (d) discussion post, (e) document page, (f) interactive content, (g) true–false questions, and (h) a Web form used for idea generation or feedback. Figure 10.2 shows a pop-up notification used in the course.

The e-mail messaging had an important role in helping learners maintain their motivation and continue their learning in the course. The adaptive learning environment sent two types of e-mails: bulk (group) mails and personal mails. Bulk mails consisted of predetermined content and sent in specific time slots, for example, at the first day of the course, the end of every course week, and so on. These messages had three parts: (a) motivational messages, (b) a brief of the course week (module), and (c) contact information of the course facilitators. The second type of emails were personal ones which were created and sent automatically by the environment while the user interacts with the content during the course. These email messages consisted of motivational messages and personalized suggestions

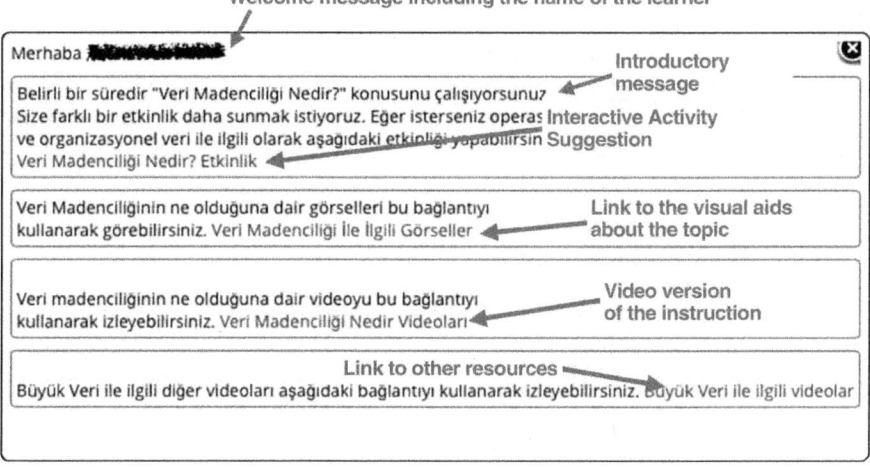

Figure 10.2 An example pop-up notification.

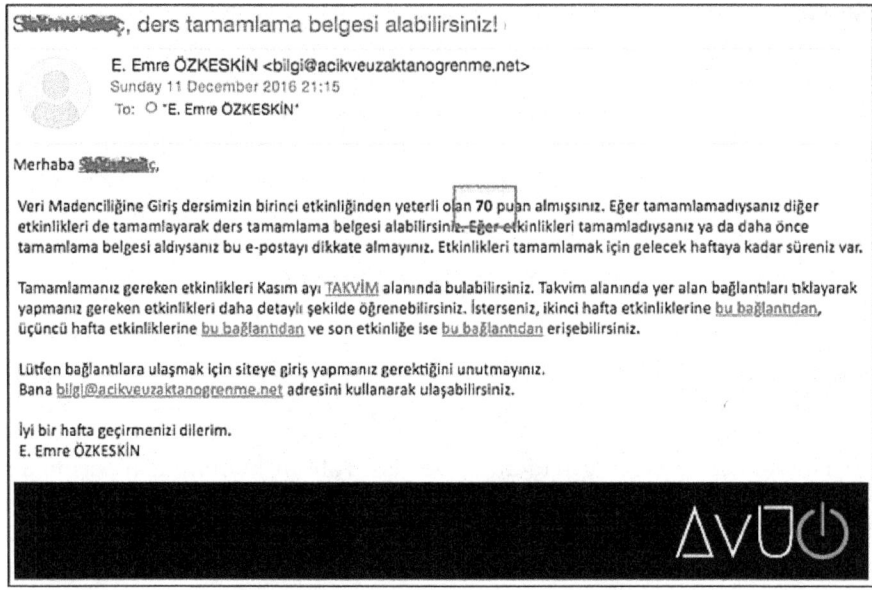

Figure 10.3 An e-mail message sample sent to a student about his/her first assignment grade and upcoming course activities.

regarding the page content they were on but inactive. Figure 10.3 presents an actual personal email message sent to a learner informing them their first assignment grade and upcoming course activities.

The reporting of the results was organized into three sections. The first section very briefly presented results regarding learner modeling and the learners' actions to the content organization provided them according to their holist-serialist characteristics. The section below actually provided a short summary of our experiences. The second section consisted of the learners' perspectives towards the environment, content, and design of the course. The last section covered the results of the survey instrument.

Learner Modeling

As previously described, the holist-serialist cognitive styles were identified to model the learners. We first reviewed the literature systematically and prepared a list of variables that could be used for learner modeling. Later, a focus group study was conducted with the participation of two international (from Canada and Taiwan) and four local experts who have experimented with learner modeling and learners' individual differences. In the end, Park's holist-serialist cognitive styles was identified as the variable to be used to model the learners. Although we have observed some differences between holist and serialist groups, we, in general, concluded that learner modeling was a very complex issue. As one or two individual characteristics were not enough for an adequate modeling, we needed more detailed analyses and combinations of different characteristics of learners. On the other hand, one of the interesting findings was about the content pages holist and serialist visited. The serialist learners spent more time in the course, and visited the pages related to guidance, such as the calendar, than the holist learners. Additionally, the number of drop-out among the holist learners gradually increased by time during the course while this number among the serialists was not stable, and in fact, in some weeks the serialist came back to course after a break.

Components

A variety of open-source tools was used to create the course environment. Figure 10.4 shows the major components of the environment. Sustainability, affordability, scalability, and compatibly criteria played an important role during the selection of the tools. As a result, the environment was built on a Linux server with the Ubuntu operating system and an Apache HTTP web server. We also used Drupal as the content management system (CMS), Percona as a database system, and Piwik and Google Analytics as analytics tools.

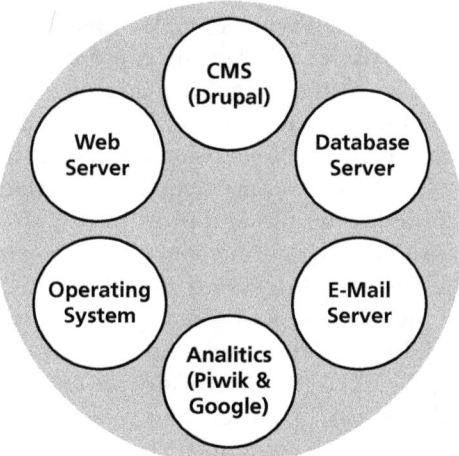

Figure 10.4 Technological infrastructure.

Learners' Perspectives

In terms of the learners' perspectives, we had very positive feedback from them not only through semi-structured interviews but also by e-mails. However, there was interestingly almost no difference among the learners' perspectives despite the differences in demographics and prior experiences of the participants. This perspective shared by the majority summarized by one of the interviewees, "For me, these things [pop-ups, emails, presentation of the content based on learners' characteristics] are obviously motivating. Because there is a nice flow in the page. I read and continue reading, then how can I say; after a while, reading from a screen makes me tired but a pop-up takes my intention and increases my interest." Emails were also regarded as motivating. The 24-years-old female participant pointed out that "emails continuously reminded me where I am in the course and what should I do.... These warnings that our teacher sent by e-mail were encouraging and helped me stay in the course." On the other hand, some of the participants found it a bit disturbing. For instance, a male 39-year-old learner expressed that "they were ok in general but sometimes I found them as disturbing. Especially when I was concentrated on the contents, those sudden pop-ups surprised and distracted my concentration." We argue that learners' preferences about receiving notifications and frequency of notifications and emails can be asked at the beginning of the course and an opportunity to change these preferences anytime during the course can be provided. This may help designers/instructors give more autonomy to learners.

The interviews and the email messages also showed that the majority of participants found the design and the content interesting. They indicated how the design helped them learn deeper. We followed an explanatory self-regulated learning approach to design the content but supported this self-regulation with regular instructor-guided activities (learner-to-instructor interactions). The content via text, video, audio was presented with some activities on the same page. A 24-years-old female participant wrote in an email message that "each unit of instruction is designed like a book chapter, which also included some thought-provoking question, and short videos. Also, activities we have to do, and short quizzes were at the end of the instruction. I liked this flow. It was easy to follow." A similar opinion was mentioned during the interviews by a male participant "there were short readings, easy to read and understand, and then a meaningful activity related to the reading...I like it...it provides an extra contribution to the understanding of the lesson." Learners also found the ability to reach out alternative presentation of the content (text, video, audio, etc.) as very beneficial. One mentioned that "instead of just text, there were also sounds, images, videos ... to provide wider information opportunities if desired."

Interaction opportunities with university professors were also found very beneficial and noteworthy. A 27-years-old male participant stated that his most liked dimension of the course was "being able to communicate with a university teacher." During the interviews and also via analyses of email messages, we found out that some of the learners did not understand that a large majority of the email messages had been created by the learning environment automatically. In fact, some responded to these automated messages as if they were really interacting with a real instructor. Some of these responses included only "thank you" messages. On the other hand, two of the study participants pointed out the lack of synchronous interaction. Since these two participants were graduate students and have had online learning experience, their comments on this characteristic of the course can be related to the widespread use of synchronous tools in many online degree programs and courses in Turkey. Meanwhile, the flexibility in terms of time and place was regarded as one of the positive characteristics of the course and the environment. Some of the common quotes included in interviews and email messages were as follows: "being flexible during working hours"; "does not overwhelm the student with lesson time"; and "providing the opportunity to learn from a distance."

It is also interesting to learn that participants noted that they transferred their learning into their workplace activities. Some of them clearly stated that the adaptive learning environment and the course content helped them gain skills that they could use in their daily work or academic life. For example, one participant noted that he used what he learned in his daily life, "I use what I learnt in this course at the company I work. It helped me a lot at work." Another participant in his email mentioned that "at work, I can make analyses easier now."

The content of the course was among one of the top reasons for the participants' enrollment in the course. We observed clearly that MOOCs should focus on popular topics and must have appealing titles to get the learners' attention but, of course, motivating them to complete course tasks is another important issue. Many participants mentioned in their interviews and emails that "data mining is interesting and very popular in the world." The participants additionally stated that the content presented was up-to-date, authentic, worthwhile, real life, and self-contained. Learners thought the variety of materials (e.g., video, audio, visual) had a positive effect on their learning.

We also observed that learners without experience in data mining benefited more than experienced ones. A 24-year-old female learner mentioned, "I have learned a subject that I did know nothing about, but I was interested in and really learned data mining and have already started to use it." Another participant also expressed similar sentences: "It was a subject I had little knowledge of before, thanks to the course. Now, I consider myself as a person who has entered the data mining field."

Along with positive perspectives, the participants also indicated some of the areas that needed improvement, one of which being about the length of the course. Some found it too short, while others too long compared to the content. Our observations revealed that those with a prior experience found the content a bit light and time as long but those with limited or no prior experience found the content and the length as sufficient. Those serialist learners also complained about the lack of progress updates. Although they received automated emails at the end of each section in the course, they still wanted to see their progress in the course. Moreover, some learners found the language a bit academic for a MOOC: "The language is a bit too academic and makes it difficult to understand because the terms we don't know much about." Another interesting point was the complaint some learners had about the frequency of emails. They found it disturbing to receive emails too often.

However, as can be observed in Table 10.2, a large percent of the emails was opened (65.63%) and the links, led to the different resources and alternative learning paths, were clicked (64.24%). We observed this trend (namely, 50–65% of the emails were opened and almost the same percent of the links were clicked) since the beginning of the course and in every cycle of the course offering (total 3 cycles). Interestingly, the analytics have shown that almost the same percent (64%) of the learners clicked on the links and 97% of the students completed the course. These figures can be considered as evidence of effectiveness of automated pop-up notifications and email messages on increasing learners' motivation and persistence to complete the MOOCs.

Satisfaction

In order to identify how the learners were satisfied with the course and the adaptive learning environment, we used the standard online, end-of-the course evaluation form and included 7-point Likert-type items to measure the satisfaction as well as questions during the interviews. These items were chosen among the most frequently used items in satisfaction scales. Regardless of the learner groups (fixed, all, or flexible), all the learners indicated their satisfaction with the course and the learning environments. Only 94 participants

TABLE 10.2 Email Messages to the Students			
	Messages Sent	Read Messages (%)	Clicked Links (%)
Total	2,322	1,524 (65,63)	979 (64.24)

TABLE 10.3 Learners' Responses to the Items Related to the Satisfaction

Items	Strongly Disagree	Disagree	Neutral	Agree	Strongly Agree	Average
I am overall satisfied with the course	3	3	5	38	45	4.27
I would suggest this course to my acquaintances	5	2	4	40	44	4.24
I would like to take another course similar to this one	3	3	4	40	44	4.27
I am overall satisfied with the course content	3	5	7	36	43	4.18
I would like to take another course related to the same topic	3	3	6	32	50	4.31
I am overall satisfied with the course environment	3	4	7	41	39	4.16
It was easy to navigate in the course environment	1	8	12	37	36	4.05
TOTAL	21	28	45	264	301	4.21

answered all the questions. As can be seen in Table 10.3, the learners were quite satisfied with the course, course content, and the course environment.

These quantitative findings actually supported the qualitative ones gathered via the personal interviews. Almost all the interviewees noticeably expressed their satisfaction with the course content, the design, and the learning environment. For example, a 45-year-old male participant noted that "lessons were well-designed, included sufficient content and activities.... The course system was easy to navigate.... we received clear instructions." Another learner stated that he was pleased with the lesson and "have already recommended it to my friends and tweeted about it."

FUTURE DIRECTIONS AND RESEARCH

Recent figures indicate a boost in the number of MOOCs during the COVID-19 pandemic (Shah, 2020). Those institutions that get involved in the

MOOCs movement have different motives. Anadolu University is one of those institutions that has been using MOOCs as a test bed environment for experimenting applicability and effectiveness of innovative technologies and strategies in its formal distance learning programs and courses. The main purpose of this study was to test the effectiveness of an adaptive learning environment and a distance learning course, which included automated notification system and content presentation based on holist-serialist cognitive styles of the learners. The study explored the MOOC participants' persistence to complete the course as well as explore the participants' reactions and perspectives to the automated course notifications. This chapter summarized the results of this large-scale study.

After a detailed systematic review of literature and a focus group study, we have concluded to use cognitive style for learner modeling. However, as it has been indicated before, modeling the learners is a very complicated and difficult process. Especially, thinking of learners' tendency to change their characteristics over time; and in instances, makes modeling chaotic. We conclude that trying to model cognitive styles for the learners is not an effective approach. Rather, we need to build environments that track learners' live activities, preferences, and other characteristics, and present the adaptive components during the learning process.

Our study has also uncovered evidence for the value of open source tools. Our adaptive learning environment was built solely on open source software which provided a sufficient, effective, efficient, engaging, scalable and sustainable learning system. The instructor (facilitator) and learners did not encounter any technical issues in this learning system. Therefore, we strongly suggest a detailed integration plan and the use of open source tools for establishing an effective learning environment in MOOCs or large online classes.

The learners' perceptions of the automated notifications both as pop-ups and email messages were very positive. The records also revealed that a big majority of those who opened email messages and clicked on the links provided on notifications came back to the course and completed. This result supported the literature on effects of personalized email messages on students' persistence. We strongly suggest integrating automated email notification components to any online distance learning environment. In fact, Anadolu University is currently working on such a project that their current learning management system, which is a custom built one, will provide pre-set and automated personal notifications to each of its distance learners. Those automated notifications will be created and shared based-on the individual behaviors and actions of the learners in the system. So, the learners will receive personalized notifications. Since the number of distance learning students at Anadolu University has reached over a million, you may imagine the scale of this project. We will be looking for the effects of those notifications on the learners' persistence, perceived satisfaction and learning as well as their performance in the exams. For the success of the university and its students, it is essential to implement data-driven research and examine effective technology tools, instructional and motivational strategies, and student support in large online classes.

In our study, we used the "time-spent on task" as a variable to send personalized notifications. It in general worked, but we felt that since the advances in technology that provides live, or physiological data about the status of learners, we should use those data for personalization. Currently, we are working on replacing the "time-spent on task" variable with "face recognition." In other words, we are working on integrating face recognition into our adaptive learning environment that will help us identify learners' engagement and provide automated notifications to them.

Moreover, we found that some learners may get distracted and develop negative attitudes against the notifications if the frequency is not set well. Thus, we strongly recommend that at the beginning the learners should be able to decide if they want to receive personal notifications, and how often they want to. They also should be able to change their preferences during the course. This will help them create a sense of autonomy in their learning processes and prevent developing undesirable attitudes against the course and the environment.

Along with all these implications, this study as well as experiences in other MOOCs in AKADEMA platform have provided noteworthy managerial and pedagogical ideas that can be integrated in the large size online courses. For instance, some prospective students may hesitate to join online courses and programs owing to various reasons, such as lack of self-regulation and online learning experience, anxiety for failure, and so on. Rogers (2003) indicated in his legendary work on diffusion of innovations that one of the five attributes of an innovation that affect adoption was trialability. MOOCs can be used as a safe trial environment and as a means for recruiting new students.

Another MOOCs-based idea is about the feedback. The more timely and adequate feedback the students get, the more they feel connected and engage with learning activities. However, it is not easy to provide feedback to each student in large size online courses. On the other hand, MOOCs have revealed that peer-feedback can be used to cope with this problem. Research shows that this type of feedback encourages students to interact with and learn from each other, and to engage with learning activities and materials (Jung et al., 2019; Kasch et al., 2020). These peer-feedback strategies can easily be used to enhance the feedback opportunities into large size online courses.

Additionally, MOOCs can be used as faculty training means. At Anadolu University, for example, AKADEMA platform was not only established to offer MOOCs but also train faculty on digital content creation and online teaching. In fact, in a recent study 82% of the participant AKADEMA instructors stated that their experience in MOOCs helped them transfer their face-to-face courses to online remote learning to a great extent (Erdem-Aydin, 2021). Before the AKADEMA, a large majority of them had no experience in digital content development. However, after the training, they asked to create their own videos and other materials for their MOOCs. The AKADEMA team provided guidelines, tutorials, templates, and on-demand support during their course development process. They reported that they have gained and improved their knowledge and skills on material design and development. A good number of the participants also expressed how they used these skills in their regular online remote courses.

In sum, this study and the MOOC experiences in AKADEMA platform clearly show that all the stakeholders of higher education institutions, such as students, instructors, administrators, vendors, and so on can benefit a lot from MOOCs. These benefits help them serve their students and community better.

REFERENCES

Anadolu University (2020). *Açıköğretim sistemi* [Open education system]. https://www.anadolu.edu.tr/en/open-education

Aydin, C. H. (2011). *Açık ve uzaktan öğrenme: Öğrenci adaylarının bakış açısı* [Open and distance learning: prospectus students' perspectives]. Pegem Akademi.

Aydin, C. H. (2017). Current status of the MOOC movement in the world and reaction of the Turkish Higher Education Institutions. *Open Praxis, 9*(1), 59–78.

Bozkaya, M., & Aydin, İ. E. (2019). Drop-out in MOOCs. *The Turkish Online Journal of Educational Technology–TOJET, 19*(3), 9–17.

Brusilovsky, P. (1997). Integrating hypermedia and intelligent tutoring technologies: From systems to authoring tools. In P. Kommers, A. Dovgiallo, V. Petrushin, & P. Brusilovsky (Eds.), *New media and telematic technologies for education in Eastern European countries* (pp. 129–140). Twente University Press.

Brusilovsky, P., & Peylo, C. (2003). Adaptive and intelligent web-based educational systems. *International Journal of Artificial Intelligence in Education, 13*, 156–169.

Brusilovsky, P., & Millân, E. (2007). User models for adaptive hypermedia and adaptive educational systems. In P. Brusilovsky, A. Kobsa, & W. Nejdl (Ed.), *The adaptive web: Methods and strategies of Web personalization* (pp. 3–53). Springer.

Çetinkaya, G. (2010). *Türkçe metinlerin okunabilirlik düzeylerinin tanımlanması ve sınıflandırılması* [Identifying and classifying the readability of the texts in Turkish]. Ankara University Press.

Diver, P., & Martinez, I. (2015). MOOCs as a massive research laboratory: opportunities and challenges. *Distance Education, 36*(1), 5–25. https://doi.org/10.1080/01587919.2015.1019968

Erdem-Aydin, İ. (2021). Investigation of higher education instructors' perspectives towards emergency remote teaching. *Educational Media International, 58*(1), 78–98. https://doi.org/10.1080/09523987.2021.1908501

Ewais, A., & Samara, D.A. (2020). Adaptive MOOCs based on intended learning outcomes using naïve bayesian technique. *International Journal of Emerging Technologies in Learning- iJET, 15*(4), 4–21.

Ford, N. (2000). Cognitive styles and virtual environments. *Journal of the American Society for information science,* 51(6), 543–557.

Freitas, A., Paredes, J. (2018). Understanding the faculty perspectives influencing their innovative practices in MOOCs/SPOCs: A case study. *International Journal of Educational Technology in Higher Education, 15,* Article 5. https://doi.org/10.1186/s41239-017-0086-6

Giannakos, M., Jaccheri, L., & Krogstie, J. (2014). Looking at MOOCs rapid growth through the lens of video-based learning research. *International Journal of Emerging Technologies in Learning-iJET, 9*(1), 35–38.

Jung, E., Kim, D., Yoon, M., Park, S., & Oakley, B. (2019). The influence of instructional design on learner control, sense of achievement, and perceived effectiveness in a supersize MOOC course. *Computers & Education, 128,* 377–388. https://doi.org/10.1016/j.compedu.2018.10.001

Kabtane, H., Adnani, M., Sadgal, M., Mourdi, Y. (2020). Virtual reality and augmented reality at the service of increasing interactivity in MOOCs. *Education and Information Technology, 25,* 2871–2897. https://doi.org/10.1007/s10639-019-10054-w

Kasch, J., Van Rosmalen, P., & Kalz, M. (2017). A framework towards educational scalability of open online courses. *Journal of Universal Computer Science, 23*(9), 845–867. https://doi.org/10.3217/jucs-023-09-0845

Lallé S., & Conati C. (2020) A data-driven student model to provide adaptive support during video watching across MOOCs. In I. Bittencourt, M. Cukurova, K. Muldner, R. Luckin, & E. Millán (Eds.), *Artificial Intelligence in education: AIED 2020: Lecture notes in computer science, Vol. 12163* (pp. 282–295). Springer. https://doi.org/10.1007/978-3-030-52237-7_23

Margaryan, A., Bianco, M., ve Littlejohn, A. (2015). Instructional quality of massive open online courses (MOOCs). *Computers & Education, 80,* 77–83.

Mödritscher, F., García-Barrios, V. M., & Gütl, C. (2004a). The past, the present and the future of adaptive e-learning: An approach within the scope of the research project AdeLE. In M. Auer & U. Auer (Eds.), *Proceedings of the International Conference on Interactive Computer Aided Learning (ICL2004).* ICAL.

Nakamura, J., & Csikszentmihalyi, M. (2009). Flow theory and research. In C. R. Snyder & S. J. Lopez (Eds.), *Oxford handbook of positive psychology* (pp. 195–206). Oxford University Press.

Nguyen, V. A. (2012). Toward an adaptive learning system framework: Using Bayesian network to manage learner model. *International Journal of Emerging Technologies in Learning (iJET), 7*(4), 38–47.

OpenupEd. (2014). *Definition massive open online courses (MOOCs).* http://www.openuped.eu/images/docs/Definition_Massive_Open_Online_Courses.pdf

Oppermann, R., Rasher, R., & Kinshuk. (1997). Adaptability and adaptivity in learning systems. *Knowledge Transfer, 2,* 173–179.

Ozgul, A. E. (2015, February 3–4). *Openness in education* [Paper presentation]. Akademik Bilisim Conference, Eskisehir, Anadolu University.

Pask, G. (1976b). Styles and strategies of learning. *British Journal of Educational Psychology, 46,* 128–148.

Rincon-Flores, E. G., Mena, J., Ramírez-Montoya, M. S., & Ramirez-Velarde, R. (2020). The use of gamification in xMOOCs about energy: Effects and predictive models for participants' learning. *Australasian Journal of Educational Technology, 36*(2), 43–59. https://doi.org/10.14742/ajet.4818

Rogers, E. (2003). *Diffusion of innovations* (5th ed.). Free Press.

Salahli, M., Özdemir, M., & Yaşar, C. (2013). Concept based approach for adaptive personalized course learning system. *International Education Studies 6*(5), 92–103. https://doi.org/10.5539/ies.v6n5p92

Shah, D. (2020, Dec 14). The second year of the MOOC: A review of MOOC stats and trends in 2020. *Class Central Report.* https://www.classcentral.com/report/the-second-year-of-the-mooc/

Sharples, M., Delgado Kloos, C., Dimitriadis, Y., Garlatti, S., & Specht, M. (2015). Mobile and accessible learning for MOOCs. *Journal of Interactive Media in Education, 1*(4), 1–8. https://doi.org/10.5334/jime.ai

Stoyanov, S., & Kirschner, P. (2004). Expert concept mapping method for defining the characteristics of adaptive e-learning: ALFANET project case. *Educational Technology Research & Development, 52*(2), 41–56. https://doi.org/10.1007/BF02504838

Truong, H. M. (2016). Integrating learning styles and adaptive e-learning system: Current developments, problems and opportunities. *Computers in Human Behavior, 55,* 1185–1193.

Wan H., & Yu S. (2020). Designing and implementing adaptive MOOCs. In S. Yu, M. Ally, & A. Tsinakos (Eds.), *Emerging technologies and pedagogies in the curriculum: Bridging human and machine: Future education with intelligence* (pp. 279–296). Springer. https://doi.org/10.1007/978-981-15-0618-5_17

Witkin, H. A., Oltman, P. K., Raskin, E., & Karp, S. A. (1971). *A manual for the embedded figures test.* Consulting Psychologist Press.

Zhang, J. (2016). Can MOOCs be interesting to students? An experimental investigation from regulatory focus perspective. *Computers & Education, 95,* 340–351.

Zhu, M., Bonk, C. J., & Doo, M.-Y. (2020). Self-directed learning in MOOCs: Exploring the relationships among motivation, self-monitoring, and self-management. *Educational Technology Research and Development, 68,* 2073–2093. https://doi.org/10.1007/s11423-020-09747-8

CHAPTER 11

BUILDING A HUMAN–AI FRAMEWORK FOR TEACHING LARGE ONLINE CLASSES

David Stein
The Ohio State University

Shen Ba
Central China Normal University

ABSTRACT

With increasing enrollments in online learning, concerns around learner interactions, learning outcomes, and overall quality of instruction also increase. A key element in quality online instruction is instructors' ability to create and sustain a supportive, intellectually challenging, and organized instructional environment. While providing timely communication, sustaining meaningful connections with students, and facilitating content acquisition are not new issues in teaching large classes, the online environment requires instructors who can quickly sense and react to the changing social, teaching, and cognitive needs of learners. This chapter explores recent developments in artificial intelligence as pedagogical agents in the online classroom. We introduce a human–AI framework about how pedagogical agents can serve learners in large online classes and help faculty manage social, teaching, and cognitive presence in large online classes.

As the scale of online education multiplies, the difficulty in maintaining the quality of the educational experience increases. A primary problem for large scale online education is the lack of interaction, which leads to low effectiveness and high dropout rate (Daniel, 2012). A large face-to-face class is defined as 35–49 learners, and a very large class exceeds 50 or more learners (Benton & Pallett, 2013). However, the definition of a large online class has not yet been firmly established. Optimal online class sizes range from 12 (Sieber, 2005) to 16–18 (Orellana, 2006) to 20 (Burruss, 2009). Parks (2017) suggested that online classes should not exceed 14 learners since an online class size of 15–30 learners resulted in lower instructor interactions. Thus, an online class is very large when enrollments exceed 30 students. In an online class, as in a face-to-face class, learner performance varies not only by class size but by course objectives, student characteristics, skill levels of instructors, and participation levels of instructors. Thus, while class size matters, other factors can account for learner performance as well.

Now imagine a moderately active large online class. Meaningful conversation with students may decrease due to multiple questions about content and instructional processes. Deep learning might be difficult to achieve (Goel & Polepeddi, 2016). Students may feel socially isolated and frustrated in large classes since instructor interactions with students are delayed (Ali & Smith, 2015). Even with help from teaching assistants, an instructor might still not be able to allocate time for securing resources, monitoring progress, and satisfying individual student needs due to routine questions and administrative tasks (Montelongo, 2019). One common strategy for teaching large online classes is to employ teaching assistants to grade, answer routine questions, and perhaps lead smaller tutorial sessions (Elison-Bowers et al., 2011).

Issues of feedback, meaningful connections with students, and facilitation of instructional interactions are not new issues in teaching large classes. Breukelman, Andrews, and Novak (1959) identified similar instructional issues comparing lecture with more active large group instruction. Critical recommendations for teaching large classes included establishing rapport with students and recruiting instructors having an interest and motivation to teach large classes. A similar emphasis on connections with learners, rather than technical solutions such as breaking the class into smaller segments, peer feedback, or self-scoring automated examinations (Shriner, 2016) seems to be related to reducing the emotional and psychological distance from the course, the instructor, and other learners (Hogan & Kwiatkowski, 1998).

Student expectations for academic support, interactions with instructors, and attitudes toward subject matter can influence performance in large group courses and the instructional design and methods used to deliver a learning experience. Transitioning to higher education and enrolling in a large group educational experience such as in mathematics can result in higher dropout rates as compared to participating in a tutorial with no more than 30 learners (Fortes & Abdellaif, 2010; Mulryan-Kyne, 2010). Russell and Curtis (2013) compared a large group online language learning experience (125 students) with a small group (25 students) online language learning experience. Learners in the large group had lower satisfaction scores. Learners participating in large group instruction expressed dissatisfaction with learner–instructor interactions as well as lack of teacher presence. Instructors in the large group environment mentioned an inability to support instructional needs due to addressing routine administrative tasks such as answering emails. The researchers conclude that large group online instruction can negatively impact learning and the instructor's ability to create a supportive and high-quality learning environment.

While online large group classes pose technical and instructional challenges, dealing with content, connections, and communication seems to be similar to conventional instructional arrangements. We respond to the challenges of large group online instruction by employing artificial intelligence technologies for increasing instructional efficiency and effectiveness. In this chapter, we describe recent developments employing pedagogical agents in educational settings. We present a model for human–AI (artifical intelligence) interactions. We also present scenarios deploying pedagogical agents in large online classes.

The term "agent" originates from computer science and refers to a computer program with autonomy, social ability, reactivity, and proactiveness (Wooldridge & Jennings, 1994). A pedagogical agent is a computer agent that inhabits a virtual learning space, monitors dynamics of educational transactions, and operates on behalf of instructors with individual autonomy such as responding to teaching and learning related incidents (Johnson & Rickel, 1997; Lester, Voerman, Towns, & Callaway, 1997). Graesser (2016) employed a pedagogical agent as a coach capable of analyzing learner's cognitive level through his/her verbal representation and providing adaptive feedback in a conversation-based learning environment. Math tutorials used a pedagogical agent as a learning companion that helps low-performance students cope with anxiety through verbal and nonverbal messages (Kim et al., 2017). Goel and Polepeddi (2016) designed and employed a pedagogical agent that works as the teaching assistant in a massive open online course (MOOC). They found that the agent can greet learners, regularly post announcements, and answer some of the routine questions without learners noticing any difference. The previous studies suggest that pedagogical agents may help address some of the challenges institutions and instructors face in teaching large online classes.

In the following sections, we will first introduce the origin of the pedagogical agent and its development. The next section will present how pedagogical agents could be implemented in large online classes to solve some of the existing challenges and form the human–AI instructional framework. In the last section, we will take a look at the future to see how teaching large online classes will differ as a pedagogical agent becoming the co-instructor.

THE ORIGIN AND DEVELOPMENT OF PEDAGOGICAL AGENTS

The idea of programming computers to imitate human tutors and achieve specific educational goals can date back to the early 1970s (Corbett et al., 1997). As Bloom (1984) proposed, learners who study with a personal tutor could outperform others without a personal tutor. However, due to limited educational resources, it is not realistic to provide every student with a personal tutor. Thus, researchers have been trying to transfer the personal tutoring model and recreate the knowledge transactions with computers. Carbonell (1970) presented the first intelligent tutoring program called SCHOLAR. Based on semantic networks, which is an organization of knowledge units and their dependent relationships, on the geography of South America, SCHOLAR was able to interact with students using questions and answers in natural language and evaluate student's understanding of the geography of South America. Another computer tutor that simulated human tutors is AutoTutor (Graesser, 2016; Graesser et al., 1999). AutoTutor consists of seven core modules, including curriculum script, language extraction, speech act classification, latent semantic analysis, topic selection, dialog move generation, and a talking head. AutoTutor can converse with students in natural language, analyze student knowledge levels, and provide feedback. Prompts from AutoTutor progressively lead students to form a deep and comprehensive understanding of a topic. Moreover, the animated talking head brought the computer tutor to a new level as the image could exhibit basic facial movements in accord with its verbal expressions. A computer tutor equipped with external human-like features is also known as the pedagogical agent (Baylor & Kim, 2004).

Intelligent tutoring systems mainly engage learners in verbal communications with computer tutors. The pedagogical agent paradigm extends this scope by including the design of nonverbal human–computer interactions (Johnson et al., 2000). One of the earliest pedagogical agents, STEVE (Soar Training Expert for Virtual Environments), was developed for the U.S. Navy training program (Johnson & Rickel, 1997). STEVE was built within a virtual learning environment to teach trainees how to operate the engine of a Navy ship through verbal and hands-on demonstrations. Similarly, another pedagogical agent, Herman the Bug, developed by Lester, Stone, and Stelling (1999) combined the intelligent tutoring model with an animated computer interface. Herman the Bug inhabited a virtual learning environment where students can learn the botanical structure of plants by building their own with provided components. During this process, Herman the Bug monitors students' operations and provides relevant advice and hints to help students solve problems.

As the research on employing pedagogical agents develops, its applications have expanded to a broader scope, with studies showing its potential to support learners' cognitive and social development (Kim & Baylor, 2016). The next section will take a closer look at these studies and establish and explain the framework in terms of how pedagogical agents might work collaboratively with instructors in large online classes.

HUMAN–AI FRAMEWORK

Pedagogical Agent for Responding to Routine Inquiries

A time-consuming instructional task is responding to routine student inquiries. Routine inquiries might include clarifying assignments, due dates, and preparing for exams. As the scale of online class increases, this challenge will only become more significant. A severe consequence might be that instructors and teaching assistants are overwhelmed by all the routine questions that they cannot facilitate discourse. Garrison (2016) established that discourse facilitation requires educators' attention to monitoring the cognitive and social dynamics of learners and ensuring that learners are progressing toward educational goals.

To address this issue, researchers from the Georgia Institute of Technology developed a virtual teaching assistant called Jill Watson (Goel & Polepeddi, 2016). Jill Watson answers students' queries and questions from the discussion board in the online class. Jill is built from IBM Watson APIs. An API (application programming interface) provides multiple toolkits for programming interactive agents. Jill Watson can process natural language and extract the main linguistic features of the questions posed by students. The agent will go through a database that contains question-answer pairs from the same online class in previous years. By comparing the semantic similarity between the new question and previous questions, the agent will retrieve the question-answer pair when its similarity reaches a specific threshold value and provide learners with the answer. Jill Watson checks the discussion forum every 15 minutes from 9 a.m. to 11 p.m. every day for new questions. Through the implementation of Jill Watson, the instructor and teaching assistants are relieved from repeated and laborious tasks of answering routine questions. Moreover, students are both satisfied and surprised to have their questions resolved in such a short time.

With the discussion forum being an essential medium for students to interact with their instructors and pose questions, helping students solve their questions as quickly as possible may increase their motivation and engagement and prevent them from feeling isolated and helpless. However, it can be extremely challenging to do this manually by instructors and teaching assistants. Employing a Q&A pedagogical agent can address most simple questions so that instructors can engage in deeper and more meaningful communication with students.

Pedagogical Agent for Personalized Cognitive Support

Bloom (1984) showed that personal tutoring could significantly improve a student's performance. The significant advantage of a personal tutor is that the tutor has a better understanding of the student's cognitive level as compared to a lecture-type class where one instructor could be facing a hundred students. A personal tutor can provide more tailored assistance to his/her tutee. Current online learning still follows a more traditional path that focuses on standardization instead of personalization (Yu et al., 2017). By providing unified learning content, instructors will be able to closely meet most students' needs with limited time and resources. However, since unified learning content may be too easy for some students while too challenging for others, there is still room for optimization. A cognitive pedagogical agent that can analyze a student's mastery of knowledge may be suitable as a complementary solution to current online courses.

AutoTutor is a series of pedagogical agents with different purposes and functions (Nye et al., 2014). The researchers and developers of AutoTutor have examined hours of human tutoring sessions and summarized the 5-step tutoring frame that could effectively engage students in explaining and discovering answers instead of directly pointing out mistakes and providing final solutions. To implement this tutoring frame, the agent first poses a question related to original learning materials. Second, students will try to answer the question by inputting their answers through text. Third, the agent will analyze answers with the purpose of understanding not only if answers are correct, but also the reasoning process that brings students to these answers. Fourth, based on the cognitive/knowledge network, the agent will provide hints or follow-up questions to guide students and improve their answers. The agent will check if students genuinely understand the specific knowledge or continue the loop and progressively provide more hints. Through the process of this tutoring frame, students will be able to master not only the answers but also the reasoning process.

Motivated by theories such as learning-by-teaching (Gartner et al., 1971), Leelawong and Biswas (2008) have developed a teachable agent called Betty's Brain. As the name implies, students will take the responsibility of teachers and teach the agent what they have learned through inputting knowledge units and relationships among these units. These inputs will gradually form a knowledge map that represents what the agent has learned from students. Then, the agent will use the knowledge map to answer a series of questions to evaluate how well it has learned. By taking the teaching role, students first can review what they have learned by teaching the agent. Second, the visualization allows students to intuitively see what they have learned and what they may have missed. Third, feedback from the agent in terms of comments helps students see the errors and review appropriate materials.

As the size of online classes grows, it would be challenging for instructors to provide a tailored learning experience. However, it is not impossible to provide students with personalized learning support to optimize learning outcomes. Pedagogical agents like AutoTutor and Betty's Brain work collaboratively with instructors. Pedagogical agents will further help students learn independently by providing personalized feedback and guidance.

Pedagogical Agent for Personalized Social Support

A recurring online learning critique is that learners do not get enough social interactions with others due to space and time difference (Akcaoglu & Lee, 2016). Social agency theory emphasized the importance of social interaction on learning performance (Wiseman et al., 2012). This theory describes a framework that includes four components, instructional messages with social cues, activation of social response, increase in active processing, and increase in quality of learning outcome. These components are organized in a three-step causal sequence. First, instructional messages containing social cues could convince learners that they are interacting with another social being (Klowait, 2018). Learners will employ social strategies for human–human interactions and become more socially engaged in the learning process. Second, during social interactions, there is an underlying consensus that the speaker is making efforts to get the listener informed by being accurate, relevant, and concise (Miller, 2018). Thus, the listener will be more active in processing information from his/her social partner. Third, learners who are more actively engaged in information processing tend to obtain high-quality learning outcomes (Liew et al., 2017; Mayer, 2017). By designing pedagogical agents with proper human traits, social interactions in large online classes might be encouraged.

Zakharov, Mitrovic, and Johnston (2008) developed a pedagogical agent that could detect students' emotional states and provide corresponding emotional feedback. In the detection of emotions, researchers focus on emotions delivered through facial expressions. Facial action coding system (FACS; Ekman et al., 2002) defines the relationship between facial muscle movements and specific emotions. In this case, the locations of outer eye corners, mouth corners, and inner brow corners are fed to the algorithm to calculate affective states. The emotional reaction of a pedagogical agent follows the rules for an event-based or emotion-based mechanism. For example, if a student correctly answers a question, the agent will respond with a praising message and a smiling expression. For the emotion-based mechanism, the pedagogical agent is set by researchers to respond with appropriate facial expressions when it detects steady negative emotions from learners' facial expressions. In the subsequent empirical study, Zakharov et al. (2008) concluded that learners, in general, prefer the proposed emotional pedagogical agent over the non-affective agent. Implementing socially and emotionally interactive pedagogical agents in the online learning environment can mediate learners' emotions and attitudes.

Pedagogical Agent for Supporting Instructor's Decision-Making

Currently, most pedagogical agents aim at interacting with students. With the size of online classes growing, another challenge faced by instructors is the increasing amount of data generated by learners, which may contain valuable information. Without proper tools, instructors will not be able to process all these data (Qu & Chen, 2015). A pedagogical agent can be a teaching tool, but it may also be an interface between instructors and data.

Although pedagogical agents can achieve various tasks, as discussed in previous sections, there are some limitations. One limitation is that pedagogical agents still need to follow a specific path or model to make decisions instead of thinking with absolute independence. It is not realistic to think about replacing human instructors with pedagogical agents. Instead, a more reasonable and promising vision is to have pedagogical agents that are designed to leverage human intelligence (Baker, 2016). That is to say, pedagogical agents should not make all decisions. A more effective approach is to use pedagogical agents to address the repetitious tasks and make lower-level decisions. The idea is to take advantage of the substantial computing power by reporting aggregated and organized results to instructors who are the real intelligent beings and domain experts. Pedagogical agents can assist instructors with data analytics to make well-informed

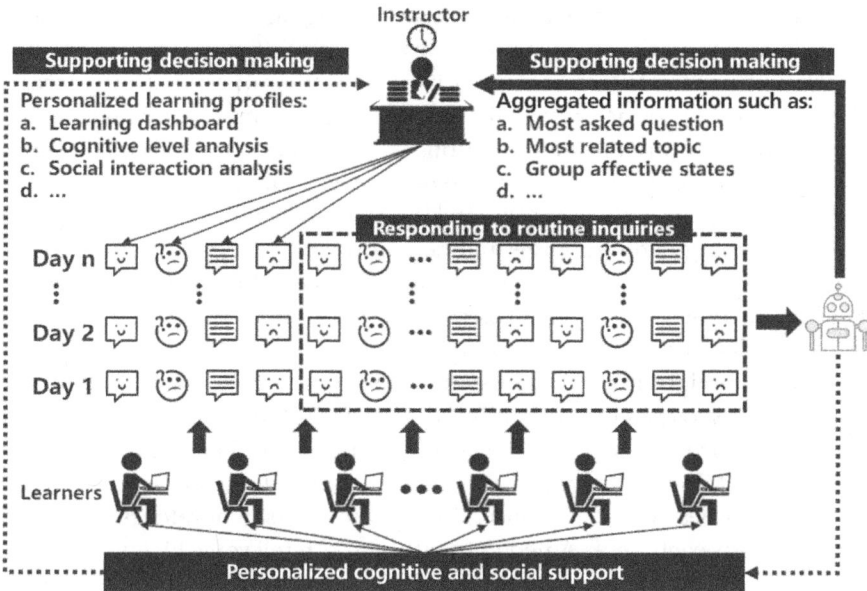

Figure 11.1 Human–AI co-instruction framework.

decisions based on their teaching strategies, domain expertise, and information from the data.

Pedagogical agents can assist in teaching large online classes by responding to routine questions, providing cognitive guidance, showing social support, and generating data analytics for instructors. A Human–AI instructional framework is illustrated in Figure 11.1.

A PARTNERSHIP FOR TOMORROW

In the future, each instructor teaching a large online class will be assigned a pedagogical agent with voice and facial characteristics resembling a human instructor. Along with the instructor's welcome message, the classroom pedagogical agent will also prepare a message inviting students to visit and communicate anytime, from any place, with any question or concern about the course. Tomorrow, instead of instructors posting office hours for routine matters or posting response times for email or ask-the-instructor questions, learner queries posted in the course can be addressed almost immediately. A pedagogical agent monitors student comments for questions about course content and procedures as well as questions for clarification and or more in-depth explanations 24/7. Feedback is now immediate, assuring learners that a presence is there listening and ready to help. There is no need to feel isolated and alone in a large digital learning environment. The classroom pedagogical agent may assist in the form of a conversation or short tutorial to help learners work through their questions and increase the learner's sense of mastery in an online environment. A pedagogical agent refers to more difficult questions back to you so that your time can be invested in helping students achieve deeper learning levels.

The pedagogical agent is also tracking students' emotional and cognitive levels. Scanning through large numbers of posts for keywords and phrases, the agent can detect those whose social presence is low and or decreasing. You might be screening posts for content or using a rubric to grade posts. Trying to detect the social-emotional aspects of your large class or trying to discern who might not be understanding the content or making significant contributions to class discussions is an arduous to impossible task for a single instructor. For example, we are teaching a mixed graduate/undergraduate course on lifelong learning in the United States, designed around weekly discussion issues. The class consisting of 34 learners generates between 133 and 192 posts each week. A pedagogical agent can tell you which learners are decreasing in motivation by assessing the learners' emotional state. To what extent do posts reflect boredom with the discussion, lack of interest in the content, low levels of engagement with content, and perhaps issues with understanding the concepts? As an instructor, you could target a personalized approach to those students at risk for non-participation or low-quality performance. A rapid intervention shows your concern for the individual learner who may otherwise go unnoticed in the large online classroom.

A pedagogical agent evolves and learns additional ways to create worthwhile learning experiences. The agent learns from quickly analyzing data generated from student comments and data generated from learner actions, including the number of responses to different colleagues, time on task, resources searched, and other data generated from the learning management system. With the guidance offered by a pedagogical agent, the instructor can focus on more productive communication and additional content and resources. Performing a high-value task demonstrates your concern for the learners by creating a high-quality online learning experience.

A pedagogical agent can help reduce concerns expressed by learners about large group instruction. Given the recent experiences in remote instruction (distance teaching and learning) that the world is experiencing, pedagogical agents can offer support and contact to learners across all levels of formal instruction just in time and only a keystroke away. Early detection of emotional issues can increase retention in large classes. Lack of perceived teacher presence might be reduced with frequent and timely personalized messages. As a subject matter expert, the instructor can invest time in curating resources and sustaining a high-quality learning environment for the whole class while supporting individual needs and concerns throughout the digital classroom experience.

The scenarios of a pedagogical agent assisting instructors in large online classrooms are derived from the community of inquiry Framework. A key concept is creating and sustaining a worthwhile educational experience created from the intersection of social, teaching, and cognitive presence (Garrison, 2016). A pedagogical agent can sense and report the extent to which learners express social, teaching, and cognitive presence. In a worthwhile educational experience, learners should be able to feel safe, secure, trusted, and engage in open and cohesive communications exhibiting social presence (Rourke et al., 2001). Teaching presence is manifested through interactions indicating areas of agreement/disagreement, seeking consensus establishing netiquette, injecting content from multiple sources, and encouraging all voices, among other indicators (Anderson et al., 2001). The third presence, cognitive presence is displayed when learners engage in critical discourse on content, connect ideas from participants to the issues, exchange personal as well as academic information relevant to the issue, test solutions, and come to have a shared understanding of the issue (Garrison et al., 2001)

A task for a pedagogical agent is to monitor balance among social, teaching, and cognitive presence to assure a worthwhile learning experience. The agent provides feedback to correct imbalances such as high social presence and low cognitive presence, which might result in dissatisfaction with the task, as well as low engagement. A pedagogical agent is always on 24/7, always working to support learners in a worthwhile learning experience. They are always there to offer feedback on ways to maintain and sustain a community of inquiry.

FUTURE DIRECTIONS AND RESEARCH

Pedagogical agents represent an innovative technological tool emerging on the edge of online learning. In COVID-19 educational environments, remote learning, increasing online class size, and parents as at home tutors are changing how adults and children participate in teaching and learning. These trends suggest a need for pedagogical agents. To prepare for post COVID-19 educational environments we recommend:

- establishing a reading program to become familiar with the current use of pedagogical agents in the educational environment;
- developing necessary skills in coding to understand how pedagogical agents are created and the functions that might be performed;

- seeking experts from computer science, engineering, and informational technology to help design and deploy pedagogical agents in your courses; and
- visualizing your instructional role with a pedagogical agent as an assistant—consider how your relationships with content, learners, might change. How might your teaching practices change with a 24/7 agent available to assist learners with tasks requiring feedback, emotional support, and additional content resources.

Employing pedagogical agents in educational environments opens research opportunities. We suggest several research considerations:

- exploring learner reactions to the combination of human and artificial pedagogical agents in a digital classroom;
- determining how pedagogical agents interact with learners in collaborative knowledge building digital classrooms;
- investigating the quality and sensitivity of feedback provided to learners and to human instructors by a pedagogical agent; and
- explaining which characteristics of artificial agents such as body type, facial image, eye movements, clothing, and voice affect learner performance.

Tomorrow, welcome your pedagogical agent as a partner in online instruction!

REFERENCES

Akcaoglu, M., & Lee, E. (2016). Increasing social presence in online learning through small group discussions. *The international review of research in open and distributed learning, 17*(3), 1–17.

Ali, A., & Smith, D. (2015). Comparing social isolation effects on students' attrition in online versus face-to-face courses in computer literacy. *Issues in Informing Science and Information Technology, 12*, 11–20.

Anderson, T., Rourke, L., Archer, W., & Garrison, R. (2001). Assessing teaching presence in computer conferencing transcripts. *Journal of Asynchronous Learning Networks, 5*(2), 1–17.

Baker, R. S. (2016). Stupid tutoring systems, intelligent humans. *International Journal of Artificial Intelligence in Education, 26*(2), 600–614.

Baylor, A. L., & Kim, Y. (2004). Pedagogical agent design: The impact of agent realism, gender, ethnicity, and instructional role. In J. C. Lester, R. M. Vicari, & F. Paraguaço (Eds.), *International conference on intelligent tutoring systems* (pp. 592–603). Heidelberg.

Benton, S., & Pallett, W. (2013, January 29). Class size matters. *Inside Higher Ed.* https://www.insidehighered.com/views/2013/01/29/essay-importance-class-size-higher-education

Bloom, B. S. (1984). The 2-sigma problem: The search for methods of group instruction as effective as one-to-one tutoring. *Educational researcher, 13*(6), 4–16.

Breukelman, J., Andrews, T., & Novak, J. (1959). A study of problems involved in teaching large classes in college general biology. *Transactions of the Kansas Academy of Science, 62*(4), 245–251.

Burruss, N. M., Billings, D. M., Brownrigg, V. Skiba, D. J., & Connors, H. R. (2009). Class size as related to use of technology, educational practices, and outcomes in web based nursing courses. *Journal of Professional Nursing, 25*(1), 33–41.

Carbonell, J. R. (1970). AI in CAI: An artificial-intelligence approach to computer-assisted instruction. *IEEE Transactions on Man–Machine Systems, 11*(4), 190–202.

Corbett, A. T., Koedinger, K. R., & Anderson, J. R. (1997). Intelligent tutoring systems. In M. G. Helander, T. K. Landauer, P. V. Prabhu (Eds.), *Handbook of human–computer interaction* (pp. 849–874). North-Holland.

Daniel, J. (2012). Making sense of MOOCs: Musings in a maze of myth, paradox and possibility. *Journal of Interactive Media in education, 2012*(3), Article 18.

Ekman P., Friesen W. V., & Hager, J. C. (2002). *Facial action coding system: The manual on CD ROM.* A Human Face.

Elison-Bowers, P., Sand, J., Barlow, M. R., & Wing, T. (2011). Strategies for managing large online classes. *The International Journal of Learning, 18*(2), 57–66.

Fortes, P., & Abdellatif, T. (2010). Dealing with large classes: A real challenge. *Procedia Social and Behavioral* Sciences, *8*, 272–280.

Garrison, D. R. (2016). *E-learning in the 21st century: A community of inquiry framework for research and practice.* Taylor & Francis.

Garrison, R., Anderson, T., & Archer,W. (2001). Critical thinking and computer conferencing: A model and tool to assess cognitive presence. *American Journal of Distance, 15*(1), 7–23.

Gartner, A., Kohler, M. C., & Riessman, F. (1971). *Children teach children: Learning by teaching.* Harper and Row.

Goel, A. K., & Polepeddi, L. (2016). *Jill Watson: A virtual teaching assistant for online education.* Georgia Institute of Technology.

Graesser, A. C., Wiemer-Hastings, K., Wiemer-Hastings, P., Kreuz, R., & Tutoring Research Group. (1999). AutoTutor: A simulation of a human tutor. *Cognitive Systems* Research, *1*(1), 35–51.

Graesser, A. C. (2016). Conversations with AutoTutor help students learn. *International Journal of Artificial Intelligence in Education, 26*(1), 124–132.

Hogan, D., & Kwiatkowski, R. (1998). Emotional aspects of large group teaching. *Human Relations, 51*(11), 1403–1417.

Johnson, W. L., & Rickel, J. (1997). Steve: An animated pedagogical agent for procedural training in virtual environments. *ACM SIGART Bulletin, 8*(1/4), 16–21.

Johnson, W. L., Rickel, J. W., & Lester, J. C. (2000). Animated pedagogical agents: Face-to-face interaction in interactive learning environments. *International Journal of Artificial Intelligence in Education, 11*(1), 47–78.

Kim, Y., & Baylor, A. L. (2016). Based design of pedagogical agent roles: A review, progress, and recommendations. *International Journal of Artificial Intelligence in Education, 26*(1), 160–169.

Kim, Y., Thayne, J., & Wei, Q. (2017). An embodied agent helps anxious students in mathematics learning. *Educational Technology Research and Development, 65*(1), 219–235.

Klowait, N. (2018). The quest for appropriate models of human-likeness: Anthropomorphism in media equation research. *AI & SOCIETY, 33*(4), 527–536.

Leelawong, K., & Biswas, G. (2008). Designing learning by teaching agents: The Betty's Brain system. *International Journal of Artificial Intelligence in* Education, *18*(3), 181–208.

Lester, J. C., Voerman, J. L., Towns, S. G., & Callaway, C. B. (1997). *Cosmo: A life-like animated pedagogical agent with deictic believability.*

Lester, J. C., Stone, B. A., & Stelling, G. D. (1999). Lifelike pedagogical agents for mixed-initiative problem solving in constructivist learning environments. *User modeling and user-adapted interaction, 9*(1/2), 1–44.

Liew, T. W., Zin, N. A. M., & Sahari, N. (2017). Exploring the affective, motivational and cognitive effects of pedagogical agent enthusiasm in a multimedia learning environment. *Human-Centric Computing and Information Sciences, 7*(1), 9.

Mayer, R. E. (2017). Using multimedia for e-learning. *Journal of Computer Assisted Learning, 33*(5), 403–423.

Miller, T. (2018). Explanation in artificial intelligence: Insights from the social sciences. *Artificial Intelligence, 267,* 1–38.

Montelongo, R. (2019). Less than/more than: Issues associated with high-impact online teaching and learning. *Administrative Issues Journal: Connecting Education, Practice, and Research, 9*(1), 68–79.

Mulryan-Kyne, C. (2010). Teaching large classes at college and university level: Challenges and Opportunities. *Teaching in higher education, 15*(2), 175–185.

Nye, B. D., Graesser, A. C., & Hu, X. (2014). AutoTutor and family: A review of 17 years of natural language tutoring. *International Journal of Artificial Intelligence in Education, 24*(4), 427–469.

Orellana, A. (2006). Class size and interaction in online courses. *The Quarterly Review of Distance* Education, *73*(3), 292–248.

Parks-Stamm, E. J., Zafonte, M., & Palenque, S. M. (2017). The effects of instructor participation and class size on student participation in an online class discussion forum. *British Journal of Educational Technology, 48*(6), 1250–1259. https://doi.org/10.1111/bjet.12512

Qu, H., & Chen, Q. (2015). Visual analytics for MOOC data. *IEEE Computer Graphics and Applications, 35*(6), 69–75.

Rourke, L., Anderson, T., Garrison, R., & Archer, W. (2001). Assessing social presence in asynchronous text-based, computer conferencing. *American Journal of Distance Education, 14*(2), 51–71.

Russell, V., & Curtis, W. (2013). Comparing a large-and small-scale online language course: An examination of teacher and learner perceptions. *Internet and Higher Education, 16*(1), 1–13.

Shriner, B. (2016, July 2). 3 strategies for teaching large online classes. *AdjunctWorld.* https://adjunctworld.com/blog/3-strategies-for-teaching-large-online-classes

Sieber, J. (2005). Misconceptions and realities about teaching online. *Science and Ethics, 11*(3), 329–340.

Wiseman, R. M., Cuevas-Rodríguez, G., & Gomez-Mejia, L. R. (2012). Towards a social theory of agency. *Journal of management studies, 49*(1), 202–222.

Wooldridge, M., & Jennings, N. R. (1994). Agent theories, architectures, and languages: A survey. In M. P. Singh, A. Rao, & M. J. Wooldridge (Eds.), *International workshop on agent theories, architectures, and languages* (pp. 1–39). Springer.

Yu, H., Miao, C., Leung, C., & White, T. J. (2017). Towards AI-powered personalization in MOOC learning. *npj Science of Learning, 2*(1), 1–5.

Zakharov, K., Mitrovic, A., & Johnston, L. (2008, June). Towards emotionally-intelligent pedagogical agents. In B. P. Woolf, E. Aïmeur, R. Nkambou, & S. Lajoie (Eds.), *International conference on intelligent tutoring systems* (pp. 19–28). Springer.

ABOUT THE EDITORS

Dr. Selma Koç is an associate professor of educational technology in the College of Education at Cleveland State University. Her teaching experience includes educational technology, educational psychology, and summer institute programs for gifted and talented high school students. Her research interests are online learning and assessment, flipped learning, immersive learning, STEM education, and technology integration.

Dr. Marius Boboc is a professor of education and vice provost for academic planning at Cleveland State University. His research interests relate to online instruction (ranging design to implementation and evaluation), assessment and accreditation in higher education, postmodern education, leadership in higher education, and teacher preparation reform.

CPSIA information can be obtained
at www.ICGtesting.com
Printed in the USA
JSHW020934200323
39140JS00001B/57